As soon as we'd fired, we raised up to confirm our kills. To my surprise, I could see nothing but dirt. I motioned our Cambodians forward. As we neared, still unsure of what had happened, I saw two shovels near the fringes of the hole, but still no VC. Then it dawned on me. They were both in the h̶o̶l̶e̶ efficient. Walking up now w̶i̶t̶h̶ ̶a̶ ̶n̶e̶w̶ ̶s̶ense of boldness, p̶ ̶ ̶ ̶ ̶ ̶ ̶ ̶ ̶ ̶w there were four V̶C̶ ̶ ̶ ̶ ̶ ̶ ̶ ̶ ̶t they were diggin̶ ̶ ̶ ̶ ̶ ̶ ̶ve for two other VC̶ ̶ ̶ ̶ ̶ ̶was now to be the fina̶ ̶ ̶ ̶ ̶ of all four.

We had no sooner finished filling the hole than shots rang out. We were under attack from the north. It was now about 1730 hours, and the first shadows of a long, hot day began to reduce our ability to acquire targets. Still, we pursued the enemy. The volume of fire told me we were at even strength, but we had the coveted M-16 rifles. . . .

HARD TO FORGET

An American with the Mobile Guerrilla Force in Vietnam

Steven M. Yedinak

IVY BOOKS • NEW YORK

An Ivy Book
Published by The Ballantine Publishing Group
Copyright © 1998 by Steven M. Yedinak

Grateful acknowledgment is made to *The Wall Street Journal* for permission to reprint an excerpt from "Vietnam Vision: Will the War Ever End?" by Philip Geyelin. © 1966 Dow Jones & Company, Inc. All Rights Reserved Worldwide. Reprinted by permission of *The Wall Street Journal*.

http://www.randomhouse.com

Library of Congress Catalog Card Number: 98-92407

ISBN 0-8041-1809-4

Manufactured in the United States of America

First Edition: August 1998

10   9   8   7   6   5   4   3   2

To my parents, family, and friends, who cared for me and who still care for me.

To my brothers in arms, those proud and dedicated Green Berets with whom I served as a member of Task Force 957, Mobile Guerrilla.

To the Cambodians—the Khmer Kampuchea Krom—who fought valiantly with the Mobile Guerrilla Force and whose families are still scattered by the ravages of war.

To all: *De Oppresso Liber*.

Contents

III Corps Tactical Zone, 1964–1971

U.S. Army Special Forces Camps in III CTZ, Vietnam, 1964–1971

1-Ben Soi
2-Bien Hoa
3-Bu Dop
4-Bu Ghia Map
5-Bunard
6-Chon Thanh
7-Dong Xoai
8-Duc Hoa
9-Duc Hue

10-Duc Phong
11-Go Dau Ha
12-Hiep Hoa
13-Ho Ngoc Tao-Tu Duc
14-Hon Quan
15-Katum
16-Loc Ninh
17-Long Hai
18-Long Thanh

19-Luong Hoa
20-Minh Thanh
21-Phuoc Vinh
22-Prek Klok
23-Quan Loi
24-Song Be
25-Soui Da
26-Tanh Linh
27-Tay Ninh
28-Thien Ngon
29-Tong Le Chon
30-Tra Cu
31-Trai Bi
32-Trang Sup
33-Xuan Loc
34-Chi Linh

Map by Shelby L. Stanton

N

0   10   20
Map Scale in miles

⊛ Saigon

War Zone D

Nui Ba Den
War Zone C

Long Binh

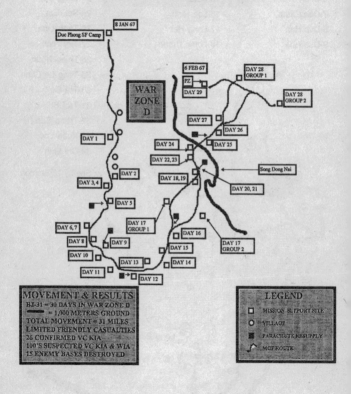

BLACKJACK-31

Guerrilla Warfare Operational Area (GWOA)

8 JAN 67

Duc Phong SF Camp

WAR ZONE D

6 FEB 67
PZ
DAY 29

DAY 28 GROUP 1

DAY 28 GROUP 2

DAY 27

DAY 26

DAY 25

DAY 24

DAY 22, 23

Song Dong Nai

DAY 1

DAY 18, 19

DAY 20, 21

DAY 2

DAY 3, 4

DAY 5

DAY 17 GROUP 1

DAY 16

DAY 6, 7

DAY 17 GROUP 2

DAY 8

DAY 9

DAY 15

DAY 10

DAY 14

DAY 13

DAY 11

DAY 12

MOVEMENT & RESULTS

BJ-31 = 30 DAYS IN WAR ZONE D
▬▬ = 1,000 METERS GROUND
TOTAL MOVEMENT = 31 MILES
LIMITED FRIENDLY CASUALTIES
26 CONFIRMED VC KIA
100'S SUSPECTED VC KIA & WIA
15 ENEMY BASES DESTROYED

LEGEND

☐ MISSION SUPPORT SITE
○ VILLAGE
■ PARACHUTE RESUPPLY
↗ MGF ROUTE

Introduction

Vietnam was a long time coming. It was not as if the United States, prior to the buildup of American forces in 1965 and beyond, had no historical record. And, unfortunately, it was not as if our experiences in Vietnam had failed to produce the kinds of evidence that would compel our leaders to reverse course.

From 1946 to 1954, the destruction of the French Army culminating at Dien Bien Phu proved that large-scale warfare in Southeast Asia was, at best, militarily untenable. More important, the French-led allied effort revealed that such a war, unwinnable on the battlefield, was divisive at home. U.S. advisers and U.S. dollars notwithstanding, the French action against the Communist Viet Minh ended in complete disaster for France and in an embarrassment for the United States. There were no winners on the side of democracy for warriors or politicians. That the U.S. first used Special Forces advisers, military men trained to assess the political and military environment, then failed to take heed of their experience, was even more ironic.

The next twenty years can be described, in U.S. terms, as five-card stud. That we continued to support efforts to spread our influence in Vietnam—a noble deed, in and of itself—when it ought to have been clear there was no war to win, was unfortunate. However, President John F. Kennedy was not to be denied. With poor input from his staff, the so-called "best

and the brightest," the vanguard of the "Eastern Establishment," Kennedy set out to teach the Russians a thing or two
about American resolve. Unfortunately, his assessment that a
few hundred well-trained Green Berets could turn the tide in
favor of a corrupt South Vietnamese government was optimistic. It soon became obvious that more troops would be
needed. How many more was unknown, but with Kennedy's
assassination came a headstrong Lyndon B. Johnson, who
would begin to find out.

Unfortunately, Johnson listened to the wrong advice. In
April of 1963, his Secretary of State, Dean Rusk, told him—
and the American people—that "the South Vietnamese themselves are fighting their own battle." And on June 13, 1963,
F. E. Nolting, U.S. Ambassador to Vietnam, told Johnson—
and the American people—that "South Vietnam is on its way
to victory." The Vietnamese general in charge, Tram Van
Dong, on October 1, 1963, told the U.S. that "I feel we shall
achieve victory in 1964." A White House statement the next
day, apparently in response to Dong's optimism, indicated
that "Secretary McNamara and General Taylor reported that
the major part of the U.S. military task can be completed
by the end of 1965." On October 31, 1963, the commander of
the Military Assistance Command Vietnam (MACV), General Paul D. Harkins, said, "Victory is just months away."
Rusk, apparently coming up for air, on February 24, 1964,
was quoted by the press as saying, "The Vietnamese can
handle this problem primarily with their own effort." Not to
be outdone by the Secretary of State, Secretary of Defense
Robert S. McNamara said, on May 14, 1964, "I think the
number of U.S. personnel in Vietnam is not likely to increase
substantially." To his credit, McNamara has already asked for
forgiveness.

Perhaps more deceptive than all others was President
Johnson's assertion on October 21, 1964, that "We are not
about to send American boys ten thousand miles from home to
do what Asian boys ought to be doing for themselves." When
Johnson made his statement, fewer than 150,000 troops were
committed to Vietnam. Four years later there were nearly

500,000 men and women in arms. In retrospect, Johnson's political statement about the war appears to have been consistent with his own personal thoughts and feelings regarding the commitment of U.S. forces. Tapes released on February 14, 1997, by the LBJ Presidential Library in Austin, Texas, revealed secret conversations Johnson had with his national security adviser, McGeorge Bundy, and close friend and mentor Senator Richard Russell of Georgia, on May 27, 1964. Almost a year before he began the large-scale buildup in Vietnam, President Johnson called the war "the biggest damn mess I ever saw" and lamented: "I don't think it's worth fighting for, and I don't think we can get out. What in the hell am I ordering [a soldier] out there for? What the hell is Vietnam worth to me? What the hell is Laos worth to me? What is it worth to this country?" Unfortunately, if Johnson, as president, agonized over Vietnam and was tormented by the prospects of sacrificing U.S. soldiers to a war he considered pointless, Johnson, as Commander-in-Chief of the Armed Forces, failed to act.

If not from the start—and I have my doubts about even that—then shortly thereafter, our leaders, intentionally or otherwise, deceived the nation. It is little wonder that this war, undeclared though it may have been, not only caused dissension in the ranks—mostly over the way it was being fought, using massive conventional forces—but turmoil at home. That said, I pray that the time has come when we can begin to listen to each other's stories about Vietnam. Not just the stories of those who went, but also the stories of those who did not serve. And the stories of those who raised our children.

Hard to Forget is a book about a young Special Forces soldier who took his green beret to Vietnam in 1966, only to discover that the real war began when the fighting stopped. *Hard to Forget* is a book about forgiveness, friendship, and survival.

I

What Price Freedom?

"Sir, Thach Son reports the second platoon is being overrun—an estimated VC company is closing on our command post," said Sergeant White, my twenty-one-year-old radio operator. "What should we do?"

My thoughts of dying were instinctive. I had always wondered what I would do when faced with the inevitable reality of dying. And now, facing death in a steaming jungle ten thousand miles from home took on a particular significance. It was as if a mechanism over which I had no control swept my mind clean of the battle that had been raging for the past thirty minutes. Our small force had been moving slowly, without enemy contact, through a clearing in the III Corps Tactical Zone (CTZ) region of South Vietnam, when sniper fire erupted from our left front at about four hundred meters. This is just about the maximum effective range of the M-3 carbines we issued to our Vietnamese Special Forces counterparts, the Luc-Luong-Dac-Biet (LLDB), and the Civilian Irregular Defense Group (CIDG) they led.

As we moved forward, cautiously, return fire from our point force was successful in dropping a black-clad Vietcong soldier. As we approached, the stark reality of this war was being confirmed as we secured our force about the bullet-riddled body of a young girl. I remember looking into her soft, warm eyes, her shredded corpse partially exposed in the mid-afternoon sun, and anxiously thinking about my own two daughters, who were fully clothed in freedom's grasp in the small northwestern city of Puyallup, Washington. It was early July, 1966, so Lori would have been nearly two and a half, and her sister Kim just ten and a half months younger. Only a few minutes passed, but it seemed like an eternity.

As we were departing the area, our faces searing with the sweat and grime of combat, the sun was directly overhead. Our two-man advisory element—White and I—walked near the front of the two-hundred-man force commanded by an LLDB first lieutenant, Nguyen Vanh Trang. Without warning, he and his forces stopped. Trang was a slight man, about thirty-seven years old, with pale yellow skin and rotting teeth. With typical American impatience, I asked him why the hesitation, speculating that it was just further corroboration of the lack of will of the South Vietnamese Army to fight a war which we, as Americans, believed was in their best interest. Without an interpreter, Trang said the sniper was trying to channel our force into a densely wooded area known as the plantation, which consisted of thousands of rows of lucrative rubber trees spaced ten feet apart. It was thought to be one of the operating areas of a North Vietnamese Army unit of unknown strength.

The LLDB believed that NVA units were trained and equipped to defeat Vietnamese self-defense forces like those being advised by our ten-man Special Forces A-team. During local search and destroy missions, it was not uncommon for the CIDG to stall at the first sign of trouble. On the other hand, they had been fighting the war for nearly twenty years, so were hardly to blame for their sense of caution. White and I continued in the direction of the plantation, alone, without looking back, hoping the CIDG forces were following. At some point we discovered that we had opened up a lead of about 100 meters. We were hoping to set an example, to build confidence in the LLDB leadership. Just as we began to think our leadership effort had failed, we glanced back to see that the units were once again on the move.

Shortly, as we closed on a small hootch near the entrance to the rubber plantation, we heard a single shot from within. We placed security forces, then entered, hoping to find some signs of occupation or withdrawal. We were quickly overcome by the sight and smell of an old man who had a gaping hole where his left ear would have been. A partially eaten meal, no outward signs of a confrontation, and a .45 caliber pistol gripped tightly in his right hand, indicated that, for whatever reason, he had either just committed suicide or had been the timely victim of an NVA security force.

I radioed our B-team headquarters in Tay Ninh that we were about to enter the plantation and would likely need air strikes as we began to identify the location and disposition of suspected enemy forces. As we began to tactically deploy our formation about the small clearing near the hootch, intending to enter the plantation itself, all hell broke loose. The sounds of combat are unmistakable, even for a young U.S. Army Special Forces lieutenant on his first combat mission. My main concern was helping Trang get his forces deployed into a tight perimeter to protect the command group, advisory element, and our radio link with the combat assets we would most likely need. The report of enemy direct-fire weapons and our own return fire rolled across the landscape as the radio squawked our initial casualties—the second platoon had three dead and six to eight wounded. Within minutes, enemy mortars thumped, moments later ripping large craters near the hootch, about twenty meters from our command post.

It was becoming increasingly clear that we were faced with a superior force that was systematically reducing the size and strength of our perimeter. "Sir," White screamed over the chaotic sounds of combat, "what should we do?"

A Prayer for the Dying

One learns in school that courage is the ability to overcome fear and persevere in the face of overwhelming odds. From where this ability comes is not well explained. Is it innate? Do we all have it? To the same degree? Is it taught? Does it just show up at the right time? At the precise moment of need? Or is courage an ability for which there is some underlying, fundamental, prequalifying presence?

Just as my thoughts of dying were instinctive, so were my thoughts of prayer. It was as if the two were born of the same emotion and competing for the same attention. Raised as a Catholic by two extraordinary parents, and nurtured through sixteen years of religious education, including four years at Gonzaga Prep in my hometown of Spokane, Washington, my turning to prayer was as inevitable as the reality of dying itself. The Jesuits, a longtime bastion of individual responsibility and personal accountability, had just about given up on me, as few, if any, of my classmates walked on the same side of the street.

Now, near the plantation, a sense of calm replaced my initial sense of fright, as I heard my mind quickly but certainly recite an Our Father and a Hail Mary over the piercing sounds of impending death.

The Dictates of War

"White," I said, "get me the fucking air request net, and lay out all of your fucking ammunition. We may die here, but we are going to take a lot of those sons of bitches with us." As White scrambled the air, we rapidly organized our position so we'd be able to quickly change magazines and use the six or eight fragmentation grenades routinely carried on such operations. While trying to assist the LLDB commander in responding to this tactical emergency, it was imperative that we take cover, consolidate our ammunition, control the air request net, and try to use tactical air power to silence an overwhelming force only minutes from our front door.

"Sir, I have Tango Six," White said as he handed me the mike.

"Tango Six, Freedom Six, over."

"Freedom Six, Tango Six. I have a flight of two being diverted from another Tac-E [tactical emergency] en route your location. Station time is two minutes, over."

"Freedom Six, roger."

"Tango Six, out."

As reports from the second platoon continued to confirm the breakthrough, and as direct fire was now screaming through our position, White and I anxiously awaited the arrival of the birds. I fondly recalled that only months earlier, when assigned to C-3 operations in Bien Hoa, I had spent a day with the U.S. Air Force Tactical Air Control Center trying to learn firsthand how the boys in blue work best with us SF ground pounders. Part of the training consisted of an actual combat mission flying in the backseat of an F-100 fighter. After two hours in the air I was totally nauseated, and developed, then and there, great respect for the young pilots who daily provided direct air support to ground units. Besides being in constant danger, the g-forces pilots sustained during high-speed turns and steep-angle bomb runs was enough to make you puke. When the day was over and we had time to share a couple of cold ones with our brothers in arms, I learned that they thought it was us guys on the ground—with the mission to close with and kill the enemy—who kept them going. They perceived, correctly, that we on the ground were often at a serious disadvantage when staring down the enemy. The mutual respect shared by fighter pilots and SF is historic, and, without a doubt, one of the most fundamental, mystifying, and rewarding relationships in combat.

"Freedom Six, Talon Three, over."

"Talon Three, Freedom Six, over."

"Talon Three, arriving grid X-ray, Tango, four-five-three-zero—how can we help? Over."

As I torched the nearby hootch with my Zippo lighter, I said, "Talon Three, I have marked my position—break break—what do you see?"

"Freedom Six, I see a fire rising from the roof of a small hootch, over."

"Roger, I'm located just south of my mark—break break—make your first run from northwest to southeast at a hundred meters. Will adjust. Over."

For the next ten to twelve minutes, using the air request net, we adjusted the 250-pound bombs and the 20mm cannon fire on known or suspected enemy positions as Trang ordered his troops to withdraw to the south two hundred meters, then west. As the last elements of the second platoon cleared our command post, we departed the area. Talon-3 reported enemy forces breaking contact and moving to the northeast.

As we began the long movement back to Tay Ninh, I felt a great sense of relief that we were able to escape, but also wondered why we'd been spared. My heart pounded, as my mind quickly recalled the young girl, the old man, my first instincts about combat, about dying, about the power of prayer, and about the ability to overcome fear and persevere in the face of overwhelming odds to the contrary. Interestingly enough, my mother always said I was lucky. As First Lieutenant Trang secured his unit for the night just outside Tay Ninh city, White and I offered him and his troops congratulations for a job well done and made our way into the B-team compound. We were exhausted and in need of a friend.

A Night at the Bar—A Night to Forget

Life at Suoi Da, the SF camp we called home, was pretty austere. There were food, shelter, ammunition, trenches, barbed wire, a communications center, and small, rat-infested living quarters. Also, a fortified cement bunker with a locked steel door for use if we were being overrun by superior forces. By comparison, Tay Ninh, our next higher headquarters and host for the night, was quite metropolitan. It contained showers, an established dining facility, far cleaner and more comfortable living quarters, and a bar. A very small bar—for ten to twelve at a time—but nevertheless, a bar. In happier times the bar could be part of a night to remember, but under the circumstances in which White and I found ourselves, the Tay Ninh bar was a night to forget.

As we walked in, we found a few B-team staffers in their clean, starched tiger fatigues unwinding after a busy day of sorting personnel files, gathering intelligence, monitoring operations, and directing the shipment of supplies. Not that those were activities without purpose, but seldom in the Tay Ninh bar did one see combat warriors in muddy boots and stinking, decaying fatigues, men with rifles, grenades, hand guns, and a story to tell. This was such a night. As round after round of "Tiger Piss"—an affectionate but typical name for the local brew—found their way to our table, White and I tried to sort out the day's events. The B-team guys were most gracious, not only because they had played an important role in diverting air strikes intended for another area, but because by nature staff pukes want to get down to an A-team, and who knows just when a few rounds of beer might be the deciding factor.

There are two reasons combat soldiers drink. First, as a reward for being alive. The second, to try to forget the sights and sounds and smells of the battlefield. All combat veterans, unfortunately, must live with the horrors of war—in sordid detail—all the remaining days of their lives. Unlike a personal computer whose memory can be erased, the human brain—the most powerful computing mechanism in existence—won't let the men and women who suffer the realities of combat forget. That's the problem for which there is often no real solution. One has only to recall the media events of the past thirty years—the movies, books, newsprint and TV stories, the Memorial in Washington, D.C., and now the Internet, to name a few—to know that there are hundreds of thousands of warriors who are still desperately trying to cope with their own versions of the war zone.

To be sure, there was not just one Vietnam War, but one war for each of the hundreds of thousands of soldiers, sailors, airmen, and Marines who participated. They are heroes, many of whom are having a difficult time blending into an American society that is indifferent at best to their suffering and to their accomplishments. They are the men and women to whom most of us owe a huge debt of gratitude for our being so well-clothed in freedom's grasp.

How's Your Courage?

As the night wore on, White and I thought we heard someone shout "last call." We'd been having a rather long philosophical discussion about courage. One of us offered that courage was the ability to overcome fear. But just how a soldier was able to accomplish that was yet another matter. We discussed the recent sad state of affairs at Suoi Da, which caused the relief of the SF A-team commander and brought me to my first command. Among other irregularities, the CIDG had not been conducting productive operations, and the leadership had lied about the results of the operations that were run. Had the U.S. Special Forces commander lacked courage? What about Trang, who was also caught up in the web of deceit? Had he been afraid? If so, he didn't show it. What about the reaction White and I had to the sniper fire, and our decision to continue on, when in fact Trang had decided to bring his forces to a halt? Were we courageous? Stupid? What if our effort had turned sour, causing unacceptable casualties? And from where did Trang get his courage to once again move out in the direction of the rubber plantation? And, when we were pinned down, thinking we were being overrun, was I afraid? Suddenly, then and there, I felt the urge to trust Sergeant White with information which I may have otherwise carried alone to my grave—my own personal fear, and the need to pray when faced with imminent danger. He said he was not surprised, that we all had our own way of conquering our fears. He recalled how the Cambodian soldier frequently carried a replica of Buddha on a chain around his neck for good luck. And, when in combat, how he placed the Buddha into his mouth for protection. The Bode believed that dying with Buddha in his mouth would assure a quick and meaningful trip to "the happy hunting ground." All this from a young but combat-experienced warrior. It was refreshing.

And then there was First Lieutenant Trang himself, who had emerged, somehow, from an episode of graft and corruption just a few days earlier. Just how he was able to overcome his fear of discovery, we weren't sure, but the method he chose to summon his courage for the military operation, his first in a long time, had been there for all to see. The more White and I thought about it, the more we had to agree that what Trang had done to prepare himself and his troops for combat in the rubber plantation was unlike anything we had ever encountered.

Positioned with the lead company, we had been walking toward the front gate of the Suoi Da compound when Trang stopped short. Startled, I'd seen a huge milk cow lying on the ground up ahead, its front and back legs tied with rope, and its exposed neck lying across a piece of wood. As we waited and watched, Trang pulled a machete from its sheath, quickly sliced the cow's throat and, with all the flair of a circus act, lowered a large glass to catch the first surge of thick red blood. Immediately raising the overflowing glass to his mouth, he gulped its contents until there was nothing left but a pinkish residue. He then turned to his troops and shouted that the blood of the cow would warm his heart and give him the courage to lead his men in combat. Apparently, the ceremony had worked, as the operation was a notable success. Trang promised there would be a "victory celebration" for the new leadership when we returned to Suoi Da.

At Tay Ninh, with the discussion about courage winding down, White and I stumbled to our feet and, with some caution, slowly made our way back to the guest quarters. The next day we would be back in Suoi Da, talking with the rest of the A-team about Operation Freedom's Price, and looking forward to breaking bread with Trang and his men.

So, where did all of this start?

II

The Beginning—
Training for War

The Reserve Officers' Training Corps at Gonzaga University was one of 287 established at Land Grant colleges throughout the United States. Entering freshmen were required to take two years of basic military education and training, and as sophomores could apply for the Advanced ROTC program, which was the basis for producing commissioned officers for entry on active duty. For most students, two years of what seemed like "Mickey Mouse" courses were enough. But almost immediately after the second year began, the cadre of war veterans who were our instructors began to identify those whom they considered had potential for active service as officers in the United States Army.

The Arm-Twisting—Decision of Logic or Feel

For me, 1960 was the year of decision. In early February the noncommissioned officer instructors wanted to know if I had given much thought to an army career. They provided details about life in the military and discussed the options for serving one's country. Most of them were Korean War veterans who already had one eye on the impending U.S. involvement in Vietnam. Military pay was relatively low, housing would be provided, and there would be opportunities for education and training, travel, and, of course, retirement.

Basically, in those days an officer who served twenty years was promised lifelong retirement pay equal to fifty percent of his base pay at separation. And, for each additional year, the pay increased by two and a half percent, to a maximum of seventy-five percent at thirty years. All in all, for a young college student that was a very strong career incentive, whether or not there appeared to be a war on the horizon. Other ROTC program incentives were more immediate. Advanced Corps students earned a monthly stipend of $47.80, and several hundred dollars for six weeks of summer training between the junior and senior years. This when college tuition for one semester was but $250. Growing up in a lower-middle-class family with two brothers and four sisters left me facing financial challenges that made any additional revenue an attractive choice.

In fact, I had many of the desirable attributes of an American soldier, and some not so desirable as well. On the positive side, I was adventurous, athletic, a risk-taker, and fearless. On the negative side, I was also headstrong, walked on the wild side, and openly displayed my displeasure with any kind of authority. The notable exceptions were my parents, whom I loved deeply and greatly respected. This was an interesting combination of traits for someone being so strongly recruited for the service. But when all was said and done, I raised my right hand, signed some papers, and took the $47.80. At that point, I became an official member of the Advanced ROTC program, taking the first important step toward serving my country on active duty as a commissioned officer.

Were They Right or Was I Wrong?

As a psychology student with mediocre grades, I couldn't understand just why the ROTC cadre wanted me to try for an officer's commission. Were they right to assume I had the basic makeup to lead men in battle? If so, they must have questioned their conventional wisdom when, during the first semester of my senior year, the school suspended me for one year for being loud and boisterous, and drunk and disorderly, on campus the night of the Mardi Gras dance. Those who knew me were not surprised, as the incident was just one of many throughout my days at Gonzaga Prep and at Gonzaga, the university that qualified for some sort of punishment. On the other hand, those who knew me well, including my parents, had always found in me something in which to believe. Nevertheless, despite six hundred student petitions to the contrary, in a school of two thousand students, the new dean of men and the new dean of women—brother and sister in real life—were eager to demonstrate the new change in direction for the small Jesuit school. Drinking on campus was not to be tolerated.

As I departed, although saddened, I was already clearing my mind for a program of recovery. I had badly disappointed my parents, especially my mother, whose tears I can clearly recall to this day, and, of course, I had let myself down as well. Within a week or two I enrolled at Eastern Washington State College in Cheney, Washington, and so lost little in the way of required credits for graduation. I also stopped drinking. For years I had considered myself to be a social drinker, but several in authority suspected I had a drinking problem. I thought I knew, but was not sure. I wanted to know, so in spite of some good-natured ribbing from my closest friends who thought worry about excess drinking was all a bunch of bullshit, I socialized for eighteen months without taking a drop of alcohol.

I was allowed to re-enroll at Gonzaga in summer school of 1962, and was back on track to graduate and be commissioned in the United States Army. When asked to state a branch preference, I chose Armor, Transportation, and Infantry, in that order.

Upon graduation, in May 1963, I pinned on the crossed rifles of an officer in the infantry, the branch known throughout the services as the "Queen of Battle." On June 22, 1963, I married Donna Simons from Puyallup, Washington, who was my rock of support throughout the entire ordeal. And did that piss off the administration: Donna was a scholarship student with an impeccable scholastic record and a picture-perfect personal life. So the school administration thought, What did she see in me? But that dramatic turn of events brought a new joy to the Yedinak family, especially to my mother, who had never allowed herself to believe that things could have ended quite so well. She always said I was lucky!

Following graduation, our marriage, and honeymoon, Donna and I were on our way to our first days in the Army together, and training at Fort Benning, Georgia.

Kennedy and the War on the Horizon

In the driving rain and darkness, it was hard for Donna and me to know just where to enter Fort Benning. I knew we were on Victory Boulevard, but I was unfamiliar with the layout of the huge training center and was unsure that we were at the right entrance to the post. Finally, I spotted a telephone booth out of the right window of our 1955 Olds Cutlass and stood ankle deep in water while trying to reach post duty personnel for instructions.

Once we signed on to the post, we were shown to an Officers' Guest House, and spent the first night in a part of the country we had both only read about. The date of my entry on active duty was September 22, 1963. I was twenty-three.

As training began, we lieutenants of Infantry began to learn a lot more about Vietnam—the war on the horizon. We spent our days and nights slopping around in the cold, sticky Georgia red mud, and then the snow, learning the basic combat skills—how to shoot, move, and communicate—for one reason, and one reason only: to close with, and kill, the enemy. That first sense of mission—taking care of our men was a vital second part—became our guiding light in everything we said and did. We studied the art of leadership—and followership—as our days and nights in the woods began to run together. We could walk in dead silence, using the existing trees and bushes for camouflage and cover from the "enemy" as we readied for various attacks or withdrawals. We could also "kill" a man-size target at 465 meters—the maximum effective range of the M-1 Garand rifle we carried as if it were a third leg. We learned how to throw fragmentation grenades, prepare small demolitions, talk cryptically on the radio, use small boats, navigate with a map and compass, prepare field rations, sanitize the battlefield, call for and adjust indirect fires such as mortars and artillery, and use air strikes. We were nearing completion of our training when it happened.

Kennedy: Where Were You?

As our canvas-top two-and-a-half-ton truck slogged its way through the rain-swollen dirt roads on Fort Benning's south forty, we suddenly came to a stop. Of course we knew not the reason, and cared little, as frequent stops en route to the training area were the order of the day. There were six such trucks in our convoy, each carrying about twenty soldiers with full combat gear and weapons. A few minutes later, a senior officer directed that we would disembark and fall into a military formation between the end of our vehicle and the one following. When we had done so, and were at strict attention, he commanded the formation to parade rest—a modified position of attention during which no movement or talking was authorized. He then said that our president—our commander-in-chief—had been shot and killed while riding in a motorcade in Dallas, Texas. We were stunned, as a group, and as for me, I was shocked to learn that, ironically, as we trained for a war ten thousand miles away—a war openly promoted by Kennedy and the Eastern Establishment—our leader was slain during broad daylight in the very streets of one of our largest cities. It was not a good sign of things to come.

Initial Inadequacies: Training or Aptitude?

As we neared the end of four and a half months of training—as graduation approached—it became clear to me that, although I enjoyed the fieldwork and was able to adapt well to the operational aspects of infantry fighting, I was near the bottom of my class when it came to scores for quizzes and written exams. I was so deficient that I had to report to a special board of officers to learn whether I would graduate and retain my commission. For one of the first times in my life, I was very nervous, and began to doubt my ability to achieve my near-term goals.

During training, it became obvious that different schools offered different training programs for ROTC students. Most of my friends from other schools seemed to know a lot more than did I about basic military operations and training. This realization had such a significant impact on me that when I learned that I would indeed graduate, I promised myself that never again would I be caught short. That near failure may well have been the catalyst I needed to persevere in the highly competitive, often combative, and potentially destructive Army Officer Corps for twenty-six years.

Airborne—All the Way!

Following graduation from basic infantry, I volunteered for Airborne training before reporting to my first assignment. Jumping from a perfectly good airplane at 1,200 feet and 125 knots seemed to be my idea of a good time. Besides, Donna and I needed the extra $110 per month jump pay I'd receive for each month assigned to an Airborne unit. The training for the next three weeks—ground week, tower week, and jump week—was very rigorous, very physical. The fact that the frost and snows of winter were setting in didn't make things any easier. Since Airborne was voluntary, the cadre didn't give a shit if you made it or not. There were no free lunches. Instructors were veterans who had previous assignments to

Airborne units, and they were as hard as nails. During the first week, they tried to get trainees to quit because of physical inadequacy or sheer exhaustion. Tower week was a test of nerves, as we dangled from harnesses learning how to land, jumped out of thirty-two- and 250-foot towers, and learned the basic air-loading procedures and jump commands. Jump week was just that. Five successful proficiency jumps, and we earned our wings.

Airborne training was so intense as to become reflexive. When jumps are completed within two to three minutes, there are a lot of things to do, and you must do them well. The different drills that one learns become instinctive, such as vigorously exiting the airplane. One second you're standing in the door with your palms on the outside of the plane facing inward, and then you're out. Honest to God, I felt at times that at 1,200 feet and 125 knots I would simply fall out of the plane. The instructors said the centrifugal force keeps you in, but several times I was reluctant to move out even one more inch than required to assume the position, lest I go flailing into the Twilight Zone, nowhere near the DZ. On the command, "Go," we were required to make a vigorous exit to clear the plane while immediately thrusting our elbows into our sides. Our hands covered the reserve parachute tied at each man's midsection.

One night during jump week, as Donna and I slept, I dreamed I was standing in the door. On the command "Go," I did everything I'd learned in training, only to awaken a few moments later to Donna's anguished cries. Apparently, while lying on my left side with Donna on her back to my right, I instinctively thrust my elbows into her stomach! At that time, she was seven months pregnant with our first child. We were both confused and scared as we talked our way back to sleep. So much for intensive training.

The roar of the engines of the air force C-123 Air Commando on the way to the drop zone was deafening. One Forty-five Company, of which I was a part, was making its first jump. Earlier, we had sat on the runway for two hours while the wings were defrosted, so any apprehension we had about clearing the door had dissipated—at least for me. Besides, I had to piss so bad I could taste it. The first sign that we were approaching the DZ was the jumpmaster's first command, "Six minutes." If there were any questions in anybody's mind about whether or not they were going to jump, it was resolved at that point; there was no turning back. Peer pressure and training would now dictate the sequence of events that would culminate in our slowly picking our asses off the hard surface below.

A few minutes later, "Get Ready" signaled that the drop plane was nearing the airborne I.P.—initial point—from which the drop would be made. "Stand up," "Hook up," "Check equipment," "Sound off for equipment check," and "Stand in the door" ensured that all jumpers would clear the door during the ten or so seconds the plane was over the drop zone.

For me, the experience was awesome! Also, my first jump was very memorable. On the final command, "Go," I made a vigorous exit, bent over slightly at the waist, and clutched hard with both hands onto the reserve parachute at my midsection, shouting—as if anyone could hear—"One one thousand, two one thousand, three one thousand, four one thousand . . ." By that time the chute was supposed to be open, a physical experience equal to if not greater than the jolt one receives when hitting the end of a bungee cord. My chute opened.

I looked up to see if my T-10 parachute was properly deployed, or if there was some kind of malfunction. I had a Mae West, several parachute lines deforming the canopy into a large brassierelike form. Well, shit! Just what I wanted to see. While not a major malfunction, the inverted canopy caused the jumper to fall much too fast for a safe landing. Possible remedies were to either deploy the reserve or cut the lines involved and hope to "pop" the chute to full deployment. There is little time to think, so one reacts instinctively one way or the other, and hopes the decision is the right one. Interestingly, during training, ours was the first class to be taught the standard of immediately deploying the reserve. But I recalled that during training, several of the master parachutists—our trainers—were somewhat skeptical of that new tack. They had serious reservations about whether or not the reserve would properly deploy under such circumstances, arguing among themselves that the newly deployed reserve would not get enough air inside the wake of the partially deployed main. With only seconds to spare—I was falling three or four times faster than my fellow jumpers—on a sixty-second jump, I heard one of the ground instructors below shout, "Number 286, deploy your reserve." Instinctively, with my right hand, I unsheathed the boot knife from inside my left ankle, and, with my left hand, grasped the six or eight lines at fault and severed the lot. Landing and living seemed to far outweigh the grumbling among instructors below who were debating the correct response. So much for training. My mother always said I was lucky! On January 24, 1964, I was awarded my jump wings.

Since Donna was about seven months pregnant, we were concerned about her health as we drove some 3,500 miles to our home state for forty-five days' leave. According to special Orders 57, I was to report NLT 9 March to Fort Ord, California, as an infantry platoon leader. Even though her doctor told us the trip would not endanger the baby or induce early labor, we took no chances, cutting short our leave and getting settled into an apartment in Seaside by late February. Only days after I reported for work, Donna gave birth to a beautiful baby girl we named Lori Ann.

Home of the Walkin' Soldier

Timmy Mears was a ten-year-old boy dying of cancer. His will to live, and his celebrated desire to become a foot soldier, sparked a national effort of support for Timmy and his family. Given the prognosis, hearing from soldiers and reveling in their stories was as close as Timmy would get to soldiering. News articles about him, and of his interest in soldiers, inspired an onslaught of letters, cards, and poems from active and retired infantrymen worldwide. They offered prayers for recovery and stories about the duties and responsibilities of the American soldier. Many shared their personal combat experiences. Timmy's kind of upper-respiratory cancer quickly took his life, but his love of soldiers lived on in the hearts and minds of infantrymen everywhere. One such unit was HHC, Third Battalion, Third Brigade, named in his honor as Home of the Walkin' Soldier by the commanding officer, First Lieutenant Eric I. MacIntosh.

As First Sergeant Myers opened the door to Lieutenant MacIntosh's office, I found myself standing directly in front of an imposing, handsome, but stern figure sitting behind a modest gray metal desk. While standing at strict attention and saluting the commander, I said in an authoritative, matter-of-fact voice, "Sir, Lieutenant Yedinak reports." The importance of the first few minutes Lieutenant MacIntosh spent welcoming me to the company, defining my duties as training officer and providing a training schedule, was lost in his final directive when I turned about to leave. He said, "See the first sergeant and take out a bond."

I Beg Your Pardon?

My initial confusion quickly gave way to an understanding that he must have been talking about taking out a U.S. Savings Bond. As I began to internalize the issue—a direct order to participate in a voluntary program—my blood began to boil. I could feel my heart pound, my anger build, and a sense of fear prevail, since I knew my response was going to be something that, while necessary, would be fraught with risk. I have always been the kind of person who needs to confront a problem, or what could grow into a problem, head-on. I looked my new commanding officer directly in the eyes and, in a measured but disarming tone, said, "Sir, I will take out a fucking bond whenever and wherever I want, and not one minute before." I faced about and walked out. Bond? No fucking way.

I was directed to report for reveille at 0545 the next morning. On the short drive to our on-post quarters, I replayed my mental "tapes" in an attempt to determine if, given a second chance, I would have reacted differently to what I viewed as a personal insult and a poor leadership tactic. No, absolutely not.

Pushing Boots

Training new recruits off the streets of San Francisco, San Diego, and points in between, was not an easy job. My outrageous entrance into the Home of the Walkin' Soldier did not lighten the load. After reveille, Lieutenant MacIntosh gave me his initial instructions: report for reveille each morning, six days per week; stay with and train the company; conduct retreat at the end of the day; plan for training the following day; and so on. Sundays would be a relaxed schedule, from 0900 to 1500.

It was April or May, 1964, and it was obvious from the intense training schedule—not only the hours, but the type of training we were conducting—that the Vietnam War was definitely on the immediate horizon. Most days were from twelve to sixteen hours long, and combat infantry tactics and heavy weapons and demolitions were being taught to raw recruits. Occasionally, it was scary; some of the kids were not very bright, and you had to keep in mind that there were those who were trying to avoid the realities of fighting by intentionally screwing up. However, the overwhelming majority were just scared, and justly scared, but gave the training everything they had. Older and better-educated U.S. draftees helped the younger and less-educated Regular Army volunteers meet the training requirements. Me? I was in great shape, physically, but starting to drain emotionally.

Adaptation to the Military Way of Life: Is It Possible?

After about six months it became apparent, even to me, that the military operated in a way of its own. Few things on the outside had much impact on the life of an officer in the Infantry. The bond issue was the first clue that just as in Tennessee Ernie Ford's "Sixteen Tons," soldiers eventually were asked to sell their souls to the company store. Training policies and methods employed throughout the sixties focused on breaking the spirit of the human psyche and rebuilding what was left in a unique mold—like an engine part that can easily be replaced by another, identical part. There was little room for individualism. There was usually just one way to do things: the army way. The answers were easy, "Yes, sir," but few if any were very concerned about the questions; everything was one hundred percent. New recruits were herded into the mess hall, seated, provided the paperwork, and told to fill out the forms, sign them, and that as a result, $6.25 would be deducted from each month's paycheck for the privilege of owning a U.S. Savings Bond. No room for maneuver. No dissension. And that was on their first day!

If officers and noncoms had more flexibility, it was probably because they were less fearful about the consequences, although for R.A.'s who were pursuing a military career, the mold held. Living with my decision to "bet my bars" on the bond issue gave me the distinction of being the only holdout in the company for several eight-week cycles. There was peer pressure, and to be sure, I was caught between thinking that I'd done the right thing for the right reason and the wrong thing for the wrong reason. Why was it such a big deal, anyway? Was it instinctive? Second nature? Would there be other such episodes for me—for my individuality—during my three years in the army? And, of course, I was getting out just as soon as my initial three-year duty assignment was over. Perhaps sooner. I was already convinced that I was not cut out to be a soldier in the Army Officer Corps. There were simply too many instances of seemingly silly policies and programs that, in good conscience, I could not support, but because of my loyalty to the army and to my unit of assignment, I knew I must.

One such policy required all officers to pay officers club dues. The dues were only about three dollars per month, but there was something wrong, in my opinion, with a service-oriented organization that was not required to be self-sufficient. So when the battalion commander, Lieutenant Colonel Ricardo Cardenas, wanted to raise the monthly club dues by twenty-five cents, I was dismayed. And when we were told that those voting no would have to report to the battalion commander, in dress greens, at 2200 hours on Friday night to explain their positions, I was furious.

I told the battalion S-3, who was collecting the votes, "Tell the battalion commander not only no, but hell no; there is no way I want to miss the Friday night meeting."

Five of thirty-three officers reported to the battalion commander, and when Lieutenant Colonel Cardenas asked me first to explain my reason, I said, "Because I was told that if I voted no I would have to report to you, in dress greens, at 2200 hours on Friday night to explain my position. And there was no way I was going to miss that. What a bunch of bullshit!"

When he asked the second officer for an explanation, First Lieutenant Menendez remarked, "Sir, I thought I had a pretty good reason, but I like Lieutenant Yedinak's answer better."

This became the rally cry of the remaining three officers. Twenty-eight officers voted for the increase, and five didn't. It was not the money, but the way in which C.O.'s typically used intimidation instead of reason to get what they wanted. Unfortunately, it usually worked, and those in opposition became known as renegades. Efficiency reports were lowered for "lack of cooperation, and lack of tact." So, in effect, the army was teaching this required way of behavior through its commanders, and eventually, to survive, one felt compelled to adapt and adjust to one's environment.

But within that environment, I learned to be as hard as nails. I eventually took out a savings bond, but was honest enough to let Lieutenant MacIntosh know that I didn't appreciate his leadership style in taking me for granted. He understood.

It became apparent that I had a lot to learn about how to deal with NCOs. In my ROTC training, and at Benning, I was taught that officers—even young and inexperienced ones—should establish their authority early on, so as not to relinquish control of their units to their subordinates. We were to take charge. Make them understand who was in charge. Unfortunately, it doesn't work that way. The platoon sergeants in our battalion had an average of ten to twelve years' experience, some over twenty years. All but a few had combat experience. None ever indicated they were the least bit interested in seizing command of the platoon. So, after a few close calls, I finally learned that a young, inexperienced officer could command the unit while the experienced NCO could run it on a day-to-day basis. Tactical maneuvers, where to place the automatic weapons, where and under which conditions the unit would eat, how and when ammunition would be distributed and controlled during an engagement, could all be easily planned and controlled by the NCO. There was and would always be a special place in my heart for the infantry NCOs with whom I had the privilege to work.

Lieutenant MacIntosh thought there was plenty of evidence that smoking caused upper respiratory infection. Therefore, the troops were not allowed to smoke during the training day. On one occasion, enforcing his policy, I gave out twenty-eight Article 15s to trainees who broke the no-smoking policy in the training area. I wondered if the commander would actually process them, and learned through the grapevine that he used the signed paperwork to scare the shit out of them—one by one—but then dismissed the charges. I guess that was one of the differences between MacIntosh and me. Had it been my choice, I would have had little sympathy, and would have maxed them out—seven days in jail, and two-thirds of one month's pay for six months. I didn't like the no-smoking policy in the first place, but when asked to enforce it, it seemed important to me to make it stick.

Because of my actions within the battalion, I was quickly

gaining a reputation as a "hardass." Hard, but fair—that was the rap! I didn't mind that, as it came naturally to me. I had no quarrels with the army's need for standards, nor the consistent application of punishment for violations. What I objected to was the veiled threat of the use of force that many commanders found more accommodating for their reputations and the longevity of their careers.

In any event, when MacIntosh was called upstairs to the division G-3 Operations office, I took over command of HHC, and the Home of the Walkin' Soldier. The date was September 1, 1964. As a commander, I would have a chance to see if it was possible to make the kind of changes I felt were needed— to eliminate some of the bullshit policies.

One such policy required that a paper tag be tied to any window, wall locker, light fixture, and so on, that needed to be replaced or repaired. The next Command Maintenance Management Inspection (CMMI) was a good test run to determine whether, and to what extent, a commander could challenge a dumb policy. When the head inspector, a full colonel, began to comment about the missing tags, I responded by saying that in HHC we didn't use tags because it was a stupid idea. He said, "You have to use tags, that's the policy." I said, "Not in my company." We used a simple log of items that required replacement or repair—I showed him the log maintained by the supply sergeant—and told him that under no circumstances would I use the tags. I reasoned that the tags themselves had become a logistical problem—worn tags, out-of-date tags, torn and unsightly tags—that expended the time and energy of those who would better be used to effect the repairs, and that our soldiers deserved life in a clean, untagged environment. He replied that he would have to write me up. I said, I could give a shit less. My NCOs back at Gonzaga would have been proud of me. I think.

Needless to say, I was somewhat surprised, on December 21, 1964, to receive a Letter of Commendation from Department of the Army, Headquarters Sixth United States Army, for achieving an overall score of 99 percent. So much for tags!

R.A.—No Way! But Wait . . .

Is it possible I was becoming one of them? Or had my ROTC instructors known something I had failed to see? Was I beginning to sell my soul to the company store? Was I destined to become just another rubber stamp, or would I learn how to create my own space within the framework of an Army that appeared to be extremely autocratic? Individuality had always been important to me. Adhering to reasonable standards was not a problem for me, but some of the established criteria seemed to be patently unreasonable. Remember, I was the high school kid who, more often than not, walked on the other side of the street. Even so, within the battalion, I was starting to be treated as if I were someone who would opt to change my Reserve status—with its one-time, three-year commitment—to that of Regular Army and a full-blown military career. Following are two typical examples of what senior officers liked about my positive attitude and concomitant behavior.

Lieutenant Colonel Cardenas, my battalion commander, needing to fill a requirement for a graduation ceremony, called to ask me if I had a trumpet player in the company. Without thinking, I said, "Sir, just look outside your window fifteen minutes from now and you will see a whole goddamn brass band."

On another occasion, when one of the battalion officers was having a hard time getting used to the rigors of basic training, Cardenas called to say, "Yedinak, he's yours, and if you can't straighten him out, he's out of the service." Cardenas had indicated that this officer was a bachelor who liked to stay in the company all hours of the night to counsel troops who were having a hard time.

When Lieutenant O'Shay reported to me, I was sitting precisely in the same chair MacIntosh had been in when I first reported to him, and was probably in the same overworked mood. I told O'Shay exactly what the battalion commander had told me. I then asked him what he thought about that, and what I could expect his behavior to reflect. He began to tell me that there were a lot of troops who needed help, and that with his background in the social sciences, he understood their difficulties and wanted to counsel those who needed help. I said that we were there to train troops, not to conduct a social experiment, and that I myself had a degree in psychology but felt neither qualified nor inclined to "mother" the troops. He disagreed, and began to detail the number of ways he could be of assistance. All this took about five minutes, after which I told him there were three rules he would have to follow if he wanted to remain in the service: (1) he would not be allowed to report to the company before the start of the training day, (2) he would not be able to remain in the company area after training had concluded, and (3) he would not be allowed to counsel troops during the training day. He reluctantly agreed. Lieutenant O'Shay and I became reasonably good friends in the process. He proved himself an effective training officer, and was able to remain in the service. A victory of sorts. But there were other events that sometimes caused me to wonder if indeed I had any place at all in the Regular Army.

One such issue involved maintaining the mess hall furniture. One day, there was a notice in the post bulletin saying that any company that wanted its tables and chairs refinished should contact the post headquarters for an appointment. We did, and when I had our furniture delivered to the collection point, our mess sergeant was told that we couldn't just leave it, but had to provide the labor detail to actually do the job. So, when he called to tell me he was reloading the furniture and would then return to the company area, he couldn't have known what I had in mind when I asked him to hand me the phone so I could talk to the post civil service representative. Screaming into the phone, I said, "Look, you motherfucker, I am going to tell my mess sergeant to unload the motherfucking furniture right in front of your doorway and return to the company without it. And I expect you to let me know when you've refinished the furniture. We're in training, there are no breaks, there are no troops who I will ask to do this, and if you won't refinish the motherfucking furniture, it will just sit there and rot."

When I hung up, I thought I'd better let the battalion commander know exactly what I'd just done, as I anticipated an angry call from post headquarters to the battalion.

The battalion executive officer—second in command—answered the phone. When I'd finished telling him what had happened, with all the graphic details, he said, "I only have one question: Was he military or civilian?" When I said he was civil service, the XO told me not to worry about it.

Nevertheless, I did worry about it. For my level of education and my Catholic upbringing, I began to wonder why it was apparently so important to behave in such a counterproductive way. I had always been my own harshest critic, and I was now beginning to think that I was coming unglued. Was the strange new environment taking its toll on me, or was I finding a more comfortable place to exercise my newly discovered brand of absolute authority?

After about a year, when asked if I'd given any thought to becoming a regular officer, without much thought I told the battalion commander: "Fuck no. Given the way you treat me, what I'm required to do, and the limited time I have to spend with my wife, there is no way I want to apply for a Regular Army commission."

But apply I did. The realities of the Vietnam War were closing in on me, and I realized that if I was going to be able to serve my country there, I would have to voluntarily extend my length of service for eighteen months while making application for Regular Army. My request for "Vol-Indefinite" was approved within six months, but an R.A. commission was a lengthy process requiring a presidential decision—or, at least, his signature. Of the many lieutenants who applied for an extension, only a few in the brigade were rewarded. Encouraged, I attributed my acceptance to my take-charge attitude, knowledge of training, uncompromising character, loyalty and support to the chain of command, my boyish good looks, and my expert infantry skills.

Applying for R.A. was, for me, almost an instinctive choice. It wasn't so much that I wanted to be a soldier, but more a reaction to questions about what to do with my life and how best to support our family. Donna disliked the long hours of military life, as did I, and I labored with the realization that I was unable to help her as much as I might have wanted. It seemed that, in spite of being in excellent physical condition, I was usually tired when I got home.

We began to train newly formed units in basic and advanced unit tactics. The incorporation of Vietnam subjects increased the normal training day from twelve to sixteen hours, with a major increase in night training. At times there were only a few hours between the end of one day's training and the start of the next day. We endured three- to five-day field exercises without a break. When I began to realize that my options were few, that my B.A. in psychology offered few opportunities in the civilian world, the most reasonable choice prevailed. Still, I had doubts that my record would support integration into the Regular Army. But in spite of my frequent outbursts, my record was mostly positive.

On September 18, 1964, on his departure from the battalion, Lieutenant Colonel Cardenas presented me with a Letter of Appreciation for "outstanding contributions to both the Third Battalion and the military service." Among those things he said warranted special commendation were my personal drive, leadership ability, willingness to work long hours, organizational abilities, and the ability to motivate my men.

The Expert Infantryman Badge

The EIB—Expert Infantryman Badge—was awarded to only a few of the several hundred officers and enlisted men who agreed to voluntarily undergo a six-week-long test of physical and tactical skills and abilities. The competition ranged from knowledge of general military subjects, like weapons, mines and booby traps, and military justice, to completing the grueling twelve-mile road march with full combat equipment in two hours or less. The combat gear, including the M-1 Garand rifle, steel helmet, and combat pack filled with rocks, weighed about forty-five pounds. The march route wound its way through the sandy hills and trails of Laguna Seca, the area of Fort Ord, California, known for racing. Temperature? About ninety degrees. All in all, the march proved to be one of the most physically demanding challenges I had ever undertaken.

Basically, to complete the march successfully, one had to jog at a fairly rapid pace for the entire length of the course. Earning the EIB was a distinct honor for any infantryman, but for me it was even more special, a single significant achievement that convinced me that, regardless of my poor showing in ROTC and the Officers' Basic Course at Fort Benning just eighteen months earlier, I had become one of the best young infantrymen in the entire United States Army. It was as if my demons had been released. I was confident in my military abilities for the first time.

Special Warfare Orientation Course

Fort Bragg, North Carolina, was the home of the United States Army Special Forces. SF soldiers—Green Berets—were the army's elite combat force. As I reported in on Temporary Duty Orders, October 25, 1964, the Vietnam conflict was beginning to occupy the American mind, and the new organization popularized by JFK was taking on a life of its own. Attendance required a Secret security clearance. During the fourteen-day course, students began to develop an appreciation for the Third World and the growing number of insurgencies therein. And, of course, they began to learn that the Russians and their satellite nations, including Fidel Castro in Cuba, had a plan to take over the world by picking off one country at a time. The so-called "Domino Theory" suggested that if Country A fell, then B would fall, and so forth. And the only way to deal with this grand strategy was to come to the aid of Country A, in our case, Vietnam. The French had fought in Vietnam from 1948 to 1954. The U.S. financed eighty percent of the French intervention. When the French troops were defeated at Dien Bien Phu after underestimating the power of the Viet Minh and the difficulties associated with fighting in the mountains and tropical jungles of South Vietnam, the civil war began to smolder. Military and political insurgency experts representing many countries spoke about and showed the resulting horrors of a Vietnam untamed.

Within the two-week curriculum it was hard not to come away with the understanding that the U.S. had a substantial investment in Vietnam, and the U.S. Army Special Forces were destined to play a major role. I have to admit that I was getting pretty psyched-up about the prospects of being on the leading edge of such an effort. Learning about the culture, religion, customs, and mores of another people was exciting. Reading Bernard Fall's *Street Without Joy* and other books, like *Two Vietnams*, gave one an insight into the nature of the struggle and the special requirements it called for. It all seemed like pretty heady stuff for a young lieutenant whose chief concern had been whether or not to stay in the service.

I left Bragg with a new sense of commitment and an eagerness to return someday soon to complete the training required to earn the Green Beret. For the time being, I was overjoyed to get back to Fort Ord and Headquarters Company in time to enjoy the Christmas holidays with Donna, who was six months pregnant with our second child, and Lori, who was about eight months old.

Training: Was the Treatment Worse than the Cure?

My return to Fort Ord left little doubt that, in training, there were two armies. One was the conventional army, the needs of which were appropriately reflected in the day-to-day regimen at Fort Ord. This army was the by-product of recruiting ordinary young men off the streets of Los Angeles, San Diego, and San Francisco, sending them to a U.S. Army combat training center, placing them under the direct control of hyperactive officers and NCOs, and systematically reducing them through torturous training to pliable but effective replacement parts for the handful of specialties requiring a "kill or be killed" mentality. Fort Ord and other such training centers were preparing men for the conventional army. The army of the masses. The soldiers whose only lifeline at the killing level was their dependence on each other. Disciplined. Unquestioning. Physically fit. Mentally hardened. Follow orders, and live—or die. We had our share of crybabies, fat boys, and mentally retarded in the Home of the Walkin' Soldier. But the eight-week training cycle reduced to a very low number the misfits who were eventually discharged as mentally and/or physically undesirable. For that army, the rigor of training was literally "on the edge." The theory of training was really quite predictable. Socratic. Young men would become more disciplined by being disciplined more. More unquestioning by being required to follow more orders. More physically fit by more physical training. And more emotionally stable by being made to endure the seemingly impossible, and living through it.

There were, however, times when this social experiment failed. One such time was when a young company commander in a sister brigade pushed a physically challenged, allegedly sick trainee beyond his endurance level. The soldier was in his fourth week of training when, on the night before the twenty-mile road march, he reported to sick-call. The captain, a former Marine enlisted soldier who had won a Medal of Honor at eighteen for falling on a live grenade during the Korean conflict, believing the trainee was "copping a plea" based on his inability to finish several shorter marches, ordered a "type code red." That night, the captain and two trainee accomplices beat the shit out of the trainee, then force-marched him around the same twenty-mile march route that would be used the following morning. Sometime after midnight, they dumped his bruised and bleeding body into his bunk. Forced to make the scheduled march, often being dragged along by "buddies" who feared for his life if he did not finish the march, the trainee succumbed. In the afternoon sun, with a fifty-pound sack of rocks and full combat gear, being disciplined, following orders, being "physically trained and mentally hardened," he died on the march. The captain tried to hide the results of his effort as simply another "training accident."

I learned this directly from the company executive officer, a friend and fellow lieutenant, who called me from his on-post quarters to tell me what happened, and to tell me he feared for his life. I admired his honesty, knew he was in danger, and told him to inform his brigade commander. The lieutenant said he would. He did. Within hours the killer-captain notified the brigade duty officer that he was on his way to the lieutenant's home to kill him. Within minutes the brigade commander ordered my friend to stay in his quarters, and to lock all doors and windows. The military police were there within minutes. The MPs intercepted the captain on the front porch of the lieutenant's quarters. He was armed with a fully loaded .45 caliber pistol. When they searched his car, they found an arsenal of weapons, ammunition, and live fragmentation grenades.

Final score? Trainee, dead. Commander, thirty years. Training went on without a hiccup following an "event" that was not highly publicized. Little wonder. A trained killer was training a potential killer using killer-training techniques. To be honest, what happened to the trainee was clearly the exception. But to be equally honest, training was torturous, and one cannot, and should not, unquestioningly dismiss all training failures as "training accidents." But for me, after having been "schooled" in the ways of the conventional army at Fort Ord, that brief experience at the Special Forces Orientation Course captured my imagination. It was then that I knew I wanted to compete with the best for the ultimate U.S. Army challenge, the Green Beret.

Special Forces Officer Course

It was with mixed feelings that I reported to Fort Bragg, North Carolina, on January 17, 1965. To be sure, I was elated to have been selected to attend the Special Forces Officer

Course, which was to run for almost twelve weeks. Unfortunately, Donna was about seven-and-a-half-months pregnant, so I would be unable to be with her for the birth of our second child.

The training was excellent. We were treated to a significant schedule of guest lecturers, and the classroom and field training were superb. It was easy to have a healthy respect for the SF cadre, many of whom had recent wartime experience in Vietnam. The first few weeks were spent digging deeper into the nature of insurgency and discussing the SF missions, including counterinsurgency and unconventional warfare. The format for training was the A-team. My A-team included an Army captain, two Marine Corps lieutenants, and eleven Army lieutenants. Part of the training was devoted to survival techniques, including how to catch and prepare snakes, fish, small animals, plants, and other jungle fare. As a special treat, one entire day was devoted to eating every imaginable morsel one might encounter in the wilderness.

Of course, a lot of training concentrated on assorted ways to effectively kill people and destroy things. We learned how to use and maintain all U.S. and most foreign weapons, and the use of silencers and special killing techniques. Most of the techniques were then, and remain, classified. There were some airborne missions, mostly at night, as we were all parachute qualified, and parachute insertion is one means of getting into enemy-held territory. Codes, setting up drop zones for re-supply, navigation, and battlefield techniques for saving lives were also taught. We learned the structures of foreign governments and how to effectively work with indigenous forces like Vietnam's Montagnards (from the French for "mountain people"). Mostly it was a matter of knowing the culture and being sensitive to local customs. And, of course, we spent quite a bit of time learning about the South Vietnamese Special Forces, and the forces under their command.

Training for the first month or so was uneventful, but very early in the morning of February 5, 1965, I received a very sad telephone call from Donna's father. Mr. Simons said that Donna had given birth prematurely to our second daughter, but that there was only about a fifty-fifty chance that the baby would live; she had a serious stomach obstruction, was jaundiced, and needed a complete blood exchange. I was devastated. There is no worse feeling than being away when your child is born. Complications make the situation worse, and when the prognosis is unfavorable, there is little to do but pray. So, pray I did, and it was comforting to know that as a Catholic I could rely on an all-knowing and all-loving God, and that whatever was supposed to happen would happen. I asked God to let me know what I could do—should I go or stay? The baby's operation was scheduled for the next morning, and Donna's dad said there was really nothing to be gained by returning to Puyallup, where Donna was staying with her family during my absence. He would advise.

Needless to say, training on February fifth was a distraction for me. I couldn't wait for the day to end, when I could be alone to think and to pray. I was looking for some sign early that evening. I was already promising that if she came through the operation, I would attend daily mass in the mornings whenever there was not a training conflict. Then I waited.

As I walked into the common area on the ground floor of our quarters that evening, several officer students were watching TV. It was about 1900 hours and "Dr. Kildare" was about to begin. The episode was about a newborn infant with a stomach obstruction for whom a blood exchange was to be performed. So I witnessed a reenactment of every aspect of the procedure that would be used the following morning on our baby girl. When the program ended one hour later, and the operation was a success, I picked up the phone to call Donna and let her know what had happened. Fate? Grace? The power of prayer? As far as I was concerned, it had somehow been given to me that our daughter would come through the operation. I began to realize that the sacrifices that Donna and I had been called on to make, and those to be made in the future, perhaps me in Vietnam and her raising small children alone, were somehow necessary and directly proportionate to the pleasures we would enjoy in our lives together as a family.

I made good on my promise to attend mass when I could,

and from that day forward training took on a new meaning for me. I began to understand where I was supposed to go with my life, and my commitment to the Army was becoming less tenuous. At that point, though without orders, I knew my next assignment would be to the Fifth Special Forces Group (Airborne), then the only Special Forces unit in Southeast Asia.

The final weeks of training consisted of deployments to the field in a major test of each student's ability to effectively operate in an insurgency environment, to survive using the skills he had learned, and to receive a passing grade on an as yet unspecified mission for which each of us would be in command. The exercise, called Cherokee Trail, began with a nighttime airborne drop deep into the mountainous regions of the forests adjacent to Fort Bragg. Some of the people who lived in and near the area role-played the partisans, and, during the course of the exercise, might be prevailed upon for mission support. Others played the role of the insurgents. Of course, SF A-teams had no idea who was who, and so had to rely on the skills learned during the training to make that determination.

About two days into the exercise, during a tactical movement, our team was caught in a firefight. During the breakout, several of us became separated and had to survive on our own. Two of us decided to go to town to see if we could locate a partisan. For that operation, we ditched our military weapons and equipment, donned street clothes, and in broad daylight walked into a neighborhood tavern. After several beers, we began to slowly establish our identities with one of the patrons who appeared to be sympathetic. The connection worked. We were told to proceed to a location underneath a bridge, where, about midnight, we would be picked up by a farmer driving an old pickup truck. We found the bridge, were picked up on schedule, and within an hour were cleaning up and sharing a much treasured hot meal with a local farm family. After a good night's sleep and a full day of rest, our partisan drove us under the cover of darkness to a drop-off point at which we were met by one of our own messengers and taken to the location of our friendly forces, where we rejoined our own A-team.

A day or two later, as darkness approached, a messenger gave me a torn piece of paper containing mission instructions. I was to assemble my team of four SF students, brief them on our mission, make final preparations, and depart within two hours toward the mission site. Successful mission accomplishment was required to qualify for the SF patch, and the coveted prefix 3 which would be attached to the standard infantry Military Occupational Specialty (MOS) code.

The mission: receive an airborne resupply at a designated location at 0200 two days following. Implicit in this mission was to place the site under surveillance, by 0200 hours the following morning, for twenty-four hours, set up and man the drop zone (DZ), and, using the correct light patterns and flashlight codes, direct the plane to drop the resupply at the designated location and time. The designated drop zone was twelve kilometers away. I directed Captain Ed Chandler to handle the navigation because he had more experience with a map and compass than the others, and because he had a Rolex watch. Timing was paramount. The drop, to be successful, had to be made between 0158 and 0202, a window of only four minutes.

We moved out within the hour, because I anticipated some difficulty in getting to the location by 0200. We walked for what seemed like hours through a huge swamp, with water up to our waists. When we broke free, we were on track for the designated spot. It was starting to snow. Wearily, we tactically walked an azimuth designed to reach our destination. At about 0100 we sensed we were in the general area. Two teams completed a reconnaissance to fix the exact drop zone location. Once satisfied we were in the right place, I established a schedule of two-man teams to keep the area secure for the next twenty-four hours. We used metal containers and gas procured along the route to establish the required eight-light set by midnight. The DZ was established and ready for use. So far, so good.

About 0155, we began to hear the drone of the drop plane as it approached the DZ. If we were right, the plane would approach our location on an azimuth of 270 degrees, and be over the DZ about 0200. At exactly 0158, I faced due east, my right foot fixed on the impact point at the mouth of the light set, and turned on the flashlight that would direct the plane on the designated azimuth over the DZ. At precisely 0200 the drop was made, and shortly thereafter we could all see the small resupply pallet, arrested by a drag chute, fall to the ground. Nothing to it.

During the final days of outprocessing, each of us met with our assignment officer to learn where we would be going after our stateside duty was completed. My orders were for the Eighth Special Forces Group (Airborne) in the Republic of Panama. I told the assignment officer I was going to Vietnam. My orders were changed, and I began to see just why some of my ROTC instructors wanted me in the army infantry.

Graduation was an important "rite of passage," but I longed to be again with Donna and Lori, and to see our baby daughter Kimberly Christine for the first time. Although she was paper thin, in the following months I learned that, if nothing else, she had a mind of her own. Aware that I might not return from Vietnam, I relaxed my work schedule in favor of more quality time with Donna and our two young daughters.

First Tour of Duty—Lasting Impressions

A young officer's first tour of duty is a major learning experience. The lessons taken away influence future behavior, and in some respects determine whether, or to what extent, the officer will prove to be a trustworthy leader. There are many situations in which a young, impressionable officer finds himself that require judgment, responsibility, loyalty, leadership, and followership. Throughout, it is important to be oneself, if for no other reason than to clearly establish who you are so others may be able to react more consistently in your presence.

In the military, particularly in combat, there is most often not enough time for equivocation. Leaders must be decisive. After my first tour of duty, I began to see in myself the things that the Gonzaga University staff saw in me that led them to support my application for the advanced ROTC program and that pushed me to eventually seek and complete a military career. I have nothing but gratitude for the professional officers who so strongly upheld their sense of trust in me even when I was beginning to distrust myself. That, of course, is the true test of professionalism. As I reread the letters of commendation and the citation for the Army Commendation Medal given to me on my departure from Fort Ord, I am overwhelmed that my fellow officers—commanders, leaders, comrades—were able to say so many nice things about me and the accomplishments achieved.

Perhaps more important were the kind words spoken by the noncommissioned officers and the lessons they taught throughout my tour at Fort Ord. I will never forget them, and there would be little doubt that they would ever forget me. Why? Because I am unforgettable. That's what the ROTC staff saw, that's what my comrades at Fort Ord saw, that is what those who will be introduced in this book saw, and that is what I see. This is not some self-serving accolade. Far from it. Remember my unforgivable behavior to the loyal civil servant who was trying to explain the post policy on the refinishing of the mess furniture? Unforgettable. They let me be me. That's the point. Oh, there were some who desperately tried to change my behavior, and to some extent, as I gained more experience, they succeeded. Good for them. But by and large, I was able to complete a twenty-six-year career with some measure of success while being myself. And that is so very important to me. So what did they say? Why were their words so important?

Just a synopsis: "His company attained excellent ratings in all training subjects; through his efforts, a new post record for basic trainees in the physical combat proficiency test was established; his company finished first out of forty-seven companies tested in the end-of-training cycle proficiency test; his careful analysis of problems and his calm professionalism led to an effective reorganization of the operations section, thereby contributing immensely to the successful accomplishment of the training mission of the 3D Brigade; his untiring efforts, dedicated leadership, and devotion to duty were in keeping with the highest traditions of the military service and reflected great credit upon himself, the organization, and the United States Army."

The demons were there. The demons were conquered. The lack of self-respect that, until then, I had so carefully reserved for myself, was gone. By seeing that, inside, there was nothing to hide, I could turn and face the light. The United States Army, the largest corporation in the world, through its representatives—the officers and men of the 3D Brigade—let me be my indomitable, outgoing, highly conceptual, decision-by-feeling, out-in-the-world self. Outrageous. Certainly, no other business venture, large or small, could afford to let its first-line managers behave in such a megalomaniacal way without endangering the bottom line. But then, no other firm has a similar mission—kill people and destroy things. Unfortunately, the army and its trained killers are inextricably linked for the duration of the contract. Unforgettable. Stay tuned!

Leaving a Family—Going to War

When going to war is your first choice, there are many questions that beg answer. God, country, family, self. Not clear enough? The price of freedom will always be high, especially for those who choose a military career. Some pay the highest price so the rest of us may continue down life's main roads, and the many side roads, in pursuit of our objectives and our dreams. While some have families, children, position, and power; others have only the soil of some small, distant field.

Well, in my mind, I never left my family. I chose to go to war so I could better contribute to whatever value we choose to place on freedom. When I was saying my good-byes, knowing full well that I might not return, I was saying my final good-byes. I wanted to return to my family, but only after I'd paid the price of freedom, whatever it turned out to be.

Also, to be sure, I wanted to establish myself within the profession I had chosen to pursue. When you start at the bottom in a large corporation, you sweep the hallways. And sweep them well you must. Or the corporate leaders will simply find someone else who is willing and able to do a better job for the same pay. We have all swept a hallway or two. Only when it has become quite clear to the corporate leadership that the jobs given have been well accomplished will that same leadership decide to give you more work and, perhaps, higher pay.

So, as a young lieutenant from Spokane, Washington, I was leaving my family and friends with mixed emotions. I did not want to go, but knew I must. Is that not what love and commitment are all about? How can you pretend to love someone if you are not able to contribute to the very condition—in this case freedom—that permits that love to continue to flourish? I left Donna, and my two daughters, Lori and Kim—just ten and a half months apart in age—to in some small way ante up, to make the pot right. To make damn sure that when the final count was taken, no one would find the Yedinak family short. We were all in it together. But I knew that for every mother who is burdened with the responsibility of raising a family alone, there is a father who has been denied that opportunity.

So much for philosophy. We are going to war! Want to ride along? Want to vicariously feel what it's like to don a green beret in the jungles of Vietnam, up close and personal? Knowing that you desperately want to return home, but that the only reasonable way that can happen is if you do your job very, very well, and have incredibly good luck to boot? If so, put on your own beret, say good-bye to your loved ones, and consider yourself booked on a large commercial airliner en route to the Republic of Vietnam. Our first stop will be Ton Son Nhut Air Base located in the III Corps Tactical Zone within the capital city of Saigon. When we arrive, we will have been flying for about twenty-four hours, and have had the opportunity—a rather cruel diversion from reality—of a short pit stop in Honolulu, Hawaii. The date is March 3, 1966.

Welcome to the Fifth Special
Forces Group (Airborne)

For those who know, there is nothing quite like stepping from the door of a commercial airliner and slowly walking down the long flight of stairs onto the hot, steamy tarmac of Ton Son Nhut Air Base. The stench of this Third World environment, the rotting flesh and slowly decaying human and animal by-products fill your nostrils in such a way that you will never be able to forget the experience. Ask anyone. They will tell you that the brain has forever reserved a special place for the initial sights, sounds, and smells of South Vietnam. There are the usual security procedures one expects in a war zone—military police augmented by local police, referred to as White Mice—but much more. Steel gates, signs for arriving service members, money exchange facilities, customs, and, if you're lucky, a representative from the unit to which you are being assigned. One of the things you should be prepared for is that, in a war zone, except on the battlefield, things happen very slowly. That's because the movement of personnel— that's you and me—is almost entirely dependent on an open jeep, bus, or, when moving within the country from city to city, a military plane on a space-available basis. I was fortunate to have been picked up by my unit, taken directly to Company A headquarters in Bien Hoa, about twenty miles from Saigon, and introduced to several of the staff. Later, I joined some of the officers in a happy hour—another cruel diversion. There, I was introduced to the commander of Company A, Lieutenant Colonel J. B. Durst.

Durst was very handsome, well-tanned, silver-haired, fit and trim, and was, of course, drinking a martini. A most engaging personality. He welcomed me to the unit and indicated that after a few days on site, I would be flown to the Fifth Group headquarters in Nha Trang for an in-briefing by Colonel Kelly, the Group commander. Durst was known affectionately in the headquarters as "old silver tongue," but to many, when pissed, he became "old stiletto tongue."

Major Ron Robinson, the operations officer to whom I was

being assigned as an assistant S-3, Operations and Training, was a tall, lanky, happy guy who ended up taking me under his wing and becoming one of my best friends on that initial tour to Vietnam. He cared about me, made me feel at home, ensured I had quarters, and offered me his hand in learning the structure, operations, and training agenda of the Fifth Group. A few days later I was taken to the Bien Hoa Air Base for a flight to Nha Trang. On arrival, I began to experience the normal anxiety of a new Green Beret.

Colonel Kelly, known throughout the Group as Blackjack, did not stand on pomp and circumstance. When I was asked to enter his office, the ruddy, rather large hulk of a soldier told me to be at ease. He reeked of experience, and I was sure he was going to say something purposeful and useful. I could hardly wait. When he began to speak, the words made their way into my brain such that I will go to my grave with a verbatim transcript of his philosophy concerning members of the Fifth Special Forces Group. With a gravelly voice, he said, "Welcome to the Fifth. There are five kinds of people I don't like—I don't like drunks, I don't like clowns, I don't like bums, I don't like men that cheat on their wives, and I don't like buglers, and by buglers I mean someone who talks badly about the Fifth outside of the Group. If I find out you fall into one or more of these categories, you will be forced to leave the Group and find your own baseball cap, do you understand?"

Well, that was clear enough for me, how about you? What Colonel Kelly meant by "find your own baseball cap" was that you would not even enjoy the courtesy of being reassigned. You would just pick up your shit, walk down the road, and look for a straight-leg (non-Airborne) infantry unit that would have you. In effect, exchange your beret, forever, for the olive-drab baseball cap worn by leg outfits. Strong measures, indeed. Had I received his transmission? "Fucking-A. Roger. Out!"

I spent a few days in Nha Trang, waiting for a flight out. Nha Trang was a relatively upscale, robust, French-cultured metropolis filled with tiny shops of every kind spawned to support its inhabitants, an odd collection of Eurasian minorities. The eastern reaches of the city are situated on the South China Sea, and it sports beautiful beaches and restaurants featuring some of the finest seafood in the world. By day, one had the impression that the war was in a state of suspended animation, as few clues were evident that, indeed, there was cause for concern. Cyclos,* bicycles, and a few European cars cluttered the streets, while entrepreneurial interests competed for the few Americans with money to spend. I thought to myself that Nha Trang would be a delightful place for a return visit someday, with dollars for large lobsters and time for the beach. As it happened, there was little time for anything except to "hurry up and wait." Sitting at the air base, waiting for a maybe flight, never knowing just when or how I would reach my next destination, had already become a way of life.

Also, while I was there, the camp was hit by indirect artillery and mortar fire, just to let us know that ol' Mr. Charles—as in VC, Viet Cong—was thinking about us.

---

*Three-wheel pedicab. Unlike in a rickshaw, cyclo drivers sit behind the customer and pedal the contraption through traffic, rather than pull it.

III

Vietnam—A War Without Boundaries

During the return flight from Nha Trang to Bien Hoa, I couldn't help but reflect on the ominous words of Colonel Kelly. Was he serious? For a senior commander to focus his in-brief on such a negative philosophy—or was it psychology?—told me that either he was trying to squelch widespread indiscretions within the Fifth Group or that he knew that combat assignments had a way of reducing man to his basic instincts. I got the feeling that his code was meant to address both issues. Being so far away from home under such uncertain conditions would undoubtedly create significant challenges. In any event, he impressed me, but I wondered whether or to what extent one could adhere to such platitudes.

Home Away from Home

I felt lucky returning to Company A, known as C-3 in SF parlance. Having met Robinson, I considered my job gratuitous, but working at "higher headquarters" would give me time to get my feet on the ground before being directly involved in combat operations. On the U.S. side, C-3 supervised USSF operations throughout the III CTZ through five B-teams geographically situated to support operations within a specified area. Normally, each B-team was assigned four to five A-teams. The A-team, consisting of a USSF commander and ten to twelve personnel, advised the Vietnamese Special Forces—LLDB (Luc-Luong-Dac-Biet)—directly charged with the responsibility for combat operations within their tactical area of operational responsibility (TAOR). Within each A-camp, the LLDB recruited, equipped, trained, and deployed a Civilian Irregular Defense Group (CIDG) consisting of five to eight hundred combat soldiers. As Assistant S-3 for Operations and Training, I was in a position to learn the nature of the operations through the daily combat situation reports, and through scheduled visits to the various B-teams and A-teams throughout the zone. The U.S. operations staff advised Vietnamese counterparts. My Vietnamese counterpart was Second Lieutenant Nguyen Vanh Song, a very bright, happy-go-lucky young officer. I was pleased.

Most C-3 personnel were quartered in the III Corps compound, a rather large, two-story, hotel-type concrete building without air-conditioning. I was double-bunked in the hallway with many others. Although each bunk had a full overhead mosquito net, they were a pain in the ass, and only marginally effective. However, without nets, you ran the risk of hundreds of bites in one night, and possible malaria. The screened hallways failed to screen out the lightning-fast lizards and snakes native to the area, and occasionally rats joined the party. March weather patterns, moderate with temperatures in the eighties but very high humidity, regularly produced intense, monsoonlike afternoon showers. Jeep transportation was available from the III Corps compound to the III Corps mess, where we ate our meals when in garrison, and to the C-3 tactical operations center where I worked.

My job responsibilities were to assist the S-3, Major Robinson, in advising our operation's counterparts in the planning, support, and conduct of military operations and civic action projects within the III CTZ. In reality, it was more difficult to establish and maintain effective working relationships with our assigned counterparts than one might think, because of cultural differences, customs, mores, and the indeterminable philosophical questions about how the war should be fought.

The Vietnamese were patient, and the U.S. usually wanted to get something done "on my watch," which meant significant progress during the one-year assignment that commanders and senior advisers normally served. Another hurdle was the Vietnamese mentality that virtually all Americans were "rich" and the reality that most Vietnamese were very poor. Actually, by Vietnamese standards, the U.S. service personnel *were* rich. But that's only because Vietnamese standards were so dismal. In real terms, most Vietnamese soldiers did not enjoy the luxury of indoor plumbing, potable water, electricity, hardwood or concrete floors, refrigeration, or shelter from the elements. Most Americans retained only about a hundred dollars a month from their paychecks, allotting the rest to their stateside spouses, families, or friends. U.S. pay was in Military Payment Certificates (MPC) to counter the huge value of U.S. "greenbacks" in the black market. During the 1967-68 period, the legal conversion rate was about 118 MPC for each U.S. dollar. On the black market, one could easily get five dollars MPC for each U.S. dollar. With these known differences, and some more subtle issues introduced as time passed, I attempted to gain the confidence of my counterpart, Second Lieutenant Song, while doing my best to serve Major Robinson, my rater, and Lieutenant Colonel Durst.

My day-to-day duties included working in the TOC, monitoring combat operations, reviewing situation reports (sitreps), compiling and briefing each morning an operational summary for the command group and C-3 staff, and, of course, spending time with Song to ensure that he was apprised of everything we had, and vice versa. The opportunity to review the results of combat operations of the CIDG camps, and be apprised through staff briefings of other issues from the field, enabled me to learn the relative strength, security, and mode of operation of each unit. Some were far more active than others. Why? Many reasons. Some USSF personnel were not able to get their counterparts in the field to conduct combat operations at all, or when they were, the operations were conducted in

areas that were not contested. Some Vietnamese SF commanders were every bit as gung-ho as their USSF advisers. Consequently, they conducted more and better-planned operations
with better results. In a few instances there were huge personality differences between Vietnamese and U.S. Special Forces
commanders. In those cases, little if anything was accomplished. Occasionally, B-team and A-team personnel would
return from the field to render personal reports of some significance, to process out on leave or "rest and recuperation"
(R&R), or to pick up payrolls for the Vietnamese strike force. I
made every attempt to debrief field personnel to learn, firsthand, what the hell was going on in their areas. You never
knew when the information might come in handy. In that way,
I became quite well informed about the various camps assigned to C-3.

My Home, Your Home

After a month or so, Second Lieutenant Song invited me to
his home for dinner. I was gratified, as many U.S. personnel
never enjoyed the kind of relationship with their counterparts
that would encourage such an invitation. Major Robinson
thought it was a breakthrough of sorts. He liked Song and was
pleased to learn about our mutual respect and admiration for
each other. As I parked and chained the C-3 jeep on one of
Bien Hoa's main streets, getting soaked in the process from
the late afternoon monsoon, I wondered how well a Vietnamese officer, wife, and little girl were able to live on the
relatively low monthly pay.

Spotting the crudely fixed home address, I was soon
standing in front of a wooden structure the size of a typical
U.S. one-car garage. I knocked, and Song opened the small,
ill-fitting front door with a wide grin. We greeted each other in
English, as I knew very little Vietnamese and he was eager to
learn as much English as possible, which was not surprising;
there was value in that within the Vietnamese officer ranks.

Once inside I could see the entire layout with a single view.

It was one room without partitions, and a hard-packed dirt floor. There was one fifty-watt bulb in the electrical outlet at the center of the flat wood-and-tin ceiling. Song's young wife and baby girl were sitting on a single wooden-based, veiled bed in one corner of the room. A small icebox with bulk ice cooled a single day's food products. A very small wood-burning stove sat in the corner opposite the bed, and in the center there was a small wooden table with four chairs.

Mrs. Song was a beautiful young woman with silky jet-black hair. The lieutenant said she was expecting their second child within two to three months. She spoke no English. We smiled a lot. A smile goes a long way in helping to break language barriers. I offered Song and his wife a bottle of wine procured from the III Corps compound store for about two dollars.

Mrs. Song prepared, from scratch, bread, soup, salad, and grilled chicken. We ate, drank wine, talked, smiled, and enjoyed the warmth of a friendly environment. I was a bit surprised by the lack of economic and industrial resources available to the young couple. Preparing a simple meal was nearly an all-day event, as even the chicken was purchased whole and alive, and needed to be killed, feathered, cut, and cooked. In addition to the wine, we drank Coca-Cola, as did all Vietnamese on occasion. Coke was available but expensive for the average Vietnamese household.

Second Lieutenant Song and his wife went all-out to make me feel as though their home was my home, and indeed I felt comfortable there. Such an event in a war zone is unusual, and as I drove back to the compound through the pitch-black night, I was grateful that I'd been assigned to C-3 and would be able to work with this young warrior.

I spent the next day, Sunday, pretty much as usual. Mass and communion in the compound chapel, breakfast, TOC duty officer, a few cold beers in the evening, and lights out. Excepting special occasions, there was not a lot of social life, particularly if you were married and cared enough about staying that way. You could go into town, and sometimes several of us did, but not frequently. First, there was security to be considered, and second, such visits created challenges such as those addressed by Colonel Kelly. To be sure, there were clubs, girls, drinks, and more, but for the most part, Bien Hoa at night was off-limits to USSF personnel.

Whose War Is It, Anyway?

Activities within the zone were increasing as more individual replacements and entire A-teams entered country. The increase in Special Forces units was directly proportional to the massive buildup of American forces within the entire Republic of Vietnam. Although President Johnson made statements to the contrary as early as 1964—"We are not about to send American boys ten thousand miles from home to do what Asian boys ought to be doing themselves"—American forces grew from late 1965 to 1968. This was a clear indication that the combined leadership of the United States and South Vietnam firmly believed that the South Vietnamese were no match for the North Vietnamese Army (NVA) and the growing bands of Viet Cong forces being put together in the South. It was felt that not only would the conflict require massive U.S. conventional forces, but there were even indications that the war might require U.S. Special Forces to revert to the highly publicized but infrequently performed role of *conducting* "unconventional operations." What a place to be. If that were true—USSF guerrilla operations within NVA secret base areas—it was possible that those assigned within the Fifth Group would be involved.

Are Regulations Made to Be Broken?

After eating with Lieutenant Song and his wife, my work relationship with him became even more friendly. He went out of his way to offer information about South Vietnamese operations heretofore unanticipated. I would learn of impending tactical plans or some nontactical issue before other members of the staff. It was well-known that we were hitting it off well together, and that helped me establish a good reputation as a friend of the Vietnamese staff. Such relationships are tough to achieve in the first place, but even more difficult to maintain. So when, on a particularly torrid afternoon, Song asked if I could buy a carton of cigarettes for him from the base exchange—an enormous cost savings for him—I had a decision to make. If, on the one hand, I agreed to take his money in exchange for the smokes, I would be breaking a regulation. The exchanges were for U.S. personnel only. On the other hand, if I refused, I would be introducing an element of danger into the fragile nature of U.S.-Vietnamese relationships. My answer was instinctive, as it is with most of my choices. I told Song that it would be illegal for me to purchase cigarettes for him in the exchange, but I'd be willing to buy all the cigarettes he wanted as a gift, at my expense. He declined, smiled, and our relationship survived its first serious challenge.

If at times military regulations appear to be counterproductive, there are usually good reasons for strict compliance. In the case of shopping the exchange for Vietnamese military personnel, several issues were at stake. Exchanges in the remote areas were small, and stocked only to support the U.S. forces assigned. Shopping for others would deny personal items to U.S. forces and tend to support black-market sales. Also, the competition would hurt fragile local businesses. In the final analysis, for the individual, the issue is one of personal integrity. Once compromised, a U.S. Special Forces officer might well be held hostage in matters of greater importance lest the lesser infraction be reported to the U.S. commander.

If It's Grass You Want, It's Grass You Get

The C-3 compound consisted of long L-shaped wooden structures. Roofs were pitched slightly and made of corrugated tin. There was electricity, as well as rest-room facilities and indoor plumbing. Nothing fancy, but adequate for the mission. A flagpole centered on the outside grounds flew the U.S. and the Vietnam flags. A cement walkway, resembling a typical American sidewalk, ran alongside the rows of staff offices assigned to Company A. There was also a gravel parking area for the company vehicles, including M-38A1 jeeps and a deuce-and-a-half (two-and-a-half-ton truck). All vehicles had to be backed in to save time in the case of an emergency evacuation. There was also a small bar on the premises, where drinks and snacks were served in the early evening. Working at C-3 was a little bit like working a relatively regular schedule at a typical stateside army post, just a bit more austere. For the most part, we were a long way from the sights and sounds of battle. Not that the prevailing attitude was cavalier, but there was not that sense of urgency, nor the reality of danger, that existed in the field.

The compound grounds consisted of about 7,500 square feet of mud. Pure mud. Given the daily afternoon monsoon rains, there was no good way to get to an office or the club without being sucked up to the ankles in the dark, gooey, cementlike, sticky mud. It was so bad that the offices themselves became but an extension of the outside grounds. We also had great difficulty in keeping the floors and modest furniture in the officers club clean. Of course, this condition had existed for years.

One day after work, several of us staff officers were commiserating in the club over a cold beer when the C-3 commander, Lieutenant Colonel Durst, joined us. He indicated that within a few weeks a well-known movie actor would visit for a few days. And, he wondered, what the shit could be done about the compound grounds? He asked my boss, Major Robinson, to analyze the situation and let him know within a day or so if there was a solution. To me, this sounded like another request for a trumpet. Without hesitation, I asked Robinson for the task. When he answered in the affirmative, I told Durst that if he would buy the drinks for a victory party the next afternoon, same time, by sundown tomorrow we would have grass. No fucking analysis, no plans, no paper, no alternatives, no command decision, just fucking grass. We all laughed like hell, and for sure, the only one in the room who knew there would be grass the next day was me. Even I wondered if it was the cold beer doing the talking. Grass just didn't seem to me like that big a deal.

I left the club immediately, walked over to Lieutenant Song's office, and asked him if he could provide twenty laborers with shovels the next day from 0600 to 1800 hours. He said no problem. I told him the mission, and that I would pick them up in the compound in the two-and-a-half-ton truck. The next morning, we drove to a field area outside town and dug up, rolled, and delivered to the compound one truckload of the most beautiful, fully matured, lush-green sod I had ever laid eyes on. The first delivery, about 2,500 square feet, took three hours. We would need three loads. I left ten of the workers at the compound to unroll, place, and water-in the sod. The rest of us departed for the second load. By 1800 hours we were finished. If I ever return to Vietnam, I want to visit the C-3 compound to see if there isn't the same grass we planted in May 1966.

The party was a lollapalooza! We had a great time, laughing, joking, sipping suds, and telling bullshit stories. Colonel Durst was in rare form. Through one martini after another, he joined in on the bullshit stories, at one time telling us again that there was a good chance we would be hosting a major Hollywood movie star within a month or so. Really, nobody gave a shit. We were just having too good a time. In fact, it occurred to me that some of us may have been behaving like drunks, bums, and clowns.

Letters from Home

As all military personnel who have ever served overseas know, it takes a couple of months before you start getting mail. But when the letters from loved ones begin to flow, they keep coming on a pretty regular basis, as long as you stay in one location. When you move, all bets are off. I cherished the letters I got from Donna, rereading them often. How she felt was how I felt. I think that's how most servicemen would characterize their true feelings when tucked away in a hostile environment in some far-off corner of the world. I'm okay, you're okay.

Unfortunately, such conditions don't encourage much honesty or spontaneity. For one or the other to characterize, in stark black and white print, the overwhelming emotional stress associated with the realities of separation, would send an unanswerable shock wave that would only tend to worsen an already challenged relationship. So there's always a bit of playacting required, confining one's comments to the routine, mundane events of daily life versus the real and potential hardships being observed. Clearly, I wanted Donna and my family to know that I was safe, well-employed, and relatively happy. That's how their letters read to me. To dwell on the personal loneliness and the concomitant urge for human warmth and companionship would indeed be cruel. There were no letters from either of us suggesting, beyond missing each other, the terrible pains of separation, the impulse to drink more than usual, or the severe temptations to find the human touch that makes tomorrow possible. She wrote virtually every day, and her strength was my strength. I tried to answer each letter, but on some days I felt that to write, given the lousy mood I was in, would not be in either of our interests. I believe we were both inclined to be faithful to each other, to accentuate the positive, eliminate the negative, and avoid those issues that might confuse or disrupt our relationship.

At about the time my letters started to arrive, I was being told that I would be reassigned to a CIDG camp in late June or July. Which one was not yet divulged. And while I looked forward to being in the field, there was a hint of uncertainty in my mind and fear in my heart, neither of which became the subject of our letters.

Let's Eat Out

There were few opportunities to leave the relative security of the III Corps compound, but one outdoor restaurant, La Plage, was not off-limits. This historic restaurant was French-owned and operated, open-air, and situated on the bank of the Bien Hoa River. Several officers piled into one of the C-3 jeeps, and after winding through some unbelievably dark back alleys, we emerged at the desired location. La Plage was known for its relative security and safe food. One look at the menu told me that it would forever be my favorite place in the whole world to eat. To this day, that is true.

Of course, you have to put things in perspective. I'd been eating in the III Corps mess for several months, so any place different would be like a raise in pay. The physical environment was dismal. Dirt floor, dim lighting, mosquitoes humming, wobbly poker-type tables, and a kitchen that would not pass any kind of inspection for cleanliness. By Stateside standards, there would be no stars for ambience, nor any for service. There would be no dollar signs ($) either, because the most expensive dinner entry on the menu was only 125 piasters, about one dollar MPC.

But the menu looked great! I was hungry. I ordered a large bowl of wonton soup, an order of sweet and sour pork, an order of sweet and sour shrimp, and a two-pound châteaubriand with a side order of quarter fries. The soup was unlike any other I have tasted. It was authentic. Large, pork-filled wontons, with pork slices across the top. It was a meal in itself. Both the pork and the shrimp entrées were superb. Large South China Sea shrimp lightly battered in a pungent but slightly sweet sauce. The pork was the same. The steak was exquisite, and the ample quarter fries filled the large plate. Total price: 425p, or a little less than four dollars. Needless to say, I ate at La Plage any chance I got. A few weeks later I returned with Lieutenant Song and his wife, doing something that, although the prices were ridiculously low on an American budget, they would not have been able to do on their own.

Dinner for three, with two bottles of Mateus, ran about ten dollars MPC.

Camp Inspections

In late May the monsoons stopped, daytime temperatures rose ten to fifteen degrees, and the nights were warm and humid. Major Robinson thought it would be a good time to begin a series of camp inspections. We were interested in finding out the relative security of each Special Forces camp within the III CTZ. In preparing to conduct the visits, I studied the regulations authorizing the camps. I was surprised to learn that only fifteen thousand dollars had been allocated for construction of each site. I was eager to see how much security an SF A-team could buy for less money than it cost for a U.S. luxury automobile.

As I made the rounds, I discovered the camps were more austere than I had imagined. Each site consisted of a wooden team house with corrugated tin roof and bunks for twelve to fourteen men, a small kitchen, a communications shack, and a tactical operations center. An adjacent ammunition bunker was used to store small arms, grenades, mines, and small-caliber, indirect-fire weapons such as 81mm mortars and the 60mm "knee" mortars, so named for their unusual method of employment.

The small USSF team house sat directly across from that of the LLDB. They were, for the most part, of similar design and construction. Both the USSF and LLDB living areas were inside the tactical barbed-wire fences designed to discourage penetration by Viet Cong ground forces. Fields of fire out to five hundred meters enabled security guards on watch in small, two-man bunkers to see and take under fire an approaching enemy unit. At that distance, mines, booby traps, and listening posts offered advance warning. Beyond five hundred meters, from sundown to first light, small patrols moved silently through the terrain to distances of up to five thousand meters, or about three miles, to locate small units and fire systems.

Normally, beyond five thousand meters, tactical operations were conducted by company-size units of 150 to 200 men to search for and destroy VC units moving within the camp's tactical area of operational responsibility. Units departing on operations or reentering the camp's basic security perimeter cautiously approached known checkpoints manned by guards who challenged, with a code, the authenticity of the unit. Unit personnel were required to respond with the correct twenty-four-hour password or be taken under fire both by the direct-fire weapons of the security force and the camp's indirect-fire weapons set to predesignated coordinates. One camp had an internal network of trenches that allowed rapid movement inside the camp and access to established concrete bunkers. The bunkers were hard-wired with telephones for requesting fire from the camp's weapons systems and to make reports during an attack.

Since the camps served as both tactical and administrative headquarters of the occupying units, they were, in actuality, only semitactical. Many were positioned in low-lying areas permitting easier access to the established road networks by U.S. B-teams that were colocated with the Vietnamese province headquarters. Unfortunately, those camps were in full view of VC and NVA units from the adjacent high ground in the mountains or hillsides and subject to frequent attack, by ground penetration and, more frequently, by long-range mortar and artillery fire. Being assigned to an A-team could be a very harrowing experience, especially when one was not in the field conducting tactical operations. Although operations targeted local VC and main-force units for destruction, and were essentially more dangerous than sitting in a campsite, units tied to the camp had no mobility and were at the mercy of a larger force that, for the lack of successful patrolling, might have managed to penetrate the camp's existing defense system.

Although the inspection results varied, most camps demonstrated high morale, an active defense system with good fields of fire, and highly trained forces capable of frequent and successful tactical operations. The best camps evidenced a good working relationship between the USSF A-team commander and the LLDB camp commander, a bonding built on mutual trust, loyalty to the missions assigned, personal integrity of key personnel, and a willingness to avoid the graft and corruption so prevalent within the general military and political environment.

A few camps were cited for poor location inviting attack, poorly constructed or poorly chosen defensive positions, poor fields of fire overgrown with vegetation that blocked view of enemy ground forces, broken and poorly maintained tactical wire, inadequate communications, water-damaged ammunition and storage bunkers, and other indefensible tactical considerations. Some camps were taken to task for being inactive, usually a symptom of more serious problems requiring a change of USSF command or other staff positions. One or two were into serious graft and corruption. All of my reports were discussed with the commander on site—and in most instances, the plans for repair were immediate—and formally submitted to my boss, Major Robinson.

Suoi Da and the Black Virgin Mountain

Of the sixteen camps inspected, one camp, A-322, Suoi Da, stood out from the rest. Built in 1964 by U.S. Army engineers, Suoi Da was one of the first SF camps constructed, reportedly for a whopping $1.25 million. Suoi Da was situated about five miles east of Tay Ninh city in Tay Ninh Province and about seventy-five miles due north of Saigon, the South Vietnam capital city, now called Ho Chi Minh City.

The camp was strategically placed just south of War Zone C, home of the VC Ninth Division, and astride the main approach route of the NVA into the South Vietnam capital region. It had long been determined by both military and political experts that if Saigon fell into NVA hands, the war would be over, Hanoi could claim victory, and the U.S. could go home.

The strategic importance of Suoi Da was underscored by

one of nature's true wonders, Nui Ba Den, located a mere four thousand meters to the northwest and rising straight up from the valley floor to a height of 4,500 feet. Nui Ba Den, known throughout Vietnam as the Black Virgin Mountain, overshadowed Tay Ninh Province, the town of Suoi Da, and the campsite itself. The Fifth Special Forces Group occupied the mountaintop with a fixed communications and radar site and, from that vantage point, except for a rather significant "blind spot," could "see" thousands of meters in any direction. VC units moved freely about the mountain, aided by the use of an extensive tunnel system with rock-hardened surface caves protruding among the forest's plants and gigantic trees, which towered more than a hundred feet skyward. The VC had good cover and concealment.

Peaceful Coexistence

Operations on the mountain itself were neither frequently planned nor often conducted. From a tactical point of view, little was to be gained. As long as we held the mountaintop, we were able to utilize the tactical significance of the region's most prominent terrain feature. Also, even daytime operations were considered dangerous, not because of any potential contacts with VC units, but mostly because of the nature of the extreme terrain itself. Huge mountain boulders gave silently and unnoticeably away to deep crevices, forcing tactical movements to be slow and methodical, even for experts in terrain navigation. On operations, all soldiers had to be equipped with standard five-eighth-inch, 120-foot-long rappelling ropes, with Swiss seats, and snap links for attachment to the main rope, and thick leather gloves to prevent rope burns to the hands during descent. Only expertise in rappelling techniques, including an extensive knowledge of ropes and knots, would enable individuals to recover ropes tied into the trees above following their use in capturing the lower piece of ground. And there was little if any daylight on the mountain. Ever. Tactically, the inherent dangers outweighed the potential results. Any operation to be conducted had to have a very specific, limited, and achievable mission designed either to capture something of significance or to deny the enemy access to the same.

Except for the top, the only mountain feature known to provide an advantage for both U.S. and VC units was a natural well with fresh running water, located a few hundred meters down the mountainside from the Special Forces team house. It was not considered to be a tactical advantage to either the U.S. or the VC forces to capture the well, as long as both retained undeniable access. Therefore, meetings by chance at the well were little cause for concern to either side, as neither force wanted to fire the first shot. For the most part, U.S. water carriers visited the well in the morning hours, VC units in the afternoon. This was the protocol that had stood for years. Denied access to water for the twelve-to-fifteen-man SF team and its equipment, U.S. forces would have had to conduct frequent expensive and relatively dangerous resupply missions, flying CH-47 cargo helicopters in and through treacherous mountain winds into the tiniest of helipads firmly fixed immediately adjacent to a towering rocky mountain ledge. Not a seat for which I would personally fight.

There was another, perhaps more significant reason why operations were infrequently conducted on the Black Virgin Mountain. As its name implies, the mountain cloaks religious sites of the Buddhist faith. From Tay Ninh and Suoi Da, one could see the many shrines that had dotted the mountainside for hundreds of years. Undeniably, to its inhabitants and those who worshiped from afar, the shrines were a cultural treasure. Any interference from military units, either directly or by indirect fire, was thought to bring discredit and disfavor from the gods themselves. Many of the CIDG soldiers in Suoi Da were devout Buddhists. South Vietnam government policy prohibited both Vietnamese and U.S. forces from either occupying the shrines or placing fires within or near their vicinity, even though we knew that VC units used the shrines as cover for monitoring U.S. deployments within the entire Tay Ninh region, particularly War Zone C just to the north.

An Impenetrable Defense of Concrete and Steel

While the living arrangements at Suoi Da were on a par with those of camps constructed for fifteen thousand dollars, the defense system was unique. An elaborate interior network of two-foot-wide by four-foot-deep zigzag trenches allowed for surprisingly rapid lateral movement to all bunkers and fighting positions within the camp. These were constructed of U.S.-grade concrete that could withstand the indirect and small-arms fire of most of the VC and NVA weapons systems. All positions were hard-wired for instantaneous communications in the event that radios were jammed. Within the camp's inner perimeter, also protected with extensive concertina wire, were three large concrete mortar positions, ringed with extensive sandbagged fortifications, which provided the camp's primary indirect-fire capability.

In the center of the camp there was an elaborate underground steel and concrete bunker to be used by USSF personnel in the event of a complete penetration and imminent destruction of the camp by NVA forces. The command bunker had enough food, water, communications, and ammunition so the A-team could survive and fight from it for up to thirty days. A sophisticated array of upward-exploding demolitions was built into the roof of the bunker to ward off enemy forces trying to tunnel down to it. All other bunkers and fighting positions within the camp were wired for command detonation and destruction, should the VC or the NVA forces actually choose to occupy the beleaguered camp.

The command bunker could withstand the force of a direct hit from 250-pound bombs, which would be ordered from within to level the camp and kill all enemy forces within its proximity. The only entrance into the command bunker was through an overhead, two-by-four-foot, five-eighth-inch steel door bolted shut with a high-density steel lock. To reduce confusion and uncertainty during an all-out attack requiring occupation of the command bunker, there was no key for the lock. Each lock to be used for the purpose of gaining entry, whether to maintain the bunker's stores or as a last-ditch effort to save the camp, had to be "shot off." All SF personnel carried weapons at all times. Once the team was inside, a similar lock secured the door from the inside. There were no plans to invite in the LLDB, nor was there room.

As I discussed the results of the camp inspections with Major Robinson, knowing that I was soon to be given command of an A-team, I couldn't help but think about Suoi Da and the Black Virgin Mountain.

The Boys in Blue and Their Fast Movers

Following the camp inspections, Major Robinson asked if I wanted to learn more about the air force mission support package for Special Forces, and he mentioned that I might be able to fly backseat during a bombing mission.

My mind flashed back to 1955, when my best friends, Mike Shanks and Denny Higgins, took me skiing at Mount Spokane. I was fifteen, and I discovered then what I know now: the shortest distance between two points is a straight line covered fast. There were fifteen towers that supported the double-chair lift over the one-mile run. In a foolhardy attempt to reach the bottom without turning, I descended from the top, an exceptionally steep and well-moguled drop for about a hundred meters. It was all I could do just to keep from falling. After clearing the cliff, I leveled off into a reasonably smooth valley, reaching speeds of 50 to 65 miles per hour. Slipping inside and outside the multitude of recreational skiers with some trepidation, I eventually reached the knoll at the third tower, which defined the portion of the hill where skiers began to traverse back and forth to the lift line. Hitting the knoll at breakneck speed, I flew airborne for the better part of a hundred feet. Only the landing stood between me and my goal. I had great confidence in my equipment. I was wearing all-leather Rogg boots from West Germany, wrapped with long leather thongs into fixed steel bindings—French wraps and bear traps, they were called—mounted on Rossignol skis. I felt my skis touch ground, and trying desperately to avoid the skiers queuing at the lift line, I screeched to a hockey stop. I had a lot of fun, but I was met by the ski patrol and quickly ushered away from the mountain toward the lodge, where I was told that my skiing days at that mountain were ended for the year.

As I found my way to the second floor of the lodge, with its large glass windows open to the hill, I found my mom and dad, who were there for the very first time to see me ski. Spotting me, my mom became very animated, asking me if I had seen "some maniac with a yellow scarf" who was thrown off the mountain for reckless skiing. I loosened the yellow scarf around my neck, sat down beside my mother, and handed it to her. Was she surprised?

I reported to the III Corps ALO (air liaison officer) in the III Corps tactical operations center about 0600, and was taken to the supply room for a flight suit, and then to the briefing room where the day's missions were being assigned to pilots. The air force wanted to expose SF officers taking field commands to the specific tactics, techniques, and procedures the fighters used in supporting ground-combat missions. The thinking was that if the grunt on the ground was first properly "initiated" in the air, mission support would be enhanced.

Weather patterns were clear and warm that day, and as I climbed into the backseat of our F-100 Super Sabre jet and donned the flight helmet and headset, the pilot said we were next for takeoff. The instrument panel indicated we hit speeds of 150 knots on takeoff; the sensation was explosive. As we were hurled skyward over the dense, jungled terrain of northern III CTZ, the pilot asked me if I wanted to "do some flying" en route to our target area. I asked him if bears shit in the woods. He helped me through some changes in speed and elevation, and then into some rolls and upside-down maneuvers, so I was becoming nauseous as we approached the western shores of the South China Sea.

As he reassumed control of the fighter, the radio squawked a mission request for 250-pound bombs followed with 20mm cannon fire in support of a ground engagement. Listening to the high-frequency radio transmissions between the command pilot and the ground commander enabled me to learn some techniques for brevity, a very important feature of tactical radio communication: clear and concise transmissions reduce air time to a minimum and eliminate confusion as to the mission parameters. They also made radio intercept by VC operators on the ground more difficult.

We were going in. You know that first big hill on some of the more advanced roller coasters? Well, multiply that by a hundred and you'll begin to understand the sensation of a bomb run over a two- to three-minute drop into the target area.

The first pass was a "smoke run" to confirm the target location and fix the desired location of flight in relationship to the position of friendly troops. The ground commander directed the fighters to fly an azimuth parallel, and not perpendicular, to the front line of his friendly units. That prevents a short round or one beyond the target from hitting any closer to the friendly unit than the minimum safe distance initially calculated. One dry run was all that was needed. We were going "hot." Our target was an estimated VC platoon preparing to attack a friendly patrol on a typical search and destroy mission. The patrol, outgunned on the ground, wisely pulled back a hundred meters or so and radioed an "immediate air request" for help from tactical air units flying the zone to respond to such tactical emergencies.

As we dove into the target area, the bombs exploded into a huge ball of smoke, fire, and scattering shrapnel. We pulled up then, the cockpit filled with smoke, and I felt a severe gravitational pull on my intestines. My stomach lurched up toward my mouth, and I sensed that my breakfast was about to fill my mask; gulping in a deep breath of air, I finally got myself under control. Only the nausea remained. We flew two more bomb runs and two 20mm cannon runs, then departed the area, as we were out of weapons and the friendly unit had been able to ward off the attack. The short flight back to Bien Hoa was none too soon for me; my head was pounding.

I learned two things that afternoon. The first was that the guys who flew the tactical air missions were the greatest! I really don't know how they did it, but they did, and they did it well. Day after day, night after night. The second? Fast down-hill skiing and flying a fighter into a target area are comparable. But to know what it's like to pull up in a fighter, the skier would have to run straight into the fucking lodge.

The Duke

It was early June 1966. As he stepped out of the jeep and walked onto the grass in front of the C-3 compound, I was immediately impressed by his enormous size. Although, like millions, I had seen him in numerous favorite movies, I was not prepared for the larger-than-life character with the rugged good looks and decidedly southern drawl. He was wearing standard lightweight jungle fatigues and a Green Beret with a Fifth Group flash.

As the officers and men of A Company gathered in the quadrangle with food and refreshments, he seemed at home. It was a Saturday afternoon, with the sun shining so brightly that most people were wearing dark glasses, but not John Wayne. He was affable. I liked him. The gentle giant wore an engaging smile that put everyone at ease. He seemed to discern instinctively that, for this moment in time, we were the "heroes" and he was the inquisitor bent on learning what the Green Beret was all about. As he walked about the grounds asking questions about the nature of the operations being conducted, and getting a feel for the Special Forces soldier, he graciously demonstrated the importance of subject knowledge to character adaptability. He was going to make another movie.

When he asked me to pose with him and to send the photo to the RKO studios in care of John Wayne, he asked if I was interested in being in the movie *The Green Berets*. I thought about it, then said, "Duke, we are fighting a real war here, and there is no fucking time for me to make a movie." He understood. As I think back, there is nothing I would have rather done than to be a part of his movie. I loved to act. Some of my friends think my whole life is an act. I had boyish good looks.

I could have learned the lines. Most important of all, I knew the subject matter. So, what was my fucking problem?

Suoi Da

In late June 1966, as a twenty-six-year-old first lieutenant, I was given command of Suoi Da. I received an extensive command and staff briefing. The S-1 covered the U.S. personnel situation, including the status of the CIDG funding program. The S-2 provided an intelligence estimate for Tay Ninh Province and offered a huge computer printout recording recent combat activities in the zone. I was aware of the operations and training problems being experienced, and so didn't require an S-3 briefing. The S-4 covered supply and logistics, and the S-5, the psychological operations and civic action programs being resourced. The command group offered an extensive, brutally honest assessment of problems of command, integrity, and trust. Although I knew the camp had troubles conducting and reporting combat operations, and I had discovered a serious weapons and ammunition maintenance problem there during the camp inspections, I was shocked to learn from the C-3 commander and staff just how fucked up things were at Suoi Da.

That night, we had a unit party in the club and said our good-byes. Major Robinson and Lieutenant Song wished me luck. Lieutenant Song's being there meant a lot to me; he'd taught me a lot about the nature of the Vietnamese soldier, and together we both learned much about the requirements of a successful USSF-LLDB relationship. I would need those lessons to survive at Suoi Da.

As I finished packing my shit the next morning, slipping my .45 caliber lightweight Colt Commander into a shoulder holster and donning a BAR (Browning Automatic Rifle) belt outfitted with an assortment of tactical items and a variety of grenades, I thought of those I cared most about and who I might never see again. I understood the vast difference between seeing the sights and hearing the sounds of combat, as I'd done during the camp inspections, and actually being *in* combat. I thought of my parents, Steve and Anna (Dugas) Yedinak, in Spokane, Washington, in the same home in which I was raised for nearly twenty-three years. There was, of course, Donna, and our two young daughters, Lori and Kim, living with her parents, Mr. and Mrs. Fred Simons of Puyallup, Washington. My brothers, Bill Yedinak, of Euphrata, Washington, and Tom, of Spokane. My sister, Anne Marie, and her husband, Dick Kirmse, in Elgin, Illinois. Alice and her husband, Chuck Moyer; Patty and her husband, Dave Brown; and my little sister, Dorothy, all in Spokane.

The helicopter ride from Bien Hoa to Suoi Da was peaceful, although one could not escape seeing bombing missions, artillery and mortar fire, and small-arms fire within the well-vegetated jungle floor below. But at three thousand feet the lush foliage and meandering rivers seemed artistically framed in nature's warm sunshine and the bright blue sky. As we approached the camp, I anticipated one final time the message I was asked to deliver to the incumbent commander. I would name him, but it has never been my style to "kiss and tell." Besides, he is not here to answer. But my knowledge of camp activities under his command reassured me that the instructions I had been given were appropriate. I just don't think that a lot of people outside of Special Forces know how brutal we must be when one of our own discredits the unit. The chopper touched down onto the small dirt landing pad in a cloud of dust. I was met by the commander.

The Huey (UH-1H tactical helicopter) blades swirled to a stop, and when the air was silent and there were only the two of us together, I realized I had to deliver my message. In my most direct, animated tone, I said to Major X-ray, "You fucker, you're fired. You have two hours to get your shit together, get back on this helicopter, and get your ass out of here. Do you understand?" He said he did, packed his bags, and was gone. That was the one and only time I ever saw him, as I was taken directly to the team house in one jeep, and he departed to his quarters in another.

The ride from the pad to camp headquarters took two minutes, three minutes, tops. The sun was blistering hot, and the scorched red earth signaled the events to follow. As the jeep slowed to a stop, I saw the welcoming committee assembled to greet the new commander of Suoi Da. Of those present, one stood out. A spider monkey. Held by one of the team members—to this day, I can't remember who, although it may have been Specialist-4 White—the monkey was thrust in front of me.

By way of introduction, White said, "Sir, welcome to Suoi Da," and as I approached to shake his hand, he delivered the primate to me, saying, "This is LBJ." LBJ then attempted to bite my face. I moved back quickly, cupped my hand, and instinctively struck the monkey's throat with a full-force karate chop, propelling it ten or twenty yards. Quickly pursuing the dazed monkey, I picked it up, detached a rope from my web gear, tied one end to the monkey's right leg and the other to a nearby stake in the ground. I then detached a red smoke grenade and a CS gas grenade from my web gear and pulled the pins, dropping them in the vicinity of the "monkey-fucker" now confined to a twelve-foot leash. I had never heard so much intense screaming in all my life. Needless to say, LBJ never fucked with me again while I remained at Suoi Da. In fact, we seemed to share a certain primal instinct.

Soon after, the team and I met in the team house to discuss our goals and expectations. I told them what I knew about the unit and asked for their input. I said we knew there had been a debilitating personality clash between the Vietnamese and U.S. commanders, that neither would work with the other, and that there was a contract out to kill the A-team's just-relieved commander. We also knew there were serious discrepancies in the CIDG payroll, but needed to learn the details. Other known problems were in weapons and ammunition maintenance, combat radios and reporting, and the infrequency of combat operations. Finally, some operations reported to C-3 were, in fact, not being conducted, and for some others enemy casualties were being grossly inflated.

When integrity and trust are at issue, many things can and

probably will go wrong. Our team meeting confirmed that the previous commander was not honest in his dealings with the Vietnamese camp commander. It is quite likely that none of the members of the A-team knew about the funds issues, as the outgoing commander was the funds officer. I would have to gather this information myself. We knew that Suoi Da was reporting a strike force strength of 850 men, and that the camp had been receiving adequate piasters each month to make the payroll. But the payroll seemed excessive. Other known and suspected problems were confirmed by one or more of the team members.

On closing, I indicated that our job was to get Suoi Da back on track. Resolve the command problems. Resolve the funds issues. Correct the maintenance deficiencies. Initiate vigorous combat operations, render honest reports, and refrain from inflating enemy casualties. When I was convinced we were all onboard, we closed our meeting and went to work.

We had given ourselves thirty days to correct those problems we knew existed, mainly delegating the requirements among the team members under the supervision of the team sergeant, Master Sergeant Bryant. Bryant was a large, jovial kind of guy with a very positive attitude. It became apparent to me during the meeting that the members had flailed about because of the leadership vacuum that had previously existed. It was Bryant who volunteered that Major X-ray hated the Vietnamese in general, and had stated during a previous team meeting that he "wouldn't give the camp commander the sweat off his balls." Bryant was the only black member on our team. I liked him instantly, not because he was black, but because he knew some serious problems existed, was forthcoming with important information regarding the relationship between the team and the LLDB, and seemed as eager as I was to find solutions.

As I walked into my small office and closed the door, I sensed that some hidden agendas had been played out in Suoi Da, and I intended to get to the bottom of them. I also imagined that Team Sergeant Bryant may have known enough to have briefed the C-team in Bien Hoa about the nature of the problems. But I don't think that anyone knew for certain the games that would come to light in the next thirty days.

It was late in the afternoon when I began to dig through the previous six months of CIDG pay records I had requested from the S-1 and brought with me to Suoi Da. That's where I would begin my investigation, but I would begin the next day. Right then, there was something of even greater importance I had to accomplish before daylight gave way to darkness and our security shifts resumed at 1800 hours until 0600 hours the following morning.

First Lieutenant Nguyen Vanh Trang was likable. In rather good English, he invited me into his office and signaled for some tea. He said he was happy to see me, and that Special Forces saw fit to replace commanders. I listened without interruption as he talked openly about his poor relationship with Major X-ray. He said the major didn't understand the problems facing the camp commander, or if he did, he was not going to help. His jeep was old and unreliable, he went on, and was a liability in making required biweekly runs to Tay Ninh, about six kilometers away. Also, the PRC-10 radios were in poor condition and seldom worked, and that was why CIDG commanders shied away from conducting combat operations, particularly near the rubber plantation where VC units were known to be.

I asked how I could help. He asked only for cooperation. I said, "Okay, you can use my new jeep anytime you want, and from now on you and your commanders can count on using our new PRC-25 radios for combat operations." I also told him that I would like to see some plans for a combat operation in the vicinity of the rubber plantation south of Suoi Da within two weeks, and that it was my intention to come along as an adviser. He agreed, we finished our tea, and as I got up to leave I said, "Together, we will make a good team—your province chief in Tay Ninh and your commander in Bien Hoa will be proud." As I made my way the hundred or so feet across the compound from his hootch to mine, I thought about the stereotypical image of the used-car salesman. I couldn't *wait* to review those pay records.

An SF team is not assigned a chef, or even a cook, so the team members often take turns cooking for the ten to twelve men on the team. When we were not on combat operations, food was airlifted in from Saigon in thirty-day quantities, stored in freezers, and used pretty much the same as in any household. The first meal I had at Suoi Da, spaghetti with meat sauce, tasted about as good as any meal I have ever had. The cold beer was a bonus. Conversation, reading, and board games were our social outlets.

I turned in early, as I was scheduled for the 0200 to 0400 security shift. I wondered aloud if LBJ had been consulted about the schedule, but felt some solace that I was now working with people who refused to practice favoritism. I was keyed up as I lay on my bunk, having a difficult time dozing off to sleep, partially because of the monumental problems we faced—although, on balance, I felt good about my meeting with Trang—and because of the rats that were running the rafters overhead, and the fact that there was no inside plumbing, and that if I had to visit the bathroom, it would be a hundred-foot walk with a red-filtered flashlight to an outdoor common latrine.

I did manage to get some sleep, but 0145 came around pretty fast. I checked into the radio net at 0200, radioing to C-3 that we were okay. Checks every two hours from dusk to dawn were required because of the number of camps that were severely challenged during darkness, and often overrun. SF camps were virtually isolated—placed in remote areas to provide security to local villages and towns. But Suoi Da had the strongest defense system in the III CTZ. H&I (harassment and interdiction) fire from the 105mm guns at Tay Ninh and the 4.2-inch mortars from the top of Nui Ba Den blistered the zone with the ominous sounds and flares of battle. As I walked the inner perimeter, I thought of Donna and imagined just how lonely she probably was. And although I had been in-country for less than six months, I have to admit my level of testosterone was pretty high.

The security watch was a slow, silent walk throughout the

camp, equipped only with a frequency-modulated radio, an M-16 rifle, and my personal handgun, looking and listening for anything unusual that might signal an attack from *within* the camp; it was estimated that ten to fifteen percent of the CIDG strike force were VC. The fact that the very forces we were working with were, in part, the very forces we were there to detect and kill, made the war a very hairy ordeal for SF. We could not be too careful. Several camps had been over-run, and most of those attacks had been assisted from the in-side. My watch was without incident, as I again radioed C-3 that we were "on the net." What could I do from 0400 hours to 0600 hours? Right! I started to rummage through the payroll records.

Money for Nothin' and Chicks for Free

In reviewing the pay records, I wanted to identify, at least on paper, how many strikers we were paying, and, in accordance with the established criteria, whether we were paying the correct amount. Soldiers were recruited into the CIDG program from the citizenry of the local area because locals would be more likely than not to invest in the security of the camp under siege, and to conduct local patrolling and so-called search and destroy operations to safeguard their families and their homes. However, due to the nature of insurgency, soldiers and their families were often displaced, and frequently had moved relatively recently into an area to find employment or the security required to raise a family. Consequently, there was no legitimate record of the political ideology of the soldier, nor was there much reliability in the size of the soldier's family. Soldiers ranged in age from about fifteen to fifty-five, a span of some forty years. Ethnic origins varied. At Suoi Da, most were Vietnamese, but other groups represented were Montagnards, a strain of Chinese called Nungs, and ethnic Cambodians. To complicate matters, it was not uncommon for several members of the same or extended family to work in the same camp. Perhaps the biggest challenge was trying to get a reliable fix on the soldiers' names, first and last. To Americans, Southeast Asian names looked alike—hell, frequently they *were* alike—with many of the same names intermingled into the soldier's total name. Trying to get a fix on a name was like trying to interpret a bar code without a scanner. Nor were the records themselves consistent, often displaying, by company, additions and deletions in random order.

Toward the end of the day, I was relatively certain of two things. The first was that, on average, we had paid an average of 842 strikers per month over the past six months. The second was that we had paid entitlements to each as if married with nine children. I was somewhat more confident of the first than of the second. As I began to think about just how to confirm what I needed to know—how many soldiers and how many "exemptions"—there was a knock on my door. It was Trang. With him were two of the most beautiful Asian girls imaginable. He was gracious as he introduced me to each, and left little doubt that the one I chose would be my companion for the duration of my stay at the camp. As I had done with Song some months earlier, I declined. I told him that the young girls were "beaucoup dep"—slang for very beautiful—but that I was married, a Catholic, and could not accept his offer. Both he and the girls smiled profusely. As he turned to leave, I asked him to hold a formation at 1000 hours the next morning, during which time we would take company pictures, and, by company, a picture of each soldier when we recorded the serial number of his weapon. As I walked the inner perimeter that night and passed the LLDB quarters, I could not help but think about the young, slender Asian girls with flowing silky-black hair and warm, soulful eyes. I wondered if I had told the truth, or had I just been too damned scared, or pragmatic, to join what to the Vietnamese was a revered cultural institution.

The next morning, Trang and I recorded the names and serial numbers of 406 strikers. There were no ongoing operations, and except for the ten or fifteen who I was told were on leave, there were no more. Four hundred twenty-five, tops. Since my initial tally was 842 strikers, soldiers had apparently been going through the pay line twice, and there simply had not been any effective method of true identification. Although I had the answer to my first question—how many strikers—I was uncertain that the camp commander was uneasy or saw anything peculiar in trying to document the CIDG strike force. Asians have a way of shielding their emotions.

Since the June payday was only five days off, I had to move fast to find the answer to my second question—how many dependents. I asked to see Lieutenant Trang in my office the following day. While extending some pleasantries, he told me that he and his commanders were putting the finishing touches on a three-day operation in the vicinity of the rubber planta-tion. I told him that was a significant step in the right direction, and as he smiled, showing damaged gums and rotting teeth, I almost forgot why I'd called for him. The camp, though inac-tive for several months, had reported some operations we at C-3 knew were bogus. Now he was telling me that they were going into the feared rubber plantation, thought to be the home of an NVA regiment. I was beside myself with pride, although there was also a twinge of anxiety as I recalled that White and I were scheduled to accompany.

However, I caught myself and asked if he could provide legitimate documentation from Tay Ninh Province regarding the family of each soldier. I explained that C-3 was trying to get a handle on the payroll and wanted each camp to bring its personnel roster up to date. Sensitive to his feelings and his cultural heritage, I noted that it was hard to believe that all of the soldiers were married and had nine children. I wasn't cer-tain at that point whether he was part of the problem or would become part of the solution, but was gratified when he said he would provide the paperwork. I wanted to resolve this issue, I told him, before I left for Bien Hoa to pick up piasters. If he seemed concerned about numbers, he didn't let on that he was aware that, even before verifying the number of dependents, the total payroll of nine million piasters would be cut in half.

Two days later Trang returned from Tay Ninh with the information I'd requested. He smiled from ear to ear as he pre-sented me with a stack of "official" records, each one containing the red seal of the province chief over his signature, and each one listing the full name of the soldier, his wife, and the names of the nine children owing to the marriage. With the trip to C-3 only two days off, and payday but one day later, I had a choice to make. As I tried to gather my composure, I sought for the right answer to what had been an elaborate scam involving the camp commander and the former SF commander. Without any conscious thought, my mind produced a clear, untethered image of the Duke standing on a plot of luscious green grass in front of Company A headquarters. I had my answer.

Stopping the payroll was not a popular decision, especially for the camp commander who would have to summon the courage to inform his CIDG strike force and save face, perhaps a greater challenge in his culture. I offered some support, reminding him that it was he who had been willing to comply honestly with all my requests for information. I also suggested that his superiors at Tay Ninh and C-3 might view his decision to correct what had been an injustice long before he'd taken command of the camp as a testimony to his courage and his leadership. I consoled him with the reality that, surely, there were few soldiers who really believed they were married with nine children. Finally, I said that although we might expect some defections, the majority of the soldiers would bravely commit to the coming operation, and that their families and loved ones would need the reduced paycheck even more than the inflated ones. He agreed.

I flew by chopper to Bien Hoa the next morning, briefed Lieutenant Colonel Durst and the S-1 about the resolution of the payroll, picked up about 4.5 million piasters in a large aviator kit bag, and returned to Suoi Da by midafternoon. I also briefed my team about the details of the leadership failure on both sides, and asked each to report on the status of repairs to assigned deficiencies. Things would be different in Suoi Da, we all agreed. There would be a commitment to excellence, full cooperation with our LLDB counterparts, interstaff training and assistance, and full advisory and logistics support during combat operations. I began to sense that we were going in the right direction, but that we had to operate at a level that would provide real security within the local area. Then, and only then, would we truly be accomplishing our mission: camp and territorial security.

Although there were some questions, and some grumbling among the troops, payday went off without a hitch. As each man passed the single table manned by myself, Trang, and our team NCOs, he had to show and recite the serial number on his weapon, and sign next to his name on the list of some 425 soldiers. Unmarried soldiers earned about 9,000p per month, about eighty-three dollars; those married with children received appreciably more. If it seems meager today, it was quite a bit of money in the South Vietnamese economy in 1966. Unfortunately, the graft and corruption existing within the camp of Suoi Da was no less than that within the Republic of Vietnam as a whole. That a U.S. Army Special Forces officer with the rank of major had been unwilling and/or unable to resist the temptation to participate was a systemic failure of the leadership then in place.

As I retired that payday evening, my heart and mind were filled with the excitement of the combat operation into the rubber plantation just a few days off. It would be the first time in months that the CIDG strike force, and Lieutenant Trang, would earn their pay. On a more personal note, that combat operation would provide my transition from theory to practice, from thinking to doing, from the known to the unknown. It would be my first ever combat operation, and I was dying to know how I would do. For reasons apparent to us, White and I decided to name the operation Freedom's Price, signifying a resurgence of pride for what, together, we had overcome in the past weeks, and, more important, a new commitment of Suoi Da to its combat mission, and the price that might exact.

A Night to Remember

White and I and Lieutenant Trang briefed our B-team counterparts on the results of Freedom's Price. The B-team staff suggested that a follow-up operation to the same vicinity might result in the capture of a local VC or two who would, under interrogation, tell us where the command posts were for the VC and/or NVA units operating out of the zone. Trang accepted the challenge, indicating that he would mount another operation within a week with the express mission of capturing a POW. That said, we left the compound in two-and-a-half-ton trucks for the hot, dusty ride back to Suoi Da, arriving in the early afternoon. Of course, we were looking forward to Trang's victory party that very evening.

As White and I entered the small canteen, we were met by Trang and led to a long table set for about eight people. White wondered if we would again meet up with the "cow of courage" Trang had killed as a prelude to combat. I said that if so, it was not immediately apparent, but even a dead cow could have been overlooked in the sumptuous feast before us. Trang seated me at one end of the table, with Sergeant White to my immediate right. Trang then took his seat at the other end. Following a short prayer by Trang in Vietnamese, young girl servers began to distribute beverages, including Ba Mui Ba (Beer 33), tea, and water. When everyone had a drink of choice, Lieutenant Trang made the first of what would become an endless series of toasts throughout the night and into the wee hours of the next morning. "To Vietnamese and Americans working together," he said, raising his glass to his lips. We followed his lead. I then responded, "To the brave soldiers who fought in operation Freedom's Price." Again, we indulged. And, so on . . .

Which Came First, the Chicken or the Egg?

The first of several delicacies was the "bloke," which brought new meaning to the American concept of the soft-boiled egg; it was more like a soft-boiled chicken. As we were being served what looked to me like an ordinary hard-boiled chicken egg, Trang explained that the Vietnamese carefully select and boil an egg between the eighteenth and the twenty-first day of gestation, and serve the egg in a leafy lettuce wrap to neutralize the intense heat. Following his guidance, I used my spoon to tap the edges and remove the top of the egg. I then spooned out, in small bite-size fragments, the fully formed chicken. In case there is any doubt in your mind that the chicken, under these conditions, is in fact fully formed, give it a try. The small red eyes and feathered beak notwithstanding, the first morsel you put into your mouth is the chicken head itself, including what is perceived, correctly, as the hard nutlike brain. The second scoop consists of the delicious young body, with the fragile wings and structure somewhat like a soft-shelled crab. Finally, the remainder is what you think is left of a chicken so described. Was it good? Absolutely! Have I had one since eating several that night? Absolutely not!

Next came boiled squid in a bloodred sauce, the substance of which I felt compelled not to inquire about. Following was the traditional cha gio or a rice-paper-roll replica of the Chinese egg roll. It was delicious, and while I was in Vietnam, it was one of my favorite dishes. Chicken and fish followed. As the guest of honor, I was served the heads of both, and I took great delight in spooning out the brains of the chicken and the eyeballs and cheeks of the fish, then downing them. I knew I had to. The cow was next, red portions of which I would grow accustomed to.

How Do You Like Your Blood?

I guess it was only a matter of time. As the servers continued to refill my glass and the glasses of each of the other guests with their favorite libation, the dessert was being served: blood pudding was traditional. I didn't have to like it. But I did have to eat it. Even if I felt myself about to puke. There could be no greater "mistake" than to refuse the rich, warm, thickened blood of the one beast that had somehow provided the necessary courage to the leader of the successful operation. It wasn't that bad, but I have to admit that by the time the blood pudding was served, I was blitzed! Thank God.

Given the events of the past three weeks, my respect for Trang was at an all-time high. I was beginning to genuinely like him, and, to be sure, he commanded the admiration and trust of the CIDG leaders. His junior officers looked to him for guidance and seemed to be at ease with him and our SF team. This rather sudden reversal spoke volumes about the philosophical differences between potency and act.

The following morning, I briefed the team on the details of Freedom's Price, and told the team sergeant I would like an increase in the number of advisers—at least two per company—we would use for the impending POW capture mission.

Mines on the Trail

About 0400, the first of three companies silently cleared the back gate of the compound. March and route discipline among the CIDG was often a problem, as even the slightest noise—a snapping twig or muffled voice—could be heard for hundreds of feet across the flat terrain leading out of the camp. Nor had I noticed the occasional flicker of light from CIDG smokers that was usually encountered along the trail. Apparently, Trang had convinced his troops that the day, and the night, belonged to those who could remain swift and silent during movement.

By the book, tactical movements were to be made alongside or perpendicular to adjacent trails and road networks, in order to avoid trail ambush placed by an alert enemy force. However, in this instance Trang led his units through an elaborate maze of trails for speed of movement and to maintain good noise discipline. Following the swampy terrain in that area, which was thickly overgrown with plants and trees, would have slowed our rate of march, increasing the amount of time for the VC to set up an ambush. In reality, both VC and friendly forces often used the trails as an effective and efficient alternative to getting bogged down in the bush.

An experienced point man was designated to navigate well out in front of the main body so as to give the enemy little clue of the size and location of the unit. We wanted to quickly get to the vicinity of the rubber plantation, engage VC forces, and capture at least one VC.

As first light approached, the long column halted. Such a stoppage might occur to recheck a plan, quickly change direction, simply take a break, or, as in this case, to signal impending danger. The point man recovered his steps backward about thirty meters, passing the security force for the command group kneeling on one knee and alternately facing outward while securing both sides of the trail. Reaching the command group, the point man said, in halting English, "VC put mine on trail." Then, through an interpreter, "He say he see beaucoup VC mine on trail, Trung-uy [first lieutenant]." Since no mines had yet exploded, our location was probably secure, at least for an hour or so. There was a heightened danger on our minds as Trang, myself, one of Trang's sergeants, and two radio operators slowly made our way to the front. The point man led us forward to where his bayonet was stuck in the ground, marking the presence of mines. They were difficult to see in the breaking dawn, just well-disguised, three-pronged, steel-wire mechanisms protruding an inch or two above the trail's surface. Carefully moving on hands and knees toward one of the suspected mines, slowly sweeping my right hand in a semicircular motion along the ground, trying to feel for prongs, I stopped about twelve inches from the first of the pressure-release antipersonnel mines. We had studied mines and booby traps ad nauseam at Fort Bragg, so it was easy for me to recognize the M-16 "tomato can" mine. About the size of a large tomato can, the M-16 has its pressure-release mechanism built on top. The self-contained mine is buried, leaving only the "detonator" uncovered. Stepping on the prongs activates the detonator, but the mine does not explode until the pressure of one's foot is lifted. When that happens, the mine explodes upward and outward, inflicting serious casualties, or death, on anyone within ten to fifteen meters.

We identified two mines on the trail for removal, as this was more tactically sound than trying to steer the rest of our force around the mines, since we could not be sure whether or to what extent Charlie had planted mines off the trail as well. For the time being, staying on the trail was the best solution. That would also speed our movement, and perhaps provide better security. Why? Because from the mines on the trails, it was evident that the VC were trying to move our forces off the trail in order to strengthen our "signature"; off the trail, we would move more slowly and make more noise. Also, if hit, we would be confined to the swampy killing areas covered by our foe.

I asked Trang to secure the area, and to pick a man with steady hands to remove one of the mines. I told him that I would remove the first one while his man watched. I also asked him to have two holes dug, each measuring two feet in diameter and two feet deep. Since the mine was self-contained, there were no extraneous wires to worry about. Using my bayonet, I etched a circle into the ground two feet in diameter from the mine's center. That defined the limits of the working area. Digging around the can, carefully loosening and discarding the dirt, I exposed the top third of the can, ensuring that the mine itself remained secure. That done, I began to loosen the dirt from the outside of the perimeter initially drawn with my knife. When the dirt was removed to a level of three or four inches, I asked one of my NCOs to hold the mine upright while I loosened the second third of the layer of the dirt in the same manner. Then I rotated the mine back and forth until it was free. Lifting the large can straight up, I walked over to one of the holes and carefully put the mine down on its side, assuring that none of the prongs touched the side of the hole. The final act was to carefully backfill the hole, "burying" the mine so it would be out of harm's way for future troops, or livestock, or people who might settle in the area long after the war would be over. As Trang's men removed and buried the second mine, we discussed plans for movement, deciding to stay on the trail for another kilometer or so and then break due south toward the rubber plantation.

In Your Dreams

Have you ever "seen" the future? Clearly? Perhaps waking from a dream, still dazed, but able to rapidly scribble down the quickly dissipating remnants of your subconscious self? Well, it was that kind of day for me. In anticipation of our operation, in my dreams I had not only heard the semiautomatic rifle shots of nearby snipers but wakened at the site of a VC ambush area with casualties in varying stages of discomfort. So I was not surprised when, not unlike my dreams of two nights before, we began to take fire from our left front. Only there it was real.

As Lieutenant Trang's middle company was in the killing zone, the intense fire from both units shut out all other sounds for a two- to three-minute period. That is typical. If you survive the initial few minutes of a firefight in your direction, it means that you were very low to the ground and/or there was some element of cover between you and the bad guys. Cover, of course, is anything that can stop a bullet, like heavy trees, thickened ground swells, destroyed vehicles. I don't think luck is involved very much during a firefight because a virtual wall of steel grazes low along the ground for what seems like an eternity. The initial burst of fire continues until the shooters have to begin exchanging empty magazines—about twenty rounds each—for full ones. Then there's a lull in the action, and leaders begin to react tactically to the situation.

At that point in this engagement, Trang began to deploy the lead company—about 150 men—toward the northernmost flank of the suspected VC company. While the middle company continued to lay down a base of fire, with the help of supporting mortar fire, Trang radioed his third company to seal the enemy escape routes to the south. With that plan in action, within thirty to forty-five minutes our superior forces and weaponry broke the enemy's spirit, causing a withdrawal from the area. Asking for a sitrep from each of his units, Trang confirmed that, although we had suffered three friendly KIA and six or eight WIA, we counted fifteen dead VC and two live POWs without wounds. Mission accomplished, we turned

for home. As Trang said, "He who knows he need not stay,
lives to fight another day."

Name, Rank, and Serial Number

When a U.S. soldier falls into the hands of the enemy, he, or
she, is required to provide no other information beyond name,
rank, and serial number. This is according to the Geneva Convention and the laws of land warfare. The rules are established
so the POW will be treated fairly and humanely and not
be compelled to offer other assistance to the enemy: where
forces are deployed, in what number, and with what weapons;
the location of communications sites, artillery positions, and
command posts; the morale of forces, plans to build up re-
serves, and plans to use nuclear weapons. Theoretically, of
course, when we capture a POW, he's interrogated "on the
ground" first, so we can get any information that will help
us destroy the enemy or keep ourselves from being destroyed. What happens beyond that, at increasingly higher
channels and levels of command, depends a lot on the quality
of the POW.

If it's a grunt, one of ours, he doesn't know shit so he's
pretty much expendable, but not until his captors get what
they want. And capturing a VC grunt is about the same. He
doesn't know shit, so he's pretty much expendable, but not
until we get what we want. If found in some local area, he can
be asked if he will lead the next operation to his home base. So
his unit, his friends, his family can be destroyed. It's almost
always a tough call for the POW. So it was the following
morning when Trang began to interrogate the two prisoners,
who were in a weakened condition due to lack of food, water,
and rest. One was an old man, the other young. Instinctively, I
knew that the young man would talk and the old man
wouldn't. That was human nature. Trang asked about the unit
to which they were assigned, its size, location, disposition,
morale, and future plans. As near as I could tell, neither said
much. That went on for about three hours, when Trang halted

the session and the POWs were taken to a holding area. He resumed the following morning, in the open, with the hot, dry, temperatures building to about 110 degrees by noon, while the searing sun bore directly into their eyes. Again, after three hours, it seemed to me that Trang's methods were not producing the desired outcome. I asked if I could give it a try. Trang told the two that I wanted to talk to them, together, as I had asked.

Through one of our interpreters, I said that I was a man of few words. I told them that we would be conducting an operation into their area soon and that I expected them to lead us to their unit. If they did, I said, they could live, and continue to fight with us. We would recruit them into the CIDG program. And pay them. And feed them. And provide them security. As I talked, I could see the reflection of their black-cloth bandannas on the inside surface of my dark glasses. I then asked each of them if they understood what I was saying. Assured they understood, I told them they would have only one chance to affirm their help. To the old man first, "Will you help us?"

"No."

To the young man, "Will you help us?"

"No."

I then had the guards separate them, along the inner perimeter trench line, by about twenty meters, but within hearing distance. I asked the old man, now that he was alone, if he would help. He wouldn't. This didn't surprise me, as older men frequently conclude that they have lived a long life, and that there is not much to gain by talking. As I pounded the old man's face with my bloodied fists, his screams could be heard throughout the camp. I then wrapped his mouth with my neck scarf, pulled out my .45 caliber Colt Commander, chambered a round, and fired in the direction of his head.

A few seconds later I asked the young man if he would help. He said he would.

The Third Time's a Charm—or Is It?

Within a week we were back in the vicinity of the rubber plantation. This time, of course, we were expertly led into the area by the two POWs we had since befriended and recruited. I had told the old man that if it was hard for him to talk, it was difficult for me to resort to violence. I think I convinced him that had I not intervened, within a day or so Trang would have become irritable and perhaps just done away with them both. He smiled the smile of a man who'd fought for years for what he considered a just cause.

Sighting the row upon row of rubber trees directly to our front, at about five hundred meters, the old man suggested we stop to check our maps before proceeding. At a certain landmark, we were to turn the unit—about 425 strong—slightly eastward and appreciably away from the trees themselves. As we secured for the night, my mind turned over and over with the anticipation of duking it out with a large VC unit. Air strikes were going in at first light, followed by 155mm artillery from Tay Ninh. Throughout the night, Trang's units moved into position, securing escape routes from the east, the north, and the northwest. Local H&I fire erupted through the night, their glowing results clearly visible from our shadowed positions along the vast tree lines of the forest.

At about 2000 hours I sent a sitrep to Suoi Da and Tay Ninh, letting them know that we were set, and to confirm the next day's support packages.

That done, Sergeant Johnson and I dug into our rucksacks for something to eat. When expectations are not high, it's hard to be disappointed. Finding a bag of rice with small dried shrimp, a packet of dried Lipton's tomato soup base, and my Tabasco sauce, I knew I had everything I would need. Concerned about showing light, I dug a hole about twelve inches deep and twelve inches wide in the soft, wet earth. I placed two sticks at the bottom, about six inches apart, then put a heat tablet between them. Emptying two cups of water into my metal canteen cup, I fired the "stove" and placed the cup on the sticks to boil. Soup base, hot sauce, and rice with shrimp, in that order. Stirring occasionally, my homemade, jungle-inspired, no-filé gumbo was ready to eat. What can I say. I have always been a good cook.

As the sky darkened I asked Johnson if he was looking forward to his return to the States in the next thirty days or so. He told me that he'd spent his entire tour living for the day he could be reunited with his wife and family. He also said that one day prior to the operation, he had received a Dear John from his wife; she didn't love him anymore and she wouldn't be there to meet him when he returned to Bragg. Go figure.

Under the circumstances, it was not hard to think about my own family and the joy I would experience on seeing them again. I could conjure up such vivid images in my mind, so lifelike, so clear, and, given my nature, so positive. In spite of my failings, my own family had always been so supportive that I knew that things for Donna and our two girls would turn out all right. I was very sorry for Johnson. There must have been a better way, a better time, a better set of circumstances under which a spouse could announce such an important decision. I mean, here was a guy ready to give his fucking life for his country, about to go into a battle from which he might not return, and he had to open that fucking letter and read that fucking news that his family wouldn't be there when he went home.

I'm not sure just when I dozed off, and really, after hearing about Johnson, I didn't much care. There was an instant when I felt his pain so deeply that I would have volunteered to take his place. You know, please Lord, let it be me.

In the bush, on operations, we didn't get much sleep, which means we didn't need an alarm to wake up. But sometime early that morning darkness began to give way to dawn, and then the ground about us thundered with the 500- and 750-pound bombs of our "predawn" strike. When you're in the immediate vicinity of large bombs, your ears go numb. And the guy who so cleverly invented the earplug for the military—you know, the half-inch diameter by one-inch length piece of something we were supposed to put into our ears—well, that's a bunch of bullshit! When you need to hear, you need to hear. You can't be casually putting this piece of garbage in your ear and then removing it so you can hear what you're supposed to hear, and then repeating the process. No way. When lives are at stake, you need to hear. Period. The recommended earplugs are just CYA—cover your ass—so the Defense Department won't have to reimburse soldiers for hearing impairment when they retire.

As the air broke, the artillery launched an all-out preparation that would have stiffened the dick of Flacido Domingo. It was show time. Still visibly shaking from the effects of the intense bombardment, our units moved into the area ready to blow away anything that moved.

Unfortunately, and to our surprise, we discovered the prize we sought had already vacated its base camp. Although there were fresh signs of a large VC unit, perhaps the 271st Main Force Viet Cong Regiment, it was equally clear that our luck had run its course. The base area was destroyed, even the underground tunnels collapsed shut, but the unit itself, perhaps alerted by the two earlier operations into the rubber plantation, had lived to fight another day. Such was the nature of a counter-insurgency. Sometimes you eat the bear, and sometimes the bear eats you. And sometimes there is no apparent outcome, except that he who knows he need not stay, lives to fight another day.

Relieving the Pressure at Trai Bi (A-323)

Trai Bi was a Special Forces "fighting camp" northwest of Nui Ba Den, in the heart of War Zone C. The camp was needed to provide a measure of security to Tay Ninh city to the south. More important, Trai Bi was a 155mm-artillery position, with a range of thirteen kilometers, that would fire in support of large-scale conventional U.S. division-size operations being planned to block NVA infiltration along the Ho Chi Minh trail across the Cambodian border into South Vietnam. During the initial stages of construction, when SF camps are particularly vulnerable, Trai Bi endured nightly enemy mortar attacks that not only impeded the engineering effort, but scared the hell out of the relatively small CIDG force recruited to secure the area. The embryonic camp's weapons emplacements were also the target of VC direct-fire weapons from the surrounding hillsides to the west. But the camp simply needed better protection if it was to withstand such attacks in the near term and be completed, to deny its part of the III CTZ to the enemy.

It was under such conditions that Suoi Da was directed to provide support to Trai Bi for a one-week period. We were to relieve the pressure until the camp could stand on its own. Upon our arrival, the Trai Bi A-team intelligence sergeant briefed us on known and suspected enemy forces in the vicinity, and provided maps designating the boundaries established for the battalion-size force Trang and I had trucked into the area. The concept of the operation was that the existing forces at Trai Bi, three CIDG companies, would operate within the immediate vicinity of the fledgling camp and airfield, out to a distance of one thousand meters, and Trang's CIDG forces would operate from one thousand meters to six thousand meters, well beyond the maximum effective range of enemy 82mm mortars. Our job was to patrol within our area to search for and destroy enemy ground forces, and to locate and destroy enemy mortar positions. Simple enough, right?

The Public's Right to Know

Since time was important, I suggested to Trang that we begin deploying that very evening, even though there was but an hour or two of existing daylight. I was able to convince him that leaving the area during darkness—our friend—would provide security not usually enjoyed during the daylight hours. I was not surprised that he agreed, and as we made final preparations, he readied his forces for movement at dusk.

At this time I was introduced to an ABC war correspondent. He was a fairly young man, but older than my twenty-six years. He asked if he could accompany our forces, to write about it and take pictures. I asked him how many operations he'd been on, and he said, "This would be my first." It wasn't that I didn't like him—I admired anyone who would put himself or herself in danger, just to ensure that the American public was getting a true flavor of this war—but I was not sure I wanted to be responsible for his safe return. I then set the conditions under which he would participate: "You can come if you understand that I will not be able to make allowances for you or your safety." I reinforced this by stating that under no circumstances would I be compelled to do one thing differently on his account than I would do were he not there, and that he would be required to observe strict noise and light discipline throughout the patrol.

"I understand," he said. "I don't expect special treatment, I will keep up, and I will otherwise be invisible."

Finally, I said, "You must understand also that your cameras, and your desire to take pictures, must not interfere in any way with the operation nor endanger our forces." He agreed. I said, "Be ready to move within the hour."

As the late afternoon sun sank gently on the hilltop to our left, we silently slipped out of Trai Bi. The order of march out of the camp was recon, Company 32, our headquarters section, Company 33, Company 34, and a small tail-gunner section for rear security. Our initial destination was the base of the distant ridgeline, at which point we would initiate patrolling operations in company sectors throughout the night. From the enemy's point of view, it was a relatively simple maneuver to get mortar crews into position, within range (four thousand meters), fire missions, and then move to another location, repeating the process again and again. The crews would have deployed listening posts to detect our movement, and established checkpoints for internal coordination. They would also have what every VC unit had in areas not secured or being contested: the timely support of the local population. The villagers often served as the eyes and ears of the VC forces living in or moving through the established villages. Kind of like a "neighborhood watch" program. Under certain circumstances, the VC sympathizers also provided food and shelter, but the risks of doing that had to be carefully weighed against the possibility of South Vietnamese government retribution if discovered, though of course there was the fear of VC reprisals if they didn't. In fact, the CIDG program was designed to relocate those villagers willing to move from the bush into the relative security of an SF camp like Trai Bi. So it could be said that we were competing for the hearts and minds of the people while providing a measure of local security.

We reached our initial objective area and without much fanfare began to deploy into company sectors. The headquarters section, with the attached recon element, remained with the three platoons of Company 32. When in sector, the units deployed on night patrols, except for one platoon designated to secure our fixed battalion command post (CP). Except for the continuous H&I fire from Trai Bi, our night operations were uneventful, though our just being there on that ridgeline may well have discouraged the VC from unleashing their nightly mortar attacks.

Can You Feel the Heat?

We rendezvoused the next morning, eager to push on over the ridgeline en route to our next objective area in the vicinity of the Bien Hoa River, about five kilometers to the northwest. Our reasoning was that the VC mortar units and their ground security elements were probably based near the river, for security, food, and water. Most likely they would bivouac on the far, western side of the river in favor of the relative security of the river itself. If our analysis was correct, the VC units occupied the high ground for good observation and firing positions into Trai Bi but traveled eight to ten kilometers each day to accomplish their mission. Accordingly, we would conduct operations on both the near and far banks of the river, and the adjacent areas, to a distance of two thousand meters, to locate and destroy the VC mortar units or seriously degrade their effectiveness.

Our movement from the high ground, back down into the valley and along the northern reaches of the Bien Hoa River, was slowed not only by the nature of the terrain, but, more significantly, by the extreme temperatures. I had never before experienced such a bizarre combination of heat and almost total lack of humidity as on that day. My face was doing a slow burn as we walked, but without the normal sweat one anticipates during an increase in physical exertion. I knew we were in trouble when soldiers with lifetime acclimatization badges began to drop along the march route. I decided then to advise Trang that we should locate a relatively well-vegetated area by the river, cease operations for the day, and care for the increasing number of dehydrated troops. As we established our bivouac about 1400 hours, the pocket thermometer I carried registered 130 degrees. We all needed water and rest. Tomorrow would be another day.

While on continuous combat operations during the hot season in Vietnam, the average soldier required about twelve quarts of water per day. Our standing operating procedure (SOP) required each man to carry four full quart-size canteens. Leaders at all levels were always conscious of the need for replenishment, and during movement they tracked on their maps the numerous rivers and streams they would encounter throughout the day. The Bien Hoa River, not a large river by Vietnamese standards, measured thirty to forty feet across in most places, and flowed at a relatively rapid six knots. After posting our listening posts and several ambushes along the trails leading into our bivouac area, leaders encouraged their men to shed their clothes in favor of a long-awaited cool bath. That was done for one company at a time while the other two companies were at the ready. Changeover was at ninety minutes until 1800 hours, at which time we would revert to full security.

As I dropped my combat gear and jungle fatigues and looked myself over for leeches, I was appalled at how lily-white I was from the neck down. I normally sported a healthy tan, reflective of my outdoor nature, but the war seldom if ever offered the time or the inclination to lie out. And although I was quite aware of the danger of skinny-dipping in the buff, I couldn't resist the river. So I frolicked, swam, dried off, swam again, and, unfortunately, got burnt. In the military, a sunburn that precludes a soldier from carrying out his mission can be a court-martial offense, and I knew I had no one to blame but myself. I can honestly say I have never felt so sick and helpless in my whole life. My head throbbed, and I never get headaches. I was vomiting, and I never get sick. I could not even put on my wet T-shirt, let alone fatigues and web gear.

As I wallowed in self-pity, a nearby explosion brought me back to my senses. For a minute or two the pain didn't matter, as I scrambled for my weapon and a nearby radio. Just about the time I was going to die peacefully, another explosion erupted. I thought we were under attack, but from where, I was not sure. In training, they teach you to listen carefully to the "sounds of combat," particularly for the first few minutes. Not hearing the report of direct-fire weapons (rifles, pistols, machine guns, RPGs, etc.), I assumed at first we were under a mortar attack. But the heavily muffled sounds were not much like the *whump* of an incoming mortar. I knew there must be another answer. Just then several CIDG soldiers ran from the river toward me and, with toothless grins, displayed two or three large fish they had stunned or killed with fragmentation grenades and retrieved from the muddy waters. For some reason, I no longer felt the intense pain of my burn, nor did I feel as sick. Call it shock therapy.

Does Anyone Have an M-60 Machine Gun?

How we managed to survive the extraordinary breach of security, I will never know. If Charlie was in the area, it would not be long until we met him face-to-face. Trang read the riot act to the troops who had done the "fishing," and our light and noise discipline improved immeasurably on the day after, but I was still uncomfortable as we looked for a safe river-crossing site. When I felt we had moved far enough away from the fishing hole, I advised Lieutenant Trang to select a crossing site that would enable us to secure both the near bank and the far bank before dark. We had about three hours of daylight to get that accomplished.

River-crossing operations are always fraught with danger. Units are vulnerable until they have secured both the near and the far banks. Once the near bank was secured, and one end of the crossing rope tied off, one of the scouts swam the thirty feet to the far bank and tied the other end to a large tree. The recon platoon then crossed without incident and secured the far bank. So far, so good. The most vulnerable period is during the crossing, when half the unit is on one side of the river and the other half is on the other. Not only are there inadequate forces on either side, but there is a lot of confusion about command and control, and when it's a wet crossing, radios and some heavy weapons are often waterproofed in nylon ponchos during crossing, and may not be available then to direct a counterattack. Such was the case at the Bien Hoa River.

Within minutes after securing the far bank, the forces that continued to cross came under attack from the near bank, the side of the river from which we were trying to cross. I quickly recovered my rucksack, my M-16, and my radio, all of which I'd put down at the base of the tree that secured our crossing line. Over the excruciating sounds of battle, up close and personal, Trang issued commands to his leaders, as I contacted Tay Ninh to report the firefight and to alert them that we would likely need support from the artillery unit and, possibly, Tac-Air.

When hit, it is important to establish communications with higher headquarters, immediately. Even though you may not be able to tell them much, your own confidence, and the confidence you demonstrate in advising and leading your troops, can made a big difference in the final outcome. There are also some liabilities. As about half of our unit had crossed, we were now seriously engaged on both sides of the river. Casualties were mounting, the sounds and the real effects of war in full swing. However, some of the initial confusion had subsided. Medics were treating the wounded, as leaders reported that we'd suffered several friendly KIA in the first few minutes.

At that point one of our M-60 machine gunners grabbed the rope to begin the crossing. I'm not sure whether it was just his turn to cross or that we sorely needed firepower on the other side. Regardless, I distinctly remember that he was a rather large Cambodian soldier, as I was kneeling on one knee near the camouflaged entrance to the river. He grasped the rope and quickly lowered his body into the water. His 7.62mm machine-gun ammunition was draped in links around his neck, the gun itself secured by the carrying handle in the firm grip of his left hand. Not otherwise secured to the rope, he jostled the MG as he maneuvered hand over hand on the sagging rope. At midpoint he slipped off the rope. I instantly used the open radio line to relay to the tactical operations center at Tay Ninh that we'd suffered another casualty while crossing. Lieutenant Colonel "Happy" Happersat, the B-team commander, apparently monitoring the operation with the TOC, said, "Recover the body." Still in contact on both sides, I said, "Negative, he's gone."

Happersat, a man I had never met, repeated, "I'm ordering you to recover that body, now."

My temperature was rising and I could feel my heart rate begin to pulse uncharacteristically fast. With the radio handset in my left hand, and my right hand engaged tightly about my M-16 rifle for self-defense, I pushed the mike to my mouth to record my transmission in order to be heard over the unimaginable noise about me. I said, "Look, you motherfucker, if you want that cocksucker so goddamned bad, just step outside your motherfucking headquarters and the fucker will be there in about five minutes, out!" Knowing that I was risking a court-martial, in view of what was happening about us, there just was not time, nor was I inclined, to debate the deep personal loss of a trooper with someone so distant from the scene. Much to his credit, Happersat never said anything to me about this incident, nor should he have.

Did You Bring Your Camera?

Even though our situation was improving—fewer rounds per minute and fewer casualties being taken—we had a long way to go. With about two-thirds of our force across the river, I felt we'd secured the far bank well enough so it made sense to complete the crossing. By then, the headquarters section, and our illustrious war correspondent, was preparing to cross. Actually, my respect for our cameraman had grown, as he'd shown some sympathy, as well as good judgment, in not choosing to capture on film my sunburned image or the dazed fish for all the world to see. He was next on the rope, just before me. As I shouted words of encouragement to him, he began the treacherous trek to the other side, his cameras dangling precariously at his left hip. I saw the cameras disappear beneath the water's surface, but was glad when he managed to get himself safely to the other side. Whether his camera strap broke under the water's force or he'd failed to properly secure his equipment really didn't matter then, nor does it today. Still, I felt bad for him that he unwittingly lost his stock-in-trade to the river wild. He was a survivor, and I hope that he has the opportunity to read this book and identify himself to me after all these years.

The images remain clear, and most of the details, but there was not a lot of time or inclination in the heat of battle to write things down, like the name of a war correspondent. Given the shit in which we daily found ourselves, and the need to remain alert and focused on the mission, we simply remembered what we remembered, and the things we didn't remember, well, fuck it! Who cared? What were they going to do, send us back to Vietnam? Whoever the correspondent is, I'm sure he had, and has, a hell of a story to tell. He was a good man, and a brave man. And I really liked him.

Let's Call It a Wrap

When we got hit during the river crossing, we were into the third or fourth day of a seven-day operation, and we were at midpoint on the map. We had a choice to make. Stay on the far bank and continue to defend a static position, or move back across the river and "didi." For instinctive reasons, we chose the latter. Confident that we had put a hell of a scare into old Mr. Charles, and that there was not a lot more to prove that time out, we resecured the near bank of the river, then headed for home.

It was one of the longest nights I would spend in Vietnam. As darkness replaced the light of day, we felt more comfortable moving away from the scene, but we had a long way to go, and the speed with which we retraced our steps was slowed by the dead and wounded we carried. We had sustained six friendly KIA and seven WIA. Our count and estimates of enemy casualties were higher. The heat of the day still lingered, as darkness alone was not sufficient to cool the air after the impossible daytime temperatures. I was extremely tired, as we had been on the move for thirty-six hours.

The next thing I remembered was reaching my right hand up toward my right eye. Apparently, we had moved about six kilometers back toward Trai Bi, but by a different route, when we just stopped and dropped into a hard-to-describe low area with serious ground vegetation and lots of moisture. The trail was pitch-black, but I could "see" that we were in a wet area, and knew we could go no farther. At that point we didn't know for sure what we were doing. We ought to have been more diligent in our maneuvers, but in war, sometimes, that's how it happens: you're so tired you're just not sure what the hell you're doing, where you're going, or that you'll survive. To be sure, and I don't think that I'm alone on this, there are times when you just don't give a shit, when your resistance is so low that you would just as soon die, right there and then, as change your course of action. No big fucking deal.

So, when I felt a slimy hardness in my right eye, I had no idea whether or not I was dreaming, or awake, or at some point in between. Slowly, I realized I was waking, and it was a leech. Leeches are common in Vietnam. In the jungle, you protect yourself against the bloodsuckers, but nothing is foolproof. As I plucked its large, warm, blood-filled body from my right eye, I squished him in my grip, wiped the bloody hand on my fatigue shirt, and began to dream of the trip back to Trai Bi. I was that tired. I occasionally woke up to the H&I fire we directed all about our location for better protection.

Then it was daylight and we were on the move once again. Without incident, we reached the ridgeline that overlooked the camp, and remained there for the night, carrying out light patrolling.

The next morning, we inched our way back to Trai Bi, aware that we'd probably discouraged the nightly mortar attacks, as the camp had not been hit in six days. It was time to rest.

Fever of Unknown Origin (FUO)

Apparently, as we approached Trai Bi, I had become weak and dehydrated, with a high temperature and severe headache. As a precaution, I was medevacked to the 93d Evacuation Hospital in Long Bien, just south of Bien Hoa. I was admitted, donned a blue overshirt in exchange for my sweaty fatigues, and was placed on a field cot next to a young black soldier. The sweat was pouring off his well-sculpted body as he lay naked on the bed, save for a cut-off pair of hospital-blue shorts.

As my temperature was being taken, I whispered to a young male nurse, "What's wrong with the trooper next door?"

"He has malaria," I was told. "We can't seem to regulate his temperature."

I asked if he was in danger of dying. The corpsman answered, "Unless we can get his temperature down—it ranges between 104 and 108 degrees—by icing his body, we're going to lose him. Unfortunately, we risk giving him pneumonia when we use large blocks of ice."

I watched from the corner of my eye, as he seemed to be in obvious pain, although I never heard him cry out.

When a female nurse returned with the preliminary results from some blood tests, I became more interested in my own medical condition. I was anxious to get back to Suoi Da. She reported that I had the countrywide catch-all, "fever of unknown origin" (FUO). They said FUO when they had no better diagnosis. My temperature was hovering at 105 degrees, but without the marked cycle of chills and sweating being experienced by my neighbor.

"When can I leave?" I asked.

She said that I was going to have to stay for observation for three or four more days, then gave me something to ease the pain in my head, and I became drowsy.

When I awoke, the cot next to mine was empty. My young black friend—a friend of the bush, the Nam, the brotherhood—had died sometime during the night. Cause of death? Pneumonia. I said a small prayer for him, and for me. A bite from an infected female anopheles mosquito, received while he was carrying out his duty thousands of miles from his loved ones, was the real cause of death.

I wanted to get out of that place, and at my insistence, I was released in two days. I was lucky.

A Date with a Lady

During the sixty-minute flight back to Suoi Da, I couldn't help but think about operations on Nui Ba Den. Like others before me, I could not get the Black Virgin out of my mind. She had held a certain fascination among the many SF A-team commanders before me. Within the past two years, Captain James G. "Bo" Gritz had launched aggressive combat operations in search of VC units on the mountain, only to conclude that such tactics were counterproductive: not only were the forays into the tree-covered boulders dangerous, but religious sensitivities were such that damages to any of the many shrines built into the mountain's face could cause local authorities to cease operations on Nui Ba Den altogether.

But, that was then. In our time, the VC were able to monitor operations out of Suoi Da from a hardened perch four hundred meters above sea level and direct their fire onto Route 13, a major road network running from north to south above Suoi Da, then west into Tay Ninh city. We estimated the enemy's strength at one rifle platoon, with one or two shoulder-fired rocket teams, for a total of thirty-five to forty dicks.

Trang and I discussed various tactics at length. We invited input from all team members on both sides. We knew that any potential target would be among the large rock caves along the eastern slope, open to Suoi Da, and at the midpoint of the saddle between the highest of two dominant peaks, Nui Ba Den herself and a sister peak, Nui Cao, to the northeast. The caves were situated about halfway between the high point of the saddle and the flat valley floor below.

After much deliberation, we dispatched the CH-47 cargo helicopter for its weekly resupply run to the top of the mountain. When the chopper landed, and the reception party began to off-load the food, ammunition, and other equipment requested, thirty-three combat-ready soldiers disembarked. We had not communicated this information to anyone, as we were certain the VC were able to intercept our regular transmissions. It was D-3, that is, three days before the attack would begin, as we completed phase one of the operation.

Our plans were to conduct a four-company coordinated attack at 1000 hours on D-Day. The mountain platoon was to rest in position for two nights, then begin the treacherous descent from the top of Nui Ba Den northeast on a straight line to the saddle. Heavily loaded with CS gas and steel fragmentation grenades, at 1000 hours they would launch a diversionary attack from their position overlooking the caves. If undetected before the assault, the unit would descend into the caves themselves to close with and destroy the VC force. If detected, the unit would do as much damage as possible without taking serious casualties, then quickly withdraw toward the saddle. That would complete phase two of the operation. Phase three, on call, would be initiated from the valley floor when either the mountain force needed help or, having retreated, was free and clear of the heavy ground and indirect weapons that would be fired in their direction.

If there is one thing that all leadership training should stress, it is that operations seldom if ever go off precisely as planned. For that reason, plans need to be flexible, and commanders need to adapt and adjust to meet the ever-changing requirements.

Paper Covers Rock, Rock Breaks Scissors, Scissors Cut Paper

Our plan was magnificent. We felt reasonably certain that the diversionary attack would not only take the VC by complete surprise, but that, having been drawn from the caves, the enemy unit would be a sitting duck for the preplanned and on-call fire we had scheduled for D-Day. I began to feel less comfortable when, during the night of D-1, a radio transmission from the scouts reported that their descent was being slowed by injuries due to the extreme terrain. Using rappelling ropes and snap links at night to tie into the steep, rocky, heavily treed slopes proved to be very dangerous. First reports indicated that two scouts were down with broken legs. A medic would care for them until all three could be recovered after the operation.

Then came more reports of serious injuries—all this without any shots being fired. More important, after nearly ten hours of daylight movement and nine hours of travel at night, the unit had completed only eight hundred meters. In the nine hours remaining, it was unlikely they would reach the saddle, some seven hundred meters away, not to mention the area surrounding the caves, another four hundred meters straight down the mountain.

After some discussion, in the name of safety, Trang ordered the scouts to remain in place throughout the night, then, during daylight, with the injured being carried out, to return to the top.

Plan B in effect, at precisely 1000 hours on D-Day, the six 106mm recoilless rifles from Suoi Da thundered mightily from their emplacement fifteen hundred meters due south of the caves. For those who know, the 106 is one of the loudest and most powerful direct-fire weapons the military has ever produced. After thirty years, I owe my M-2, high-decibel hearing impairment to the report of the 106s firing that day, as our command and advisory element was located behind two of the gun positions.

The 106s are also highly accurate. Using hindsight, given the disastrous results of Plan A and the unexplored dangers of fighting the VC on terrain familiar to them, from positions directly above the caves, we were back in the ball game with only a few injuries and no real casualties at that point. We had to be encouraged.

Hoping to have drawn the VC from the caves with the 106 bombardment, we initiated the thirty-minute preplanned indirect-fire program: 105mm artillery and 81mm mortars from Suoi Da, 81mm mortars from the mountaintop, and the much heavier 4.2mm mortars from Trai Bi. Under cover of those, we moved two companies along the mountain floor, just inside the woodline adjacent to the caves, and another two companies frontally from southeast to northwest. Trang and I were with the second group.

As we began to receive return fire, we established that we were engaging a worthy target, and that our suspicions about the VC occupying those caves were correct. We were now engaged in an intense exchange of various types and sizes of weapons. We may have underestimated both the size and the will of our enemy.

What Is the Price of a Casualty?

The two companies in the woodline directed their fire toward the VC encampment from an established base, semi-perpendicular to their target. As the 106 gun jeeps were advancing along a trail toward our friendly base, a loud explosion

occurred. When the smoke settled, we were able to confirm a
direct VC hit, destroying the gun jeep, killing both the driver
and the gun crew chief, and seriously wounding the assistant
crew chief. The remaining five gun jeeps quickly pulled into
the woodline, established a hasty firing position, and returned
fire toward the caves as our ground forces closed to within
three or four hundred meters from the cave area. Phase three
of our operation was well under way.

From the continuous barrage of sitreps being radioed from
the leaders in contact, we learned we were taking some pretty
heavy casualties. Within minutes one of the medevac helicopters loading wounded for the ten-minute flight to the field
hospital at Tay Ninh was also struck with direct fire, but it
managed to clear the area safely. The intensity of the battle
rose as I directed flight after flight of Tac-Air over the target
area, using combinations of 250-, 500-, and 2,000-pound hard
bombs, and napalm. Hard steel bombs explode on ground contact, creating large earthen craters while spewing hand-size
chunks of steel fragments about the killing area. Anyone
caught uncovered within a hundred meters or so was in imminent danger of being killed. Napalm was much more insidious. The napalm containers, about six feet long and eighteen
inches wide, break open on contact but tumble over and over
for hundreds of feet, all the while releasing massive amounts
of highly volatile, burning, boiling hot, thickened fuel that
clings to the body like tar. Not only is the pain that napalm
inflicts real, but the psychological effect is horrible as well,
because those not in the killing zone witness the screaming,
tortured, burning bodies of their comrades being slowly but
effectively charred beyond any recognition. Those not directly
hit by the burning jelly are often sickened by the residue and
rendered ineffective for battle. Medics find it nearly impossible to administer first aid to those hit.

The battle raged for hours as friendly casualties mounted.
Although we enjoyed the advantage of superior firepower, the
VC had the high ground and the plunging fire. While we were
not, nor would we ever be, in a good position from which to
estimate enemy casualties, we could be relatively certain that

we were not only inflicting serious casualties, but making a clear statement that had needed to be made for some time. And that is, if you want to fuck with us, there are times that we will stand and fight, and pound sand up your ass with a baseball bat.

Though we had little cover on the grassy valley floor, our command group and advisory element remained outside the maximum effective range of VC small arms. The maximum effective range is defined as that distance at which a well-trained rifleman, given the weapon at issue, would expect to inflict continuous casualties on his intended target. For the French-made MAS-36, AK-47, and other known VC weapons, that distance was about five hundred meters. Of course, that doesn't mean that we were out of danger, as rifle experts, particularly those using sniper scopes, can, and do, repeatedly kill targets well beyond a thousand meters. The bullet itself will fly up to a mile, consequently, with so many rounds being fired, lots of soldiers deployed beyond the maximum effective range of enemy weapons are routinely killed or wounded in battle. And with so much chaos, it was hard that day to keep those not wounded from prematurely escaping the battlefield, while ensuring that those who were hit, and who required treatment at the field hospital, actually were safely loaded onto the medevac helicopters.

From my position near the command post, I was closely monitoring the medevacs coming in and leaving. I was concerned not only that the wounded were evacuated, but that the choppers were not overloaded, which would endanger the safety of the pilot, the helicopter, and the wounded. It was this concern I felt as one chopper, ready for takeoff, hesitated as one of our troops ran across the marshy field toward an open door. Judging by the distance he ran and the speed with which he moved, there was little indication that the soldier was wounded. The door gunner waved the hyperactive soldier away from the crowded door in anticipation of an immediate takeoff. The helicopter was near the maximum load, but the trooper nevertheless continued to scratch and claw his way onto one of the helicopter skids. In the interest of safety, and fair play, I intervened. Although I could see no visible wounds, I instinctively trusted the soldier, helping him through the door. I climbed aboard to see how our wounded and dead were being treated. As the two medics aboard administered first aid—stop the bleeding, clear the airway, protect the wound, and treat for shock—to the more seriously wounded, my new friend sat up straight in one of the brown-nylon seats fastened to its tubular aluminum structure. He had a smile on his face, apparently happy that he hadn't been left behind.

I gave him a knowing glance as I patted his right knee with my outstretched right hand, mouthing that he would be all right. The noise of the chopper and the intense screams of the wounded all but drowned out the shouted instructions of the medics and the attempted communications by the patients. Blood was everywhere. Body parts were broken open, attached loosely to larger parts, and in some cases chunks of blood-soaked flesh were being bandaged with sterile gauze and green tape. When a large, open wound is gushing blood, well-trained soldiers and medics will often try to stop the bleeding by wrapping the three-inch-wide, army-green duct tape around and around the wound. This puts maximum pressure on the wounded area while trapping massive amounts of blood that would normally escape.

The flight to Tay Ninh was uneventful. Flying at fifteen hundred feet ensured that we were in little danger from VC snipers, who occasionally got lucky in trying to down a U.S. or Vietnamese helicopter along its flight route. Since choppers could be heard from several hundred meters, the VC had time to adjust their positions so they could fire from directly underneath the flight path. In cases where there was little vegetation, or in large open areas, the VC had a better chance of striking their targets, but also faced the risk of having their positions marked for air attacks or indirect fire like artillery.

As we began to lose altitude, turning sharply downward, I saw the large, bright-white X marking the center of the landing pad. My eyes were fixed on several medical jeeps lined up just off the pierced steel planking of which the pad was constructed. After we touched down softly onto the hardstand, the pilot in command informed me, through the headset attached to the flight helmet I was wearing, that we were on the ground and it was safe to begin off-loading. As the on-ground medical crew approached, I glanced up behind me to ensure that my friend was being unbuckled from his safety belt secured to the seat. He looked pale. I reached my right hand up to his chin strap to unfasten his steel helmet. His eyes were dim. Without talking, thinking that he'd lapsed into a coma, I reached up my right hand behind his neck to support his loosened head. I felt a sticky substance on my fingers where the top of his neck met the hairline. Exploring cautiously with my fingers, I found a small hole, and noticed a trace of blood dripping onto the collar of his fatigue shirt. Apparently, his hyperactivity had been caused by a bullet that entered his head at the top of his neck but had failed to exit, remaining lodged in his brain. I knew then that he was dead.

While war is something of a science, it is not a precise, predictable one. There may be some artistry involved, particularly at the higher levels, where the blood of the killing fields gives way to the sleepy sounds of briefings and other staff activities, but ground combat is different. For those whose job it is to close with and kill the enemy, the war is measured, day to day, by their actions and the feedback they receive as a consequence. Whether we were successful in our effort to reduce VC interference with our operations into War Zone C by attacking a surprisingly strong defensive position on Nui Ba Den is a matter of perspective. We suffered three KIA and twenty-six WIA that day. And three helicopters were damaged as those brave medevac pilots made repeated trips to the valley floor to retrieve our seriously wounded troopers for treatment. And, although we lost no fighter aircraft, the pilots who flew low and slow about the target, to ensure that they hit enemy positions and not friendly soldiers, routinely put their own lives on the line in support of their comrades. What they did at Nui Ba Den that day required courage, stamina, and a sense of honor of which all Americans can be proud. God bless the United States Air Force.

Tiny

Soon after returning to Suoi Da, I interviewed a new non-commissioned officer who had arrived a day or two earlier from Bien Hoa. He said, "Hi, sir. I'm Tiny." From his appearance, it was not hard to see the connection. Tiny was a huge hulk of a man, well overweight by anyone's standards, particularly Special Forces'. Initially, I was taken aback, wondering just how he had managed to escape the fitness police. On the other hand, he was friendly, good-natured, and open. After no more than a few minutes, he indicated that he was serving his third tour of duty in Vietnam and that "the third time was a charm."

I bit at this English idiom, reinforcing the notion about just why our language was so difficult for the Vietnamese to understand. I said, "What do you mean?"

"You know, sir, 'the third time's a charm to buy the farm.' My luck has run out."

I said, "Bullshit, what we do here is not based solely on luck. Whether you are on your first tour, second, or even a third, has little to do with your chances of survival. If you do what you're supposed to do here, you'll be fine. But if you start looking for something to do when it's none of your business, you can get into trouble." This tough talk was important, because some U.S. soldiers—whether reassigned or volunteering—were returning to the war zone more frequently than anticipated, because as the war spooled up and we received new people, there was always a need for tested, experienced personnel to guide, train, and lead them. I reasoned with Tiny that, although the third time was particularly precarious, for a number of reasons—some due to overconfidence and a sense of invulnerability—it would be his attitude and experience that would help him survive. Still, as I left him I couldn't help but wonder if his statement would become a self-fulfilling prophecy. In retrospect, I now wonder whether some soldiers, little understood and poorly treated at home—whether by their families or by stateside commands ill-prepared to deal with combat vets who'd had little peacetime military experience—didn't sign up for repetitive tours as a way of "going home" to the only place they felt safe. Home to the killing fields, where their skills and abilities were appreciated and rewarded. Home to rest.

The War Was Heating Up in War Zone C

For several months there were indications that the NVA would likely contest the growing U.S. involvement in the Vietnam War. By mid-1966 more conventional American divisions were arriving on the scene, eager to tear into an enemy thought to have inferior firepower and poorly trained soldiers. The U.S. press was starting to surmise that what began as a relatively small U.S. effort to assist the Vietnamese in securing the urban areas was spreading out into the countryside. People back home were already being "asked" by the politically motivated news media, "Will the war ever end?"

Theoretically, the large, well-equipped, and expertly trained American units were more self-sufficient and had more staying power. Under the circumstances, it would be only a matter of time before the NVA would try to muster its forces at one time, in one location, and attempt to dispel the American belief that such forces were invulnerable. There was at this time no more deserving battleground than War Zone C, where U.S. conventional forces were more frequently beginning to conduct search-and-destroy operations. Heretofore, because U.S. units had at their disposal the best weapons money could buy, whenever NVA units observed divisional-size elements rummaging near their secret bases, they withdrew, avoiding the large battle, quietly slipping back into neighboring Cambodia. There they would wait since, politically, the U.S. had no authorization to penetrate Cambodian soil. But the day would come. Our small-force operations within War Zone C had managed to stir up a hornets' nest or two. Eventually, to gain a measure of respect, the NVA would be compelled to stand and fight.

The fact that Suoi Da was on the edge of War Zone C was

not lost on me nor on the men that made up our twelve-man A-team. It was becoming quite clear to us, by our own instincts and by the reports we were receiving from C-3, that if there was to be a large conventional operation, Suoi Da would have a role to play.

The Little-Understood Nature of Intelligence

Historically, wars have been won and lost by adequate intelligence or the lack of it. "Intelligence" is the product of systematically processed combat information. As we were conducting our operations around Nui Ba Den and Trai Bi, we reported through intelligence channels all we gathered about the enemy—size, activity, location, unit identification, time, and equipment (known as a SALUTE to infantrymen). The intelligence staff processed our reports, along with many others (and other types of intelligence—communications, intercepts, aerial photography, agent reports, etc.), trying to reasonably conclude where, when, in what strength, and with what intention the enemy was operating. Reports were "graded" as to their value, from A-1—accurate source and reliable information—to F-6—inaccurate source and unreliable information. Seldom does there exist an A-1 report, one based on an undeniably truthful source and conclusively corroborated material. The next best thing is a B-2 report—about as good as it gets. So when C-3 received from another intelligence agency a B-2 report that remnants of six NVA regiments (1,200 to 1,500 men each) were marshaling twelve kilometers north of Suoi Da, we could "take it to the bank." Lieutenant Colonel J. B. Durst immediately ordered Captain Tom Myerchin to deploy within two hours his Mike Force from its base in Bien Hoa to the area north of Suoi Da to confirm the existence, size, and locations of enemy units. Tom's staging area and support base would be Suoi Da. Myerchin's five-hundred-man, three-company battalion of Nungs—fierce soldiers of Chinese ancestry—arrived in Suoi Da within the hour and immediately deployed its three companies in a fanlike formation, one due north in the center, with the remaining two on either side. It was essential that the NVA regimental forces be located and disrupted before they could gain strength while moving south through Suoi Da, possibly to Saigon.

Suoi Da itself became a major center of activity, as it was strategically located to serve as the staging area for elements of the U.S. 196th Light Infantry Brigade, the unit ordered to deploy a rapid-reaction force when, and where, the Mike Force got in trouble. C-123 and C-7 cargo planes began landing in a whirlwind of dust onto Suoi Da's unimproved, relatively short, dirt airstrip. Helicopters swirled in from all directions, unloading troops who began procedures for an immediate deployment.

By about 1400 hours, as the broiling sun bore down on the poorly shaded camp, the first field reports provided the grim news: Myerchin's center reconnaissance element, about 250 strong, had made contact with the lead elements of the NVA regiments. Initial friendly casualties were extremely heavy. KIAs were put at more than two hundred, with the remainder of the force being defeated in detail, leaving U.S. leadership responsibilities to a young Specialist-4; all other U.S. leaders were dead. Myerchin radioed that he was on his way from his position on the left to reinforce his center unit's demise. He also officially requested the deployment of the 196th's rapid-reaction force. The time was about 1700, as the sun was quickly moving behind the elongated mountainscape of Cambodia toward its full decline. About two hours of daylight remained.

Tiny and the Hat Trick

The seriously wounded were arriving at Suoi Da for treatment by medical personnel, and there was a never-ending flurry of helicopter activity into the 196th's base camp, which was being established a few hundred meters north of Suoi Da's main entrance. About 1800 hours, I learned through SF radio channels that the commander of the 196th Light

Infantry had decided not to send in the reinforcements to rescue Myerchin's badly defeated unit. Although darkness was
falling, Myerchin went ballistic. Who could blame him? He
had sent his own highly prized unit into the teeth of the enemy
to disrupt a major advance south into Tay Ninh, Suoi Da, and
most likely on to Saigon. And now, just a few hours later, there
was to be no rescue effort on his behalf? Under the circumstances, the 196th's avoidance of combat was highly questionable, and, I thought, it bordered on cowardice.

In all the commotion, another sitrep came in from the field,
from the location of Myerchin's decimated company. One of
the few remaining soldiers reported that an SF sergeant had
been found sitting up against a tree. It was Tiny. He was dead.
Apparently, he had gotten flown out to the site on one of the
medevac helicopters, to help with the wounded. Then, real-
izing that there were no return seats except for the wounded
and the dying, he sacrificed himself for his friends. Smart? Not
necessarily. Brave? Courageous? Absolutely. Predestination?
Who knows. Self-fulfilling prophecy? Perhaps. Whatever the
real motivation underlying Tiny's death, I was deeply saddened to learn that one of America's elite soldiers had been
porked up against a tree, the result of a combat action not
assigned to Detachment A-322, Suoi Da.

Attleboro

The following morning, the U.S. 196th Light Infantry
Brigade made its ignominious entry into the area where Tom
Myerchin's Mike Force had waged a ferocious battle with
regimental-size NVA units. Within the weeks and months that
followed, it became apparent that the NVA had not only established a major secret base in War Zone C, but that they also
intended to remain. Soon after discovering a large jungle
redoubt, the 196th itself requested, and received, timely reinforcement from the U.S. 25th Division, followed by the Big
Red One, the U.S. Army's First Infantry Division, under the
command of Major General William E. Dupuy. Operation

Attleboro, later redubbed Battle Creek, escalated into the largest U.S.-NVA confrontation of the war to date. On both sides hundreds were killed and thousands wounded. The tactics employed by our conventional forces—stand and fight while wielding overwhelming firepower—turned out to be the prescription that would kill the patient. A war fought without boundaries on one side was beginning to take on the dimensions required by overweight U.S. divisions on the other. In time, four and one-half U.S. divisions would duke it out with six NVA regiments. For what? By that time, I was back at C-3 in Bien Hoa preparing to recruit and command a mobile guerrilla force, but Philip Geyelin, a news correspondent, wrote about Battle Creek from Suoi Da in the November 23, 1966, edition of the *Wall Street Journal*:

VIETNAM VISION: WILL THE WAR EVER END?

It was late in a long, hot day at this Special Forces encampment on the edge of War Zone C when all the pieces seemed to fall in place, presenting—as in some surrealistic tableau—a chilling vision of how the war in Vietnam could ultimately evolve if it follows its present course. The vision was of a never-ending conflict in a Vietnam suffused and supported by a growing U.S. military presence; of a Vietnam engaged fitfully and inconclusively in endless "civic action" programs for "revolutionary development" and shaken periodically by recurrent domestic political crises, Fourth French Republic–style; of a Vietnam increasingly dependent for its safety and survival on "pacification" efforts, whether by the big battalions in the jungles or squad-size patrols in the hamlets—but in any case by U.S. troops. It was only a fleeting vision, but curiously compelling—and not entirely removed from reality.

Geyelin was writing about what he had witnessed at Battle Creek. The large-scale operations. The larger-scale egos of those who commanded the conventional combatants. He surmised that no territory was at stake—at least not permanently. No population was involved. Rather, the day's maneuvering had in it more of the French strategy at Dien Bien Phu—the tiger shoot, enticing the enemy into a fray to inflict a devastating defeat.

Geyelin surmised that if the VC, for their part, chose to pick up the First Division's challenge, their cost would be heavy. A Dupuy aide said, "We can handle anything they throw at us. While the infantry holds them, we pound them with artillery and air support, close in. That's the way to kill VC." In the command post huddle, the generals and the colonels were already talking of plans to pick up their battalions, drop them deeper into Zone C's forbidding hinterlands, and continue the hunt if the VC faded away.

Geyelin concluded, "The question raised at Suoi Da is not whether the techniques are sound or expertly executed. The real question, perhaps unanswerable, is whether the U.S. will not become more than ever the indispensable support and savior of South Vietnam, while American staying power erodes at home." Of course, history, reliably honest, provided the answer.

Task Force 957, Mobile Guerrilla

If there were substantial differences between the way large conventional forces and Special Forces fought the war in Vietnam, these differences were no more remarkably evident than in the creation of the mobile guerrilla forces. That I was asked to contribute to that historical event was an honor for which I was singularly unprepared. Not that I had not witnessed my share of combat actions in the few months in the field since leaving C-3, but there were hundreds of more experienced Green Berets who could have donned that mantle, the significance of which, at the time, was unknown even to Colonel Kelly, the Special Forces Group commander. Colonel Kelly had just received authorization for the creation of a mobile guerrilla force from General William C. Westmoreland, Commander, U.S. Military Assistance Command, Vietnam (COMUSMACV). And I had been promoted to captain only weeks earlier.

The mission outlined to me by Major Jim Archer, Deputy Commander, Company A, Fifth Special Forces Group (Airborne), was to recruit, organize, train, equip, and command an ethnic Cambodian guerrilla force using unconventional warfare tactics and techniques against VC guerrillas and major NVA units. The force would be clandestinely deployed into NVA secret base areas for extended periods without the normal support—heavy ground weapons, artillery support, and medevac of wounded forcemen—enjoyed by conventional forces and routine SF operations within Vietnam. Also, the missions were to be classified secret, and, if they were prematurely discovered, the U.S. would disavow all knowledge of their existence. The results of two such missions, Black Box and Blackjack-31, have been declassified and were made available under the Freedom of Information Act.

From an army perspective, the move was militarily significant. The establishment in October 1966 of Detachment A-303, later designated Task Force 957, Mobile Guerrilla, signaled a departure from the traditional advisory role, marking the first attempt to employ the United States Army Special Forces in a guerrilla warfare role in the conduct of the Vietnam War.

When Major Archer asked if I wanted to accept such an assignment, I unhesitatingly said yes. After signing a document attesting to the above conditions, I began to outline the organization of such a force.

It seemed to me that the mobile guerrilla force should be a balanced team consisting of intelligence, operations, medical, weapons, communications, and demolitions skills. Messages were sent to all III Corps Tactical Zone Special Forces camps for American volunteers. More than eighty-five Green Berets responded, reporting for interview to a III Corps Mike Force compound office to maintain a measure of secrecy. Sincerity, cooperation, enthusiasm, skill, imagination, and experience

were personal qualities most heavily weighted in interviewing
applicants. It was important that such missions not be compli-
cated with personal problems. I asked few direct questions,
but they were important indicators of the type of soldier I was
recruiting. I wanted to know whether the applicant would be
comfortable operating as a lone American with a small band
of Cambodian guerrillas within the heart of the NVA secret
base areas for periods of from thirty to forty-five days without
the support of heavy weapons or artillery, and without the possibility of medical evacuation. It was not surprising to me that
about sixty of the eighty-five declined. Remember, these men
were seasoned Green Berets. For their honesty I thanked those
who declined. Simply put, these missions were not for every-
body. Of those who met the criteria, eleven were selected,
rounding out a twelve-man team.

A Baker's Dozen

As I was finishing up the paperwork of the recruiting effort,
very pleased about the quality of the selectees, Major Archer
called me to his C-3 office and informed me that I was being
replaced as the A-303 commander. I was stunned. He offered
that this in no way reflected on my actions to date, about
which he said he was pleased, but rather that the Group commander, Colonel Blackjack Kelly, wanted this first-of-a-kind
opportunity in the hands of a more experienced soldier. I told
him that I understood. He said the officer coming in to assume
command was a very experienced Green Beret who had been
in Special Forces all his service life, beginning as an enlisted
man with the old 77th Special Forces Group. I said he was
lucky to have such a man and that I would gladly step down.
He said the new commander was Captain James G. "Bo"
Gritz. He then made me an offer I couldn't refuse. He offered
me command of Suoi Da, or any other A-team in III Corps. Or
I could stay with the mobile guerrilla force, as deputy commander. My response, burned in my mind to this day, was,
"As much as I want to command at Suoi Da, I believe in the

Second Lieutenant Yedinak, Airborne!

Cadre at headquarters and Headquarters Company,
Home of the Walkin' Soldier.

The author, a handsome devil, as HHC company commander.

The author and classmates in Special Forces Officer Training.
Note their disheveled state, for which Special Forces types
are justly famed.

Lori, eighteen months old, in her father's uniform.

The pointer rests on Suoi Da Special Forces Camp.

The 81mm mortar position at Suoi Da.

Author with John Wayne during the actor's visit
to C3, 5th SFGA.

LBJ walking his pet Special Forces first lieutenant.

Author conducting class at Ho Ngoc Tao, 1966.

Author (right) and Capt. Bo Gritz (left) demonstrating holds and throws at Ho Ngoc Tao.

The author sharing a gourmet meal and a vintage brew with S.Sgt. Joe Cawley at Ho Ngoc Tao.

Captain Yedinak
and the
"black box."

The author at Duc Phong
after Blackjack-31.

Bo Gritz (left) and the author (right foreground)
at Duc Phong.

The author with Kim Lai at the Khmer Krom Convention in
Philadelphia, November 22, 1997.

mobile guerrilla concept, and if Gritz is as good as you say, I have a lot to learn. I'll stay." I have never regretted that decision.

A-303, Mobile Guerrilla, consisted of a detachment commander (a captain), a deputy commander (also a captain), a team sergeant/main force platoon commander (master sergeant), operations and intelligence specialist (sergeant first class), communications specialist (staff sergeant), recon platoon commander (first lieutenant), heavy weapons specialist/ platoon commander (sergeant first class), and a light weapons specialist/platoon commander, two team medics/deputy platoon commanders, a demolitionist, and a recon section leader/ communications specialist, all the latter staff sergeants.

I met Gritz the next day, and liked him immediately. In the first few minutes, I could tell he was a smooth operator, gave a shit about what we were doing in Vietnam, had plenty of experience, and that our personalities would mesh perfectly. In all my dealings with Bo, in Vietnam and in the "real world," I have had nothing but admiration and respect for who he is, what he has done, and whoever he may become in his remaining days. I'm not altogether sure that, in spite of our friendship, he ever was told the whole story described above. I know that I never told him, and that he had no reason to ask. I do know that my decision that day cost me a seven-day R&R to Hong Kong. I had been booked for several weeks on a flight to Fantasy Island, but given the urgency of our schedule, I had to decline. I can't say I was disappointed, as I was put in charge of recruiting the Cambodian force we would come to know and respect. And it was Saturday night.

When Is a Flight Not a Flight?

Mass at the chapel was a hit-and-miss deal. Even as a practicing Catholic, I was neither over- or underexercised about making mass; also, I was seldom in a location where mass was offered. On this particular Sunday, about 1000 hours, I was giving thanks for being fairly treated in Special Forces, and for being alive. I was also asking for protection for me and our force, knowing that our missions would be very dangerous. Just then I was startled to hear a voice in the chapel call out for Captain Yedinak. I responded, grabbed my gear, and within minutes was en route in a C-130 cargo plane to Bu Dop, a Special Forces camp northwest of Bien Hoa. This was our first major recruiting opportunity. I'd learned during camp inspections that there was a heavy Cambodian contingent in Bu Dop.

About halfway into the forty-five-mile trip, an alarm went off. Then another. It was clear that the flight crew of three or four was trying to respond to a set of unusual conditions. But I did not ask what was going on, nor was anyone in a rush to tell me. It seemed we were in the middle of an air emergency, and that the plane was listing badly first to one side and then the other. Then the plane banked very sharply and made a sharp U-turn. I suspected we were heading back from whence we came. Just as I thought that the crew was getting the situation under control, a third alarm sounded, there was more scurrying about, and flames shot from one of the outboard engines. A few minutes later I was informed by the crew chief that we had feathered *three* of the four engines, and were about ten minutes out from an emergency landing on a foamed runway at Saigon's Ton Son Nhut Air Base. I said a small prayer, then assumed a good crash position. Fortunately for me, I was the lone passenger sitting on the four-engine cargo bay, and the only cargo as well. So much for the power of prayer.

Another Night at the Bar

The distinction of living and spending the night in Saigon was somewhat overshadowed by my night at the bar of a local advisory unit. After being shown to a dilapidated hotel, I asked where I could get a cold beer and was directed to a club. Once I found the bar, it was obvious that I was the only fatigue-clad, armed combat soldier there. Before too long an overweight sergeant major approached and asked if I was aware of the dress requirement. I said, "In Vietnam?"

He said, "No, Captain, in this bar." I responded in the negative. He said that I would have to change, and give up my .45 caliber lightweight Colt Commander. I told him that was stupid, that I could not, would not, and that I just got off an airplane and would only spend one night in his pussy club. In all of the commotion, I don't know to this day if he understood what I was really saying, because before he could get his dick out of his mouth, I turned, walked away, and ordered another beer. It occurs to me now that G. Gordon Liddy would have been right proud of me. Within minutes I was in a conversation with a full colonel (for civilians, a captain is pay grade O-3, and a colonel is an O-6, that is, God) who was trying to tell me that his ten-man infantry squad could do anything that a ten-man SF A-team could do. Again I walked away, but not until I told him that he was full of shit.

What a crock! It's really scary that some line officers believe that kind of drivel. Unfortunately for Green Berets everywhere, pukes like that colonel were sitting on promotion boards and ruling on school assignments.

What a fucking disaster. Little wonder that Dave Hackworth's favorite book was *Once an Eagle*. Hackworth, an Infantry tiger who retired a colonel, knew how fucked up most things were in Vietnam, and was not afraid to push for major change. When it became obvious, even to him, that he was being shouted down by the senior brass and the liberal press, he had the balls to go on the record with his story, that is, before he went away to Australia to begin a second life. Amazingly, just about the time you start getting bored out of your ass by being around combat, and killing, and dying, you end up in some weenie den like that O-club bar talking to assholes who, at the very least, are a little light in the loafers. We may be talking about the CSB (combat sounds badge—as opposed to the Combat Infantryman Badge awarded to those who actually fought the enemy), for the sergeant major whose club assignment was close enough to combat to hear it. But for the colonel, it would have to be the CDB (combat dumb badge), for those who have no fucking idea about the things of which they speak. As Dennis Miller is fond of saying, "I don't want to get off on a rant here," but since when does a gracious host try to make an unintended guest for the night feel bad about being a proud member of *any* United States service, let alone the fighting part of the army, and not to mention those who volunteer for hazardous duty so that misfits can quote dress regulations in a war zone. But that's only my opinion.

Recruiting a Guerrilla Force

Within the next day or so, Bo Gritz and I went back to Saigon to visit the headquarters of the Khmer Serei, the friendly Cambodian movement in Vietnam that was aligned with U.S. interests. We sought authorization to recruit from within III Corps, primarily from the CIDG camps under C-3 control, Cambodian soldiers for the mobile guerrilla force. We obtained that authorization, without conditions. There is a major untold story about Cambodian assistance to the U.S. effort in Vietnam. Basically, the established Cambodian government supported the U.S. involvement in Vietnam, providing soldiers and access to certain Cambodian territories during the conflict. For its efforts on our behalf, those who were known or suspected of providing such political or military assistance were hunted down and killed by the Communist Khmer Rouge following the end of hostilities. By some accounts, as many as eight million were killed by the Khmer Rouge. Some avoided capture, and some, though fewer, have realized their dream by being offered asylum in the United States.

Aside from the politics of the time, there was never a doubt in our minds about why we wanted to recruit, organize, train, equip, and fight with Cambodians. They were superior physical specimens, considerably larger than most Vietnamese. They were in good health, with strong, white teeth. They were honest and could be trusted. They were ferocious fighters, not afraid to sacrifice one, or a few, for the good of the many. They were clean spirits who could laugh. Finally, they were devoutly religious Buddhists who were able to understand that there was more to life than living and dying. Personally, I would have had little trouble either dying with or for our Cambodian soldiers.

Bu Dop was a major center of our activity for the next few days, since the camp was not only an important recruiting center but a drop-off location for Cambodians of other camps who desired to be considered for the task force. Our goal was to identify, recruit, select, and move to training about 250 strikers. When the camp commander had assembled all who were interested, I stepped up onto an ammunition box placed front and center to the formation, opened ranks, and, through an interpreter, shouted, "Special Forces needs 250 Cambodian freedom fighters for Rangerlike operations; soldiers will fight special missions; we prefer soldiers without family; we will train and equip like guerrilla; good pay—three times pay CIDG soldier; hard work, dangerous work; long jungle operations; Special Forces command Cambodian; we have best training; we have best U.S. equipment; we have M-16 rifle; we live in jungle like VC; we kick VC fucking ass; some U.S. die, some Cambodian die."

The immediate roar from the group told me all that I needed to know. At that point none of the Cambodians knew the true nature of Task Force 957, nor did they know where or when the missions would begin, and we did nothing to reduce their speculation that the freedom fighters would be training for deployment within their homeland, Cambodia. The next morning, we moved the new recruits by cargo plane to Bien Hoa, then by truck to our secret training base at Ho Ngoc Tao.

One Last Night

I stayed in Bien Hoa that night, while most of our NCOs traveled with our new troops to Ho Ngoc Tao. It would take them a day or two to get a camp established, as Gritz, Buck Kindoll, and I put the finishing touches on the training program. Gritz was a tough taskmaster. He also scared hell out of those in C-3 who unwittingly wandered into the TOC without authorization. We were working late in the day, with the area of War Zone D, our initial AO, depicted in red grease pencil on a large map, when one unsuspecting colonel from the III Corps compound walked into the unsecured area without warning. Gritz, in his usually calm, unfettered voice, told the colonel that he was not authorized to be in the war room. In fact, he said, "If you had any idea about where we were going, you would probably shit your pants, Colonel." When the colonel tried to explain why he was there, Gritz told him to "get the fuck out before I call security."

As the startled officer was leaving, a thunderous *boom* blew out one of the TOC windows and we all scrambled for our weapons. We began to secure ourselves, expecting the worst but having limited firepower. After a few minutes, when there was no other indication that we were under attack, we emerged onto the grass, which by then had taken on a life of its own, only to learn from the security force patrolling the compound that the VC had blown up the ammunition storage dump at Long Bien depot. Never a dull moment.

Anyone Have the Password?

About 2000 hours, we retreated to the bar for a cold beer. There, I heard the most amazing story. It seems that a Special Forces captain and an SF sergeant were mistakenly killed near Nha Trang while trying to enter the perimeter of the CIDG force they were advising. Apparently, they both worked in Supply but had wangled their way onto an operation toward earning the coveted Combat Infantryman Badge. For the CIB, which was not taken lightly, an infantryman had to participate in a minimum of five combat operations. In their haste, the two men had failed to confirm the correct challenge and password for the night in question. At darkness, as the CIDG commander was setting out mechanical ambushes (claymore mines), the two Green Berets slipped outside the perimeter to check the location and disposition of the security forces. When challenged upon their reentry, they were unable to respond properly to the security post. After they failed a second attempt to confirm they were not the enemy, the security guard fired at relatively close range, blowing Sergeant Hubard's head off and putting four rounds from his M-16 into the heart of the captain. What was amazing was that the captain, Kent Miller, was in my training company at Bragg, and on graduation had been voted—tongue in cheek—the person from our company most likely to do something impetuous that would cost him his life. I learned later that Miller was not that unlucky. He spent the better part of two years in a hospital, but lived.

Bo and I finished our beer, leaving the club at closing time. We then packed our shit for the duration.

Ho Ngoc Tao

Ho Ngoc Tao was little more than a road stop on the right side of one of the few paved "superhighways" that ran from Bien Hoa to Saigon. Approximately six miles from the approaches to the capital city, it was the home of another Special Forces secret unit, Project Sigma. We were made to feel most welcome, even though there was limited room and we could divulge little more than our title.

Even in mid-October, the days were long and hot and the ground was hard dirt and dusty. We took up semipermanent residency in two large and fifteen General Purpose Medium (GPM) tents made of canvas. The American team bunked in the field in tents and canvas cots much like those of the Cambodian recruits. Even though the sides of the tents were rolled up to allow cross-ventilation, the tents were hot and steamy by day. They were appreciably more comfortable at night.

As "pay officer," I had several million piasters for the payroll, food, and "seed" money. Most of the funds were paid out immediately to the troops for the first month in training. But I needed to locate some relatively safe place for the remainder, three or four hundred thousand piasters, the equivalent of about $3,400. Most of it was in small bills, so the little cash-

stash was more than could be hidden in a bread box. Gritz suggested using one of the extra refrigerators as the bank. And so
it was. An elite fighting force, handpicked for dangerous missions deep into enemy territory, hiding its money in a refrigerator with only a lock and key. Sears would have been proud.

There was some confusion and unrest during the first few
days due to an unanticipated delay in the receipt of clothing,
equipment, and rations from Nha Trang. For me, it was interesting just to see how Bo handled the situation. When the
flights failed to show on the first day, by radio and telephone
Gritz pressured the G-4 staff responsible for logistics. That, in
itself, was difficult, as Nha Trang was a couple hundred miles
from our base, requiring long, frequently disrupted radio
transmissions late at night; trying to get through on the telephone was futile. And, unfortunately, there was no way we
could leave Ho Ngoc Tao for face-to-face discussions.

Assured that the cargo was to arrive on the second day, we
informed the Bodes that they would have new tiger fatigues,
web gear, rucksacks, and the coveted M-16 rifles on day three.
At that point, the unit in training looked more like the Mon-
tana militia than a highly valued guerrilla force. The former
CIDG soldiers brought with them a variety of uniforms, field
equipment, and rifles. However, despite the initial supply
snafu, neither the soldiers nor the SF team lost its sense of purpose, nor its sense of humor. Training continued, but some
things on the schedule had to be moved back for the issue of
new weapons and equipment. When the shit failed to show on
day three, Gritz exploded, about the same way I had exploded
at Fort Ord about the mess hall tables and chairs. The evening
of day three, late at night, I heard Bo tell the G-4, "Get off
your fucking ass—if the supplies do not arrive by 0600, I will
have no other course of action but to file a detailed, failed-
support mission report to the Group commander."

About 0200, we were awakened by the mighty roar of four
C-123 sorties from Nha Trang onto the dirt-field strip just off
the northwest corner of Ho Ngoc Tao. Using flashlights and
the headlights from our two jeeps and two cargo trucks, we

off-loaded the eight-by-eight-foot steel resupply pallets, then moved the contents near our staging area for distribution. The next day was consumed by the issue, to each soldier, of two new sets of tiger fatigues with bush hat, two sets of jungle boots, a complete set of field gear, and the M-16 rifle.

The importance of the M-16 for the Bodes, which I think was the most effective jungle rifle on the market, mostly because of its light weight, was underscored by the fact that they were in such short supply that they had yet to be issued to many of the American units. We ruled out steel helmets because of their weight and propensity for making loud noises when soldiers moved through jungle growth. For our missions, body armor was out of the question, for the same reason. Better to have the advantage in tactical movement, with a soldier or two silently greased, than a whole unit endangered. There were also many "specialty items" to be used in training and to be selectively issued to those who earned them or merited them by their yet-to-be-assigned position. Color-coded neck scarves were issued for ease of recognition and as a sunscreen from the sweltering heat. Master Sergeant Jim Howard's first main force platoon wore yellow. Staff Sergeant Dale England's second wore black. The third, commanded by Sergeant First Class George Ovsak, had red. And First Lieutenant Ken Chilton's recon platoon wore blue scarves. The headquarters section wore black. Deputies and attached medics donned the color of the unit to which they were attached.

The normal training day of fourteen hours began at 0600 with physical training. Discipline, physical fitness, teamwork, techniques of fire, battle drill, and night operations were stressed throughout. Combatives were taught for two hours, four days per week. The U.S. team participated in demonstrations and practical work, as we wanted the Bodes to know that we were all in the fight together. Very little mention was made of rank. They knew who was in charge by the nature of the exercise. The setup worked well, and to this day my ideal fighting army would wear no rank, and the responsibility and

authority for its operations would rest in the hands of those
holding a leadership position.

Among the skills we thought would play an important role
in successful guerrilla operations were medical, mining and
booby-trapping, sniping, sterilization of routes and bases,
aerial resupply techniques, communications discipline and
innovative communication techniques, and patrolling techniques. We developed and rehearsed one special squad-level
technique combining rearward fire and movement while
employing claymore mines and CS gas to break contact. All
squads learned to initiate the drill within fourteen seconds. To
lighten the troop load for the extended operations anticipated,
we substituted a secret-formula, homemade gas mask for conventional masks, and used ski goggles to preserve the soldier's
eyesight when they were exposed to the CS gas. Training was
planned to last forty-nine days. Our methods of instruction
were similar to those used in stateside training centers except
that we were under no obligation to observe the rigid stateside
rules involving live fire.

Interpret This, If You Can

One of the challenges we faced early on was the creation of
an effective personal communication system—leader control
of both training and ground combat actions by word of
mouth—for troops that had little understanding of the English
language. Of course we would need interpreters, and because
we could offer three times the going rate with an equivalent
combat bonus, we had many of the best interpreters in
Vietnam from which to choose. Since a misspoken command
during the heat of battle—whether due to a lack of understanding, or with different words to lessen the bite—could
cost lives, we took those who were able to demonstrate a high
personal sense of trust, honesty, and courage. Most were hired
before we moved to Ho Ngoc Tao.

The recruitment and selection of interpreters was vintage
Gritz. In English, Bo first described the requirements of trust,

honesty, and courage. "Do you understand that you must say exactly what the leader says, even if you don't completely understand what he is saying or why?"

"Yes, Dai-uy [captain]," the supremely confident applicant said.

Gritz continued, "You cannot change the words, the tone, or the temperament of the commands, even if you don't like them."

"No, Dai-uy."

"You mean if I say to a Cambodian platoon sergeant, 'Fuck you, and the horse you rode in on,' you would say exactly that?"

"Yes, Dai-uy," the man said.

Gritz pulled a fragmentation grenade from his web gear and handed it to the interpreter. "Do you know what this is?"

"Oh, yes, Dai-uy."

"Go ahead, pull the pin," Gritz said.

Beads of sweat started to trickle down the cheek of the man called Rinh, but he nervously pulled the pin with his left hand, clutching the explosive device in a death grip with his right.

"Drop the pin," Gritz said.

When Rinh dropped the pin, a most confused look, one that betrayed any confidence he had shown to that point, appeared on his face.

Backing up slightly, Gritz said, "Drop the grenade."

"Oh no, Dai-uy," Rinh said, as if to seek from the proven warrior the respect one might gain for sparing his life.

"Next man," Gritz said.

Are You Afraid of Heights?

Project Sigma had a dangerous mission. Something like trolling for alligators in the Florida Everglades with a man on one ski. They flew by chopper at treetop level into a contested area, dropped a four-man recon team at point A, then sped to point B for the quick extraction. Wearing lightweight gear, the recon team jogged the several hundred meters in a straight line to the planned extraction site. If all went well, the Sigma team would excite an enemy unit into disclosing its location, then continue to run toward the extraction zone. Once the recon team was at the pickup site, the C&C (command and control) element would direct on-call air and artillery fires on the disheveled enemy force. About halfway through our training, one of the Sigma missions failed completely, resulting in two friendly KIA. The eager response from the Sigma leadership was to rerun the same route the next morning, but with two teams seemingly disconnected, in an effort to capture one or two prisoners for revenge. That mission was successful. The two VC POWs were flown to eight thousand feet, to their own extraction zone. If you're wondering how I felt about this episode of "You Bet Your Life," I was saddened by the loss of the recon element. But I certainly didn't give a shit about the other guys, who were given an unparalleled opportunity— albeit an unwelcome one—to learn how to fly.

Cabin Fever

Training for twelve hours a day in the hot sun was a bitch. Night training was more comfortable, but by the end of the first month or so, the days ran into the nights. As a unit, we were coming together, or at least I thought we were, until one evening Master Sergeant Howard, double-slotted as the team sergeant, approached me. "Sir," he said, "can I talk to you?"

"What's up, Top?" I said.

He said that several of the men were beginning to show signs of frustration with the length and pace of the training schedule. He added that there was no "free time," and that a kind of cabin fever was beginning to set in. Howard said, "The men want some time to themselves."

I said, "You mean to get fucked?"

"Well, sir," he replied, "I'm not sure what they want to do, but you know, just to get out of this place for a few hours on a Friday night, knowing that you don't have to train the next

morning at 0-dark thirty, that would be a help." He finished
by asking me if I would talk to Captain Gritz. Howard was
the consummate professional. He was also a religious man, a
very sensitive man, a very hardworking man, and above all,
a very fair man.

I valued his opinions and welcomed his confidence in me. I
said, "Of course I'll talk to Captain Gritz."

When Gritz and I were together that night, reviewing the
day's training and previewing training for the next day, I told
him of Howard's concern. He asked me, "What do you
think?"

I said, "Bo, given the relative danger of this type of mission,
even for units that are ready, I see nothing on our schedule that
we can omit."

He called a team meeting. It was about 2000 hours, Friday
night, and I witnessed one of the most brilliant leadership
forums that I would see in twenty-six years of service. When
everyone was settled into the small team house we had on loan
from Sigma, Gritz said, "It has come to my attention that several of you think that we may not be taking this training seriously." He continued, "I have tried my best to provide the
subjects we need, with some details on how best to accomplish the training. We are currently training an average of
twelve hours a day for five days, six hours on Saturday, with a
rest on Sunday. Hell, we have to have some time to prepare the
next week's training instructors, right? Well, I'm sorry that I
have failed you. Beginning tomorrow, Saturday, we will train
sixteen hours a day, Monday through Friday, twelve hours on
Saturday, and six hours on Sunday. I will never let you down
again. Are there any questions?" The room was silent. There
were no questions. When the meeting broke, we all had a
better understanding of just who Bo Gritz was, and just why
he was handpicked to lead the missions. In all my years of service, at the tactical level, he had no equal. I will always feel
privileged for having had the chance to work with him. He
was the professional's professional.

He and I stayed up well into the morning, adding this drill

or that, hoping that when the missions ran, it would make a difference.

Just When You Thought the Money Was Safe

It happened suddenly. One morning I opened the refrigerator door to withdraw some funds for food, and the money was gone. About 150,000 piasters, or $1,300. No one was in the tent. There were no clues. I didn't think it possible that a team member was involved. I knew we couldn't prove whether or not one of the Bodes took the money. I knew we didn't need an investigation of any sort. So I made a unilateral decision. Given the circumstances, I said out loud to myself, "Fuck it. Just, fuck it! I will simply restore the funds during the next payroll cycle, render no report, and move on. Case closed." It never happened again.

Graduation Week

From the first day of the increased training, it became obvious to me that, as a unit, we were coming together in a way suggested by the kind of men we'd chosen to be a small part of history. Our group was tight. The Bodes were awesome. The last week was spent with a somewhat relaxed schedule, making damn sure that all the drills we taught could be performed, on cue, day or night. Eyes closed. It was then that I began to feel a sense of personal pride about my role on the team. Also, I truly began to feel the importance of self-sufficiency, flexibility, resilience, and the power of a positive attitude. Graduation week was the time we used to award the specialty equipment, like scopes, which went to those who could, from a hundred yards, knock down a long-necked goose buried beneath the surface in a wooden ammo box with a hole in the top. There were other contests that provided some sort of comic relief while fulfilling a needed function. But none was as remarkable as the Greased-Pig Contest.

This Little Piggy Went to Market

It was late Thursday evening, about two hours from sunset, when Ken Chilton and I, and David, one of the interpreters, drove an open-top jeep to Bien Hoa. Mission? Find, buy, and bring back to Ho Ngoc Tao the biggest, ugliest, meanest motherfucking hog in Vietnam. Saturday would be graduation, a full day of planned activities, including a stirring, patriotic, but conventional passing of our Bodes from raw recruits to fullfledged, professional guerrillas. Other events would feature more contests to award special merits and an assortment of more technical weapons. But for several weeks I had this thought in my head about giving the Bodes a unique look at American culture. And I decided, what would be more representative for that group of mostly young male graduates than a greased pig contest? I had been baiting our troops all week. "Do you think you could catch a greased pig?" I would ask. At first I got nothing but a few hearty laughs. But as the questions became more focused—"How would you organize your platoon to both fight off the three other platoons and catch the pig?"—it became obvious that I was not just bullshitting them. There was a lot of talk about it, and everywhere I walked, I heard the faint squeals of a pig. So they were ready, and most said no fucking problem. The only challenge remaining was to actually locate a suitable animal on such short notice. But I'd lived in Bien Hoa, and had a pretty decent idea about where to find a pig. Of course, we were not looking for just any old pig.

"Do you have any hogs for sale?" I asked the old man, through David. He quickly led us to a pen chock full of large hogs. "Which one is the biggest?"

Carrying a large stick, the old man shuffled his way through ten or twelve hogs, pushing all aside except one.

He said, through David, "This is the one."

I asked if he was mean, did he have spirit?

The pig farmer struck the grossly overweight swine with the end of the stick. Menacing grunts and squeals, a shuffling of ham hocks, and a meaner-than-cow-shit stare followed.

With a most pleasant expression on his face, the old man said, "This is the one. He is the meanest one."

I paid him the equivalent of two hundred dollars, and the four of us bound the hog's legs, inserted a long, sturdy pole between them, and loaded him into the backseat of the jeep. Amid onlooker stares, we began our return trip with our prized possession. The grunts and unearthly groans of the huge hog could be heard in every corner of Ho Ngoc Tao as we entered the front gate. It was pitch-dark when we finally got the hog firmly tied to a steel stake in the middle of our football-field-size training area.

One day before graduation, the Bodes were wild with excitement over the pig, and each platoon was speculating, in earnest, about how it would deploy its forces to accomplish two things: (1) capture the pig; (2) fight off the other three platoons while moving the large animal to the platoon's corner of the field, to deposit it into a foxhole built for the occasion. They couldn't wait. Nor could I.

Graduation Day

About 1000 hours, we began a fairly solemn march onto the parade field for formal graduation. With the troops in position, looking every bit like respectable fighting guerrillas, from their well-oiled green and black jungle boots to their fully camouflaged tiger fatigues, BAR belts with ammunition pouches, laundered neck scarves, and jungle hats, Gritz told them of their proud accomplishments. He spoke of dedication, pride in self and unit, trust in each other and their own abilities, decency; of well-trained fighters and true professionals.

As they marched slowly past a small wooden platform, Gritz shook their hands and handed each man two pieces of cloth that would become one of the least known but most widely respected and highly coveted arm patches in the world, a patch worn by only fourteen Americans. Gritz had designed the patch, and had them sewn under a secret agreement with a local agency. About four inches high, the patch replicates an

Indian diamond head signifying resourcefulness and stealth. The black background, bordered in yellow, represents the nature of guerrilla warfare and the importance of fighting at night. A bright yellow lightning bolt on the black background strikes fear into the heart of the NVA empire, represented as a red star. A tab at the top signifies the unit, Task Force 957, Mobile Guerrilla. We all received our patches from Captain Gritz and reveled in the glory of the occasion. Now for the fun and games.

Fun and Games

If you ever got the idea that Gritz was all business and no pleasure, I'm sorry for misleading you. Work hard, play hard. That was his motto. The work was over for the time being. We had recruited, selected, organized, trained, and equipped 255 ethnic Cambodians, transforming them in the process into a mobile guerrilla unit, one that would be tested in the weeks and months to come. But it was time to let our hair down, step back a few paces, and celebrate our accomplishments. Because of the nature of the exercise, I can only truly remember two things that day—and night: the greased pig contest and the American celebration.

The Greased Pig Contest

With each platoon of about sixty Bodes—dressed only in boots, shorts, and neck scarves—positioned near its own fox-hole, about seventy-five meters from the center of the field, and the pig, the contest was about to begin. We opened several quarts of motor oil, kneading its sticky substance into the short bristles on the hog's body. That done, and the Bodes—and the Americans, as well—waiting in anxious anticipation for the starting gun, I had another idea. To make it interesting, I asked one of our medics to inject the monster hog with a preparation

of wintergreen, right up the old wazoo. The result was predictable, as the pig immediately let us know that we were not
his friends and that if cut loose from the steel stake, he would
prove it. The moment was approaching.

Bang! The hog ran in one direction, toward the third platoon. At about midfield one of the Bodes, an impressively
muscled black-scarf soldier, flew about fifteen feet in the air,
striking the hog at the shoulder. The hog, dazed and down,
shook the blow off, got to its feet and turned in the opposite
direction. By then, there were seventy-five or eighty soldiers
on his tail, and as they got close, the hog kept changing directions. Within minutes several troopers representing the second
platoon, their black scarves in evidence, secured the pig. As
they attempted to carry the hog into their territory, they were
attacked by blue scarves, Chilton's dreaded recon platoon.

Of course, the Americans had all kinds of side bets going.
As deputy commander, I was also the deputy for the second
platoon, so I had bet about a hundred dollars with Chilton on
my black scarves.

Red scarves intervened, then yellow, and finally, after about
thirty minutes of good-natured fighting, both with each other
and with the pig, the recon platoon persevered. Throwing the
monster into their foxhole, they raised their banner, let out a
monstrous *"Yahoo!"* and claimed their prize. Of course, the
pig was the prize, and was featured on the menu of the recon
platoon that afternoon.

An American Celebration

The party started in earnest at about 1500. The bright afternoon sun slowly began to slip its way westward, the sky now
overcast. The Bodes had set up a GP Small tent with a round
table in the center and about ten or twelve gray metal folding
chairs. Positioned near the tent was a pallet of beer. Maybe
that's where I really got my taste for beer. There were eighty-
six cases to a pallet. More than enough for the thirteen of us
and some of the Bode leadership. There were no women pre-

sent. Just male bonding, friendship, and craziness. There was food fit for a king: boiled lobster; beefsteaks covered with peanut sauce; huge, South China Sea shrimp. We drank. We talked. We laughed. We told stories. We drank some more. We told more stories. We treasured the moment. It soon got dark. We set up a light and continued throughout the night. The last thing I remember, it was about 0400. I was alone. I must have had a good time. I slowly got up from my chair, walked away from the tent, found my bunk and went to sleep.

What Did You Say You Lost?

It was early in December 1966. Our training mission accomplished, we struck camp and began preparations to move to our new staging base about forty-five miles northwest of Saigon. Duc Phong (A-343) was selected because it had the kind of terrain we anticipated finding in War Zone D and because of its proximity to the war zone itself. After saying our good-byes to the folks at C-3, then under the command of Lieutenant Colonel Tom Huddleston, the task force settled into its new camp without much fanfare. Our relatively high mission priority enabled us to "shop" in the Saigon warehouse for a thirty-day supply of fresh-frozen food, including large boxes of steaks, chicken, potatoes, bacon, eggs, and vegetables. We also hijacked a pallet of soft drinks from the huge warehouse located near the docks in Saigon. We were well received by the USSF A-team on the ground at Duc Phong.

However, as we moved the Bodes from the airstrip toward the camp itself, our task force banner flying high on a long bamboo pole, we sensed some friction between the resident CIDG force, made up mostly of Vietnamese soldiers, and our ethnic Cambodians. Weapons were drawn and at the ready, and even a few shots were fired, as if the incumbent force felt threatened by the presence of the Bodes. Apparently, the CIDG had not been told that another force would be moving in for a short duration, and, as we later learned, there was speculation on the part of the local CIDG that the Cambodians had gone there to start an uprising that would result in the local CIDGs' dismissal from the camp.

Gritz quickly invited the camp commander to join him, and, through an interpreter, he told the assembled forces that we intended no harm, that we were friends, and that we would be there only a short while before moving out. Even though asking for their understanding, he was in no position to relate to them, or to our own forces, the exact nature of our operations or the operational area.

Early the next morning, we deployed the MGF to the northeast and began to practice what we'd learned. We were back in contact with the VC within the first day or two, and so had an excellent opportunity to reinforce the principles we'd spent so much time teaching and training at Ho Ngoc Tao.

Rather than stay and fight, and risk becoming engaged, we marked our sightings and withdrew. We mainly operated at night, and chose to hide and rest during the daylight hours. We began to be more aware of the signature we created as we operated—things like footprints, litter, smells from waste, and so on. We carefully brushed the entry and exit points of trails, to disguise our movements. We began to frequently change directions to compound the problem for trackers, and also to employ mines and booby traps near and on the trails to discourage being followed too closely. We broke down into small operating patrols, so that at any one time we would be seen by the enemy as a very small force operating independently, one that did not constitute much of a threat. And, of course, as our name implied, we were highly mobile, never staying in one base location more than ten to twelve hours, and departing at irregular times using irregular routes, down the center of a stream, for example.

One of the issues that surfaced during our tryouts dealt with the routine resupply of the task force. On the third or fourth day, we scheduled a resupply using air force Air Commandos flying C-123 cargo planes. We knew that they were the best, and that they had plenty of experience working with SF. With the DZ secured, we watched the huge cargo plane get on track about three miles out at an altitude of twelve hundred feet. As the camouflaged fuselage drew closer, we began to hear the roar of engines. The plane then descended to treetop level, made final corrections on direction, and lowered itself toward the semiopen area we'd selected as the drop zone. When on target, the cargo plane released a standard eight-foot pallet, then drew skyward for its departure from the area. This technique, newly developed by the air force in concert with the army, was called the Computed Air Release Point (CARP) system.

As we watched the drop, which was restrained by a series of large cargo chutes, we were impressed. But we were also uneasy, about both the noise and the signature of the aircraft itself. We were also concerned about how to disguise the fact that we were receiving a resupply, as in, what the fuck to do with the steel pallet. We immediately realized that the new technique would prematurely disclose our location to VC units within our operational area. We had configured everything else in our favor—the fighting loads were light. Communications with higher-ups were secret. We carried no heavy weapons. There was no artillery support. We had opted to die of our wounds rather than disclose our position by using helicopters for evacuation, and so on. So why were we using this most predictable, obtrusive means of resupply? That would have to change. We notified both C-3 and Nha Trang that the system was unacceptable for a guerrilla force conducting clandestine operations within enemy territory. We asked them to look for another, less obtrusive, less predictable, but equally effective method.

Following the resupply, we continued to operate within assigned areas. The second platoon seemed to be humming, working closely together with good communication and excellent fire discipline. We had another contact, slipped out of it and moved on. I have to admit, it felt good to be in contact with real VC again rather than Bodes posing as VC during training. We got several KIA during the morning of the fourth day, but were abruptly told to wrap up the patrol and return to the base camp.

Since we were operating in the nearby highlands, our trek

back to Duc Phong was completed within a few hours. Without discussion, Gritz and I, and Staff Sergeant Buck Kindoll, our operations and intelligence specialist, boarded a waiting helicopter for the thirty-minute trip to Song Be (B-34). On arrival, we were quickly ushered into a small briefing room full of important-looking people of various ranks and service. There were also some civilians. We learned, then, that on October 8, 1966, an aircraft of the Strategic Air Command Operating Location 20 had crashed approximately four miles southeast of Song Be in Phuoc Long Province. It was subsequently discovered that extremely sensitive electronic equipment had been lost during the crash and was very possibly still in good enough condition to be compromised. The USAF briefer said that a compromise of that particular instrument would gravely affect U.S. national security. The Fifth Special Forces Group, commanded by Blackjack Kelly, who was present at the briefing, was being asked to provide an organized search of the area for the lost instrument.

The search was to take place in practically impenetrable jungle, deep in Viet Cong territory. Throughout the briefing, the air force was trying to say what they could not say. In spite of our questions that they clarify what we were looking for, and where, the briefer, and then the commander of Operating Location 20, Colonel Charles D. Rafferty, were evasive. We began to appreciate the profound position in which the air force, and the United States, found themselves, when they indicated that the so-called black box was thought to be intact; that somehow, the instantaneous destruct mechanism attached to the instrument had failed to self-destruct; and that the release of the coded frequency on its transmitter would compromise the entire U.S. strategic reconnaissance system. I was thrilled at the thought of conducting our practice missions as a live scenario. At an appropriate interlude in the briefing, Captain Gritz, in the booming voice for which he is respected and known, said, "Oh, great! You mean you want us to go into an unknown area to find something we have never seen before and which you are reluctant to describe in any detail?" Just then, an air force briefer pointed to an area on the map as the most likely general location of the aircraft. The cone-shaped area encompassed hundreds of square kilometers. When asked again to describe the black box, the briefer divulged more than he had in his earlier statements. He did say that it looked like a radio much larger than a PRC-10, to which we could all relate. But it could be anywhere.

After conferring with Kelly, Gritz told the air force that we would accept the mission. He said that we were organized, equipped, and trained for success on such missions. At that point, someone raised the concern that the VC, or the NVA, would undoubtedly be looking for the wrecked plane to record the sequence of numbers that would reveal the code. We all recognized that the likelihood of finding the relatively small piece of electronic gear was improbably small. Not impossible, but almost. And we who would lead the task force clearly thought that, if anyone could accomplish the mission, it would have to be us. We were excited by the opportunity, but understood the risks as well. We also knew that such an opportunity would constitute a good shake-out of the Mobile Guerrilla Force before being committed to Blackjack-31.

Black Box

Thirty years later, the extremely sensitive mission, now declassified, can be described straightforwardly. Simply put, Operation Black Box was briefed as a United States response to locate, secure, and extract the electronic "friend and foe" (IFF) device from a U-2 spy plane. Since time was a critical factor, we moved the MGF from Duc Phong to Song Be the next morning, and spent the rest of the day getting our shit together, marking maps, and briefing the leadership. The Bodes were excited.

About 0600 the next morning, we deployed the truck to a staging area near the foothills of the densely jungled mountains of Nui Ba Ra. Our first challenge was to locate the downed aircraft, independent of the search mission to follow. It was important to learn whether the piece of electronic equipment was still in the plane or nearby. Within a few hours we were in contact with VC trackers, who broke contact and withdrew to the northwest. Apparently, we were not the only unit looking for the crash site. Fortunately, we had no friendly casualties to slow our pace—we may have wounded or killed a few VC, but did not consider confrontation one of our priorities—so we continued to move quickly toward the objective area. Sporadic enemy fire interrupted our round-the-clock patrolling, but because our mission argued against an engagement of any kind, we continued to slip and slide our way through the dense underbrush while looking for the downed aircraft.

The second platoon was commanded by Staff Sergeant Dale England, a most professional warrior from West Virginia. I was his deputy. From the first time I met England, I liked him. He not only looked like he knew what he was doing, but his slow southern drawl seemed to signal his familiarity with the woods. He also had a lot of combat experience, and was the kind of personality we were looking for when recruiting the American force. He broke down his assigned area along well-defined terrain features, and split the second platoon into two patrols. We were able to work on parallel paths, facilitating mutual reinforcement if either of us got hit, and making it possible to share information by word of mouth as the search progressed.

As my patrol inched its way out of the staging area, I was very aware that, as a unit, we needed to stay focused and disciplined. Also, that my group, like the others, would have to do its part for the good of the whole. The nature of the terrain varied from dry, somewhat mountainous high ground to low marshy areas with occasional streams.

Through one of the interpreters, I told my patrol of about fifteen Bodes that to accomplish our mission one of our patrols must first find the downed aircraft. While this mission was critical, I knew that it also gave us some time—working as lone Americans with a small ethnic contingent—to strengthen our grasp on the operational concept for BJ-31. As for me, I felt comfortable with the Bodes, and I suspected that they had a similar respect for me. In all, we had allotted eleven days for the operation, December 18 to 28. We would then prepare for deployment on BJ-31, which had been put on hold until after the IFF mission.

Fortunately, the weather was perfect, temperatures in the mid-nineties, with a clear sky. The only noises we heard were the crackling of leaves beneath our feet as we moved slowly along the undulating contours of the hilltops, valleys, and an occasional extended ridgeline. As the terrain became more extreme, we slowed to almost a stop, thoroughly searching, at times on hands and knees, the small indentations and changes in direction, to ensure that we did not overlook anything. The excitement of the mission was sufficient to keep my adrenaline up even though we had worked straight through the first two days without locating the U-2. When England and I stopped for the second night, we coordinated our routes for the next day and had some time to get to know one another a little better. Our contact with Gritz was limited to a brief report, "Fox Two, negative."

Day three began with a brief firefight with a couple of VC trackers. We also heard explosions within the area, which indicated that other patrols were fighting off VC elements. Fortunately, nothing big. As slow and methodical as we were required to be, I was beginning to wonder if we'd be able to complete the mission in the eleven days allotted.

We discovered the broken remains of the fuselage midmorning of the third day. The impact of the plane had left a huge crater, offering an immediate opportunity to quickly investigate the wreckage. Built with long, straight graceful wings—almost delicate in appearance—the U2 was by then in total disarray as we anxiously searched for the top-secret instrument. After scanning a 100-meter radius in vain for almost two hours, we concluded that we'd have to continue the search the following morning.

Captain Gritz conferred with the platoon leaders and their deputies about his plan. He indicated that if we were to have a chance of locating the equipment, we would have to systematically search every square meter of ground within the cone-shaped area indicated by the air force and marked in red grease pencil on our operational maps. There would not be enough time to search the same square meter more than once. He noted that the mission required focus and discipline. If, for any number of reasons—tiredness, darkness, lack of focus, VC disruptive tactics, complete burial of the black box in a marshy area, of which there were many—we "missed" the device, the mission would be a failure. Accordingly, when he laid out the assignments in thousand-meter squares with hundred-meter overlaps, it was with the thought that if the equipment was actually there—had not first been recovered by the VC— if it were seeable, and if we stayed focused, we could not help but locate the black box. How could we lose? Ingenious. In order to create as many supervised elements as possible, ensuring that each was squarely in the hands of one responsible American leader, we broke our platoons down into two, and in some cases three, recon elements. By Bo's instructions, we were to search by day, stop at dusk, render situation reports by PRC-25 tactical radios, mark our maps methodically— crossing off those thousand-meter squares already searched— get some sleep, and begin anew the following morning.

I Caught a Fleeting Glimpse, Out of the Corner of My Eye

Skeptical that we could locate something so small, I gathered my Bode contingent, reiterating Bo's plan that we would walk on a straight line, tactically, slowly, about ten meters apart, never losing sight of the man to the right or left. Really, much like a stateside "police call," where troops looked down for small bits of refuse, especially cigarette butts, to sterilize the company area. If contact was initiated with the VC, we would mark our location, fight as we must, or withdraw and then return to resume the search.

Sometime about mid-morning of day four, our patrol descended slowly down the side of a small but perceptible ridgeline into a low area with some standing water. Where vegetation thickened, for instance, near a small seasonal stream, we were forced to drop to our knees to maintain sight coverage of the marshy ground below. Ten to fifteen minutes after reaching the area, a low voice ten or fifteen meters to my right front said, "Dai-uy." One of the Bodes gave an arm signal for me to approach. I stood up, looked down, and was surprised to see the Bode with a wide grin, pointing to a rather large, blackened electronic instrument buried deeply within the marshy bed just a few feet from where I was standing.

Rock fans, especially those with a thing for Pink Floyd, are familiar with the movie *The Wall*, and the passage that relates to the words above. The instant I saw the black box, I knew it was, indeed, the black box. I also knew that, like the young boy, Pinky, surprised one night by the sight of a woman undressing in front of her window, I would never be able to erase that image from my mind. We worked the piece of equipment out of its sucking hold, lifted it from the thick vegetation that seemed to have a stranglehold on it, and carried it to higher ground fifteen to twenty meters away. We were overjoyed, knowing instinctively that the only reason we'd found the box was because God wanted us to find it. I said a small prayer of thanks.

We drew our forces together, secured a small perimeter, and notified Staff Sergeant England and Captain Gritz that we had recovered the black box. We then made our way, tactically, back up over the ridgeline, retracing our movement back to the established MGF command post. For reasons that never escaped me, the return trip seemed as if we were walking on air. Once Gritz saw the equipment, he was convinced that it was the genuine article, and so requested a helicopter extraction from a pickup zone to be designated. He notified the other platoons that the equipment had been recovered and to return to base. Once we were all assembled, we established a tight perimeter to secure the equipment while a patrol was dispatched to locate a suitable PZ, no small task given the nature of the terrain, and the heat and humidity, which would tend to decrease the performance of the helicopter used for an extraction.

Did You Bring a Rope?

As the afternoon sun was beginning to fade, about 1600 hours, I heard the faint sounds of a Huey, presumably flying toward our location. I personally had doubts about the capability of a chopper to drop into the only semblance of an extraction zone we could find. The area we selected was a bomb crater. On arrival in the area, we monitored the radio traffic of the air force Forward Air Controller, who was flying a small observation plane while directing the helicopter belonging to the army's 281st Aviation Company. The FAC was indicating that the mission site would not be suitable for a landing due to the high trees in and about the entire area, confirming my earlier concern regarding the heat and humidity.

Once over the PZ, the helicopter held a "steady platform" while lowering a 120-foot nylon rappelling rope into the base of the bomb crater. As the instrument was being secured to the rope, the downward draft of the Huey's large blades created a small twister on the ground, making the pickup hazardous for both the ground forces and the pilot-in-command (PIC). When the black box was inside the helicopter, an intelligence coordinator determined that it was definitely the correct instrument.

It Was Only a Matter of Coordination

For the uninitiated, I should explain that few operations are successfully conducted that are not well-coordinated. The U.S. team brought into this recovery mission reads like a who's who in the clandestine operations business. The MGF anticipated that its senior commander would be on the scene, so when the black box was verified, this information was passed to Lieutenant Colonel Huddleston, commander of Company A, Fifth SFGA, and his sergeant major, Richard D. "Micky"

Finn, who were flying in their own C&C ship as airborne coordinators. We later were informed that the daring 281st Aviation Company mission was flown by First Lieutenant Robert J. Reynolds. His four-man crew was rounded out with Chief Warrant Officer (CWO2) Thomas E. McElhinney, PFC Wilford P. Paye, and Specialist-5 Charles R. Clark. The Intelligence Coordinator from the Fifth SFGA was Captain Robert J. Weinfurter. The MACV Coordinator from B-55, Fifth SFGA, was Major Clarence M. Hooper. The 19th Tactical Air Support System was comprised of Lieutenant Colonel James E. Poore (ALO—air liaison officer—Fifth Infantry Division, ARVN), Major Joe W. Carr (ALO, A Company, Fifth SFGA), and Captain Charles L. Pocock (FAC, Phuoc Long Province). We got to know Pocock pretty well, as it was he who most often flew FAC for us on the BJ-31 mission. His experience and complete dedication to our mission requirements were essential to mission accomplishment.

Was There Anybody on the Ground?

Detachment A-303, MGF, Fifth SFGA, consisted of Captain Gritz, myself, First Lieutenant Chilton, Master Sergeant Howard, Staff Sergeant England, Sergeants First Class Kindoll and Ovsak, Staff Sergeant Dennis H. Montgomery, SFC Patrick D. Wagner, Sergeant James C. Donahue, Staff Sergeant Joseph J. Cawley, and SFC Lowell T. Glossup.

Black Box—A Historical Perspective

Black Box was one of those missions that, had it not been true, would have been eventually fictionalized by Hollywood as a blockbuster movie, perhaps starring Chuck Norris. But it was and is true, so nothing that glamorous will come of it. However, when the black box was verified to be intact and uncompromised, President Lyndon B. Johnson was immediately notified. From a historical perspective, the Black Box mission has been described, in general terms, in many other books and magazines. Most of these sources were written many years ago, by honorable and well-informed military men, but when information was sketchy and the facts of the mission were highly classified.

Through declassified reports, we were able to surmise that the air force's reference to a "friend and foe device" must have been a cover story. In reality, the black box, System 13A, was designed to fool enemy radar into thinking that the U-2 was something it wasn't. Unlike the ECM (electronic counter measures) systems that filled enemy radar screens with clutter, the System 13A device gave no indication to the enemy that the information displayed on the radar screen was false, it just identified the U-2 as an NVA aircraft.

Recently, in his *Mobile Guerrilla Force*, award-winning author James C. Donahue described the Black Box mission. His account is authentic, as he was a young task force medic on the mission, code name Fox-3. The account I have provided marks the first time the mission has been publicly discussed in any detail by the lone American who, by the grace of God, was present when the equipment was first discovered. In the final analysis, an unknown Cambodian soldier, paid little more for his services than a fast-food employee in the States, was the first person to locate the elusive instrument. To him and to all the Cambodian strikers who made up Task Force 957, MGF, I want to publicly convey my long-delayed gratitude for their courage, focus, discipline, and good fortune. Our MGF could not have been without them. Someday, I hope that this account, and others, can be translated into their language so that they and their loved ones will begin to realize the credit they deserve.

Fortunately, all Special Forces soldiers in the MGF were issued Penn-EE half-frame cameras to record important events. See the photo insert for the picture taken on the afternoon of day four, December 22, 1966, just prior to extraction, to record the existence of the black box. As near as I know, it is the only (unauthorized) photo of its kind.

In the Wake of Black Box

Following recovery of the black box, the MGF vacated the extraction area immediately to reduce the risk of being discovered in the aftermath of a very noisy, but superbly coordinated mission. We set camp in an operating base near a more suitable PZ, and on December 24, I was flown out of the operational area to coordinate with the air force a newly designed method of resupply. About midnight, Christmas Eve, during a presidential cease-fire, the MGF was bombarded by a Vietcong mortar attack as they slept. There were several casualties, but no one was killed.

The unit returned to Song Be on December 26, flew to Bien Hoa for three days R&R, then back to Duc Phong to make final preparations for BJ-31. The air force showed its appreciation for saving its bacon by flying most of the U.S. team to Nha Trang, courtesy of Blackjack's three-day pass.

As we departed the plane, an air force representative offered us each piasters that came to the equivalent of $150. I have to say that the air force really does know how to reward good performance. We took the money, of course, anxiously awaiting a few days off while anticipating yet another American celebration. At Francois', a French-owned and -operated restaurant on the South China seacoast, several of us discovered the "2000p lobster," a huge hybrid crustacean fit for five or six people. Those who know me will not be surprised that I ate one myself. The next day, we languished in the beautiful blue waters of the South China Sea, and that night enjoyed huge charbroiled steaks at Frigots', one of the premier restaurants in all Vietnam. Not having to worry about drinking and driving, we continued to develop the trust that would later pay huge dividends. Even though I missed my R&R to Hong Kong for the MGF, no one in Nha Trang was more pleased than I.

Military Downsizing

Long before the term made its way into the defense establishment's lexicon, we experienced our own form of military downsizing after Black Box. For religious reasons—it was a religious holiday for the Chams of certain sects of Islam and Hinduism—some of the Bodes did not return. And some of the Khmer Serei and Khmer Kampuchia Krom (KKK) may have learned, through the back door, that we were not going into Cambodia to overthrow the suspicious government of Norodom Sihanouk. One or two may have had other leanings, although I think that unlikely. Some may have "simply overslept." Whatever the reasons, we configured the MFG downward from a robust 185 to 108 Bodes. Nothing was lost in the translation.

When Is a Fighter Not a Fighter?

One of the problematic issues we had to quickly resolve before our deployment dealt with just how we were going to be resupplied during the extended BJ-31 mission. Based on our evaluation, and a hard-fought decision by Blackjack Kelly, General William E. Westmoreland, the commander of all U.S. forces in Vietnam, announced to the Seventh Air Force that it must accept the mission to resupply the MGF using a fighter plane—specifically, the A1-E Sky Raider, delivering napalm containers, prepackaged with man-size portable loads and pre-rigged with a T-7A reserve parachute. The air force dug its heels in on this one, arguing that fighters were only about delivering ordnance, and that they scarcely had a sufficient number on hand to meet the planned and on-call mission on a day-to-day basis. Not to mention the TAC-E (tactical emergencies). I could see their point. On the other hand, the concept became a reality and served as a living testament to how well the army and the air force were able to coordinate support operations. Historically, the concept took on a life of its own, and is today used to support special operators on the ground.

The resupply issue decided, we again said our good-byes to our friends and thanked our major supporters at C-3, especially Lieutenant Colonel Tom Huddleston, the commander, and Sergeant Major "Micky" Finn. They may never have known just how much we needed their all-out effort to make these missions successful. When you're young, and full of piss and vinegar, you think you're invincible, and you take for granted the accomplishments of others. Without the concern of C-3 and Blackjack, the MGF would not have gotten off the ground. It took a well-coordinated, concerted effort on the part of the existing leadership to make the MGF a reality.

I'll See You in My Dreams

Few letters from home reached me from the time I left Ho Ngoc Tao, deployed on Black Box, and until the 1966 Christmas season had come and gone. That did not, of course, mean I was alone. I had the precious pictures in my wallet to look at, so that I could remember what it was like to hold the ones I loved. To be with them. To be one, again. I missed Donna terribly. I could see her warm smile, and feel her gentle touch as she reached out to take my hand. Her deep, soulful eyes met mine as we frolicked in the morning sun. My vivid images of Lori and Kim, neither of whom had yet reached the age of three, were constant reminders that indeed I was there for a purpose—to fight a war that, although controversial, would stem the tide against Russian and Chinese aggression on the Asian continent.

Vietnam and the Green Berets

On June 10, 1776, General George Washington established the United States Army. He authorized ten companies of infantry, of 150 men each. The job of the infantry was to close with and kill enemy soldiers and destroy their weapons and equipment. To this day, the basic infantry mission remains intact. There have been some doctrinal changes—how the infantry fights—and some tactical improvements, mostly brought on by innovations in technology. But, historically, the more power you could generate, the better were your chances of achieving a military victory. A three-to-one tactical advantage became a major teaching point, and the War Department's force structure was characterized by big units, big weapons, and big dollars. Unfortunately, World War II encouraged few changes in strategy. Although there were some secret operations and some less well-known units, like the Office of Strategic Services (OSS), by and large, the Army was properly characterized by recruiting posters depicting tanks, artillery pieces, trucks, engineering equipment, and mobile troop carriers.

Nor was the thinking of other armies much different. From 1948 to 1954, during the French-Indochina War, the French Army deployed to Vietnam and spent its life's blood fighting Communism. The French, bankrolled eighty percent by U.S. dollars, and under the counsel of U.S. advisers, wrestled with Viet Minh insurgents who they thought to be poorly trained and undermanned. Underestimating their adversary, the French opted to fight the "big war," choosing to deploy massive ground forces to a small village named Dien Bien Phu. The French thought they would be able to pin down the Viet Minh major forces against the ridgeline of a nearby mountain range and, using their advanced weapons systems, quickly secure a military victory. As history records, the Viet Minh labored for weeks, disassembling their own artillery and, using long sections of rope and hundreds of determined guerrillas, pulling the weapons up the steep mountain slope, piece by piece, to the top, where the pieces were reassembled. When the French Army made its final movement into the valley below, the results were predictable. But the military defeat paled in comparison to the loss of will and political resolve within the French government. The war was over, and the French left Vietnam, embarrassed.

After the stinging French defeat, the U.S. maintained a small contingent of Special Forces, CIA, and others in Vietnam. The mission focused on trying to dissuade the numerous, largely uncommitted mountain tribes from joining the Communist revolution, and better yet, to encourage them to join the government effort in putting down the insurrection. That relatively small, unnoticed, low-cost approach was moderately successful into the early 1960s. But that was then.

After his inauguration, in early 1961, President John F. Kennedy visited Fort Bragg, North Carolina, home of the Army's Special Forces. Although only a few operational units existed at that time, he liked what he saw. He became enamored of the Green Berets and their success in Vietnam. He studied their training and education. He admired their skills. Their cunning. Their field craft. Their sense of volunteerism. Kennedy learned that SF recruited for training only the best, and maintained a significantly high attrition rate throughout training. Of those who tried, about one in one hundred earned the Green Beret. Those who made the grade possessed not only a commanding range of tactical skills—weapons, demolitions, communications, and medical—but were also well-educated in the "soft skills" and the attitude necessary to counter an insurgency.

Not coincidentally, Kennedy had a war on the horizon. One of his own making. He wanted to respond to the growing threat of Communism in the Southeast Asian area and what was believed to be the Soviet empire's goal, world domination. According to the so-called "Domino Theory," Vietnam was destined to become the primary testing ground—the lead domino. It was postulated that if the Russians were unchallenged and, by default, successful in Vietnam, the whole Asian continent was up for grabs. Mindful of those possibilities, Kennedy immediately authorized the establishment of several Special Forces operational groups. He wanted Special Forces to form the basic building block of the U.S. foreign policy response.

So, with President Kennedy's support, the 1960s became the glory years of Special Forces. What would become known to most Americans as "Green Berets" (because of the lyrics to Barry Saddler's song) had a mountain. With renewed interest, manpower, and money for innovative weapons, equipment, and training—no expense was spared—SF and associated others began anew the workload that had been carried since the mid-fifties by a much smaller contingent. The mission was to counter the insurgency. Vietnam was being viewed by scholars as the test case of American will and of its commitment to a growing global foreign interest. The counterinsurgency mission was aimed directly at the root of the problem. Its tactics included advising, engineering, training, medical assistance to the outlying villages, and getting the crops to market. Winning the hearts and minds of the people. Helping to moderate the expectations of the people.

Unfortunately, John F. Kennedy had surrounded himself with poor advisers. And when Lyndon B. Johnson took the oath of office in 1964, following Kennedy's death, those liberal-minded products of the Eastern Establishment, like then–Secretary of State Dean Rusk, who had "helped" Kennedy get the U.S. into Vietnam, were advising the new president that the United States could win in Vietnam with more forces. Just send in the big units with the big weapons, and pay out the big dollars for an easy military and political victory. This played directly into the hands of LBJ, who was just dying to teach the Russians a thing or two. You know, "get us a couple of coonskin caps." Unfortunately, during the impending buildup of U.S. forces, as early as 1964, U.S. strategy was weak, and U.S. resolve was weaker. Unbelievably, then–Secretary of Defense Robert S. McNamara, another member of the Eastern Establishment, ruled against the military's desire to destroy war-making equipment positioned in large staging areas in North Vietnam. The destruction of the NVA missile defenses, fuel stocks, rail transits, ships and docks, bridges, communications, and ammunition deposits would have systematically starved the Communists' effort to wage war. In spite of the military's repeated insistence that those targets be destroyed, the weak-knee crowd repeatedly ruled them "out-of-bounds" and the military's desired strategy as "provocative." Had those types of targets been allowed, as they were in Desert Storm some thirty years later under President George Bush, the SF role in the South might have been sufficient. The United States might not have had to commit millions of troops over twelve to fifteen years, or to suffer 58,000 killed, hundreds of thousands wounded.

Well, that didn't happen, and by 1967, with the in-country presence of American forces sitting at over 300,000 and growing, it was becoming obvious that Vietnam was an American war seeking an American solution. This response seemed to trigger a like response from the Soviet and Chinese sponsors of Hanoi, so more NVA troops were recruited and deployed to South Vietnam. Oh, we killed many more of them than they killed of us, but they never gave a shit how many they lost—or would lose—and we did. It was that simple. And we never seemed to understand that, although most of our soldiers on the ground were never in doubt. The reckless experiment, begun by Kennedy and continued by Johnson and his ignominious staff, went sour.

Blackjack-31

On the morning of January 8, 1967, Ken Chilton's recon platoon slipped out of Duc Phong, moving eleven kilometers due south into the heart of War Zone D, a known enemy stronghold. Chilton maintained radio silence except for two secret transmissions per day on the PRC-25 radio. The following morning, about 0600, wearing our black scarves, Staff Sergeant England and I followed, using a different route of infiltration. Our first task was to rendezvous with Chilton and, together, establish a clandestine base area for the remainder of the force. Our entry into the area was without incident. Using some of the high-speed trails, we reached our destination by nightfall.

Small, Quiet, and on Foot

One of the advantages of writing about major life experiences when you're older is that, because you are older, you not only have had more life experiences but also, you're better able to connect important events. Thirty years after meeting up with Chilton's recon platoon, waiting for the rest of the MGF to close, my thoughts focus on one of the childhood experiences I cherished the most: fishing with my dad. From the time I was a small boy growing up in Spokane, I looked forward to the weekend fishing trips with my dad and, on occasion, my older brother, Bill, and at times some of my dad's friends. As almost a ritual, we dug for worms—night crawlers—on Friday nights, placing them in a large tin can filled with dirt. Dad would show me the location on his map—usually Blanchard Creek, his favorite place, I think—and I would fall asleep in my downstairs bunk bed dreaming about the next day's fun. When we arrived in the area, Dad would slowly move his right forefinger to his lips, saying, "Now, Steven, we need to be quiet. Otherwise, the fish will hear us." My six-year-old heart would pound with excitement as Dad quickly prepared my pole with a shiny silver spinner and put a worm on the hook. Patiently, he would help me get my hook into the trickling water and let out some line. Until I was older, Dad never left my side by more than a few feet. When I was six, my dad was like a god to me. If I became too anxious, or began to lose patience because the fish were not biting, he would calmly reconfirm the plan by again moving his forefinger to his lips. When it became obvious, even to him, that we were fishing a dry hole, we slowly and quietly walked upstream. This was an exercise with which I became very familiar: move slowly into an area, quietly set up, and patiently wait for the fish to bite. It wasn't long before I learned to prepare my own rod and reel, bait my own hook, cross the stream on my own with Dad's knowledge, and of course catch, clean, cook, and eat the variety of trout with which we were blessed throughout eastern Washington and northern Idaho.

More important were the lessons my dad taught me over the years. Learn about and respect the environment, don't break tree limbs, don't litter, step lightly, don't scare the fish, and, when you're certain the fish are elsewhere, relocate. Those lessons, once hard to endure, became habit. So much so that when fishing the Saint Joe River with my own son Jeff many years later, I slowly crept up on a fourteen-inch rainbow sunning in shallow rocks, quietly bent down so as not to cast a shadow over its eyes, and, when I was sure I was ready, with lightning speed snatched him just below the gills with my right hand. I wasn't surprised, but I can't say the same for the fish as he struggled for survival. I felt so lucky, I let him go. When I later told that fish story to my dad, he also was not surprised.

War on the Ground Can Be Gruesome

As the rest of the MGF closed on our base camp, two things were evident. One, we had managed to infiltrate a known enemy secret zone without being challenged by any of the large units being counted by our intelligence sources. The only evidence that we were not alone consisted of the sporadic warning shots reporting the location and disposition of VC trackers. We were unimpressed. Two, one of our medics reported low resistance in some of the Bodes, and at least one American. Sergeant Jim Donahue, our twenty-three-year-old field medic, code name Fox-3, was concerned that one of our communication specialists, Sergeant First Class Wagner, was showing symptoms of latent malaria. The third platoon commander, SFC George Ovsak, was also feeling "punky." This was not good news, as we anticipated being in the secret zone for up to thirty days, perhaps longer. If we were to be slowed by disease and suffering, the risks we faced would multiply. Our medics and leaders were told to brief the troops, and were cautioned to be on the lookout for cold, clammy skin, high temperature variations, and extreme headaches.

The next morning, we assigned platoon-level missions, and

began to operate in squad-size patrols, usually one American and ten to fifteen Bodes. On January 10 the recon platoon reported a small contact with an undetermined number of VC resulting in one friendly WIA, one VC KIA, and one VC CIA (captured in action). I learned later that the wounded Bode, bleeding profusely from gunshot damage to his upper arm, which sustained a compound fracture, died of an overdose of morphine as a result of his being treated by three separate Bode medics. If there is a downside to small unit operations with ethnic guerrillas, it is that trained medics are at a premium. Unfortunately, recon's Joe Cawley, although cross-trained as a medic, was not with the patrol that suffered the casualty. What might have been only a minor medical emergency turned on the availability and competence of medical judgment and treatment. Do you still believe in fate?

Aware that the accident was the exception that proved the rule, I recalled with American pride the quality of our SF field medical training. When pressed, guys like Donahue, our 91B4S field medic, could perform miracles, quickly applying sound field-based medical procedures in the most austere environments, where infection was a principal concern. During the glory days of Special Forces, the field medic selected for SF received fifty-two weeks of advanced field medical training. I had personally witnessed SF medics performing amputations, working on the head and stomach, and treating and closing gaping wounds gushing massive amounts of blood. Of course, they were also expert in administering the appropriate drugs to enable seriously wounded soldiers to fight the pain while continuing to operate or waiting for evacuation. SF medics were simply the best combination of fighting and healing. Unfortunately, such a medic was not always available at the time and place of the serious wound. We had seriously considered taking a doctor with us—an SF doctor—but that plan was dropped since, collectively, we didn't think the doctor would be able to keep up with our schedule and still be able to care for the wounded. Also, if a doctor, how many? Fitness and fighting aside, we were operating on such a small scale, it was thought that two medics would provide better coverage than a single doctor because our medics were killers first, medics second. For MGF missions, we could approve no other concept. Both Sergeant Donahue, deputy commander of the third platoon, and Staff Sergeant Dennis Montgomery, the task force medic, carried rifles, used fragmentation grenades and command-detonated claymore mines, set up mines and booby traps, established ambushes, and closed with and killed VC soldiers.

It was important to the VC that they be able to account for their dead and wounded, not so much for the sake of numbers, but to ensure a proper burial. So, using parachute cord, we tethered the bodies of VC KIA to nearby trees and left them on the trail as bait for the huge, jungle-born and -bred wart-hogs that would eventually pick up the scent of rotting flesh. In other words, we porked 'em. If you're wondering how I felt about that practice: at the time, it didn't seem to matter. The VC soldier was killed while trying to kill us. Although under normal circumstances I would not personally deny another human being from reaching his or her own form of spiritual reward, these were not normal circumstances.

Good Prisoners and Bad Prisoners

For a Mobile Guerrilla Force without standard evacuation capability even for its own wounded, prisoners were a liability. Usually, the information they could provide had less value than the danger they represented if we were to allow them to remain free in the secret zone. Accordingly, prisoners were classified as either "good prisoners" or "bad prisoners." Good prisoners talked within three days, and were then porked, with their mouths taped shut to preclude premature screaming. Bad prisoners maintained their silence for up to three days and were then porked. In either case, prisoners were treated as human beings, being offered cigarettes, food, and water. Nor were they tortured.

MGF prisoner-control techniques were fail-safe. After the

capturing unit escorted the prisoner to the task force head-quarters, a forceman placed a noose made from a six-foot length of det cord around his neck, and attached a six-inch fuse lighter to the end of the remaining three feet. An identical necklace was fixed to a small tree adjacent to the bewildered VC insurrectionist. An interpreter told the VC to visualize the damage to his neck as he witnessed the total destruction of the neck-size sapling. He was warned that if he even looked like he was trying to escape, the guard would pull the fuse, causing the detonation cord to explode within six seconds at a rate of 26,500 feet per second. In case you're wondering, dynamite explodes at a rate of ten thousand feet per second.

There's No Place Like Home

The recon platoon contact excited my senses. From a brief examination of the VCs' clothing, weapons, and equipment—their basic fighting load—Chilton reported that they were caretakers for a nearby way station. The way station was a permanent base camp used to temporarily "house" NVA and large VC units moving through the area. Such secured bases allowed a unit infiltrating from the north to the south, via the Ho Chi Minh trail, to move into, rest, and move out of the area with guides, information about enemy forces, and local secu-rity forces. Interior fighting positions and large crude cooking pots placed over fireplaces cut from earthen banks near the center suggested that this particular way station was estab-lished for a regiment-size unit consisting of three to five hun-dred men. Recon marked the area for destruction by air strikes—Sky Spot missions flown by F-4 fighter-bombers—early the next morning. Destroying way station base camps was part of our mission to disrupt the even flow of VC and NVA units being introduced into South Vietnam to engage large American units. The loss of the way stations presented the enemy with a huge logistical problem. Nowhere to go. Nothing to eat. No guides or security. No sense of direction. And finally, a knowledge that enemy forces had somehow

penetrated and were operating in their secret zone with relative ease. I don't know about you, but that would scare the shit
out of me.

As daylight gave way to complete darkness, amid the intermittent cries of the spider monkeys, our second platoon settled
for the night into a well-concealed hillside security position.
England and I reminisced about the third platoon's good fortune, marked our maps for upcoming operations, and verified
the coordinates of the DZ designated for our first resupply.
Incidentally, only two maps reflected the MGF's entire operational game plan, including specified coordinates for the resupply drops and the general route structure. I had one, as task
force deputy commander. Gritz had the other. We were on our
third of four days' rations, so we were expecting a resupply on
day five. As I feasted on rice tomato soup with chicken and
Tabasco, canned fruit, and black coffee, I was anxious to learn
how well our new aerial resupply concept would work in a
triple-canopied jungle with some trees as high as a thirty-
story building. Asleep or awake, sometime between 0100 and
0300 I was jostled by an enormous explosion some seven hundred meters to our southwest. That would have to be the VC
way station. Sky Spots were deceptive. Silent entry, pinpoint
radar bombing from fifteen thousand feet, with a ground
circular-error average of fifty feet. We never heard them
coming, but the shock value from the strike was much like
being at the epicenter of a mild earthquake.

What Color Are the Leaves?

Our plan for the day was to feed off the recon platoon's initial contact near the way station. It was reasonable to conclude
that the destruction of a large base camp would invite a
follow-up investigation. Someone within the VC infrastruc-
ture would want to know what happened, when, where, how,
and why. We wanted to hurt them. Toward this end, we centered the destroyed way station on a 1:50,000 topographical
map and assigned four quadrants, one to each platoon. Within

the second platoon quad, from 90 to 180 degrees and a distance of two thousand meters, England and I studied the map to determine the most likely routes into and out of the base area. We then split the area of operations in two, and broke down the Bodes into two groups. All of that completed in a matter of minutes, fifteen Bodes and I slipped out of the Bo Chi Huy on a northeasterly azimuth running alongside a small, intermittent stream. We reached our destination within one hour. It was nearly 0700 when we established our ambush position.

Waiting in ambush is at least as exciting as fishing. Positioned near the intersection of two trails, in the shape of an inverted, elongated L, and facing southeast, we watched and quietly listened for any signs of life. Since we were wearing masks and goggles, it was not long before sweat began to trickle down the side of my face and into my mouth.

M-16s off safe and ready to fire in the fully automatic fire position, we controlled both trails from either direction without endangering friendly troops. I lay out in a covered position near the base of the L, facing almost south, able to control the southeast-northwest trail with one claymore mine and the northeast-southwest trail with another. The claymores were positioned about twenty-four feet to my front. Thick vegetation concealed our ambush site from ground observation, and tall trees loomed overhead throughout the area.

As my body temperature rose, my goggles began to fog slightly as the warm morning turned hot. The ambush requires silence, patience, and focus. The slightest unexpected sound or movement can cause an enemy force to sense that something is not quite right. The previous day's activities were enough cause for enemy skittishness, so we had to be perfect to make it work. Even then, the VC might have been too smart to soon return. We would wait.

A good ambush enables several in the ambush force to see one another, and everyone to be seen by at least one other guerrilla, so that hand and arm signals can be used to relay information. It was about 1030 when I slowly raised my right forefinger to my lips. I thought I was picking up human sounds moving toward our position from the southeast. My heart pounded as I rechecked the claymore clackers at my side. As the sounds grew stronger, the singsong noises of Vietnamese, I slowly picked up the command detonator for the claymore covering the suspecting trail. Within seconds I clearly saw two bright blue fatigue shirts exposed in the mid-morning sun. Closer, closer, none the wiser, then total eruption! The claymore mine triggered the mechanical ambush, the detonation telling the guerrillas to empty their weapons in their assigned directions of fire, whether or not they could see anyone or anything. The result was catastrophic for those caught in the ambush. All that was left of the two VC trackers could be viewed high above in the translucent discoloration of the leaves on the trees. Unfortunately for me, it was something I would not soon forget, if ever.

Manna from Heaven

Somewhere to the north, in the midafternoon of day four, we were debriefing the combat activities of the MGF. All units had been in ground contact, with no friendly casualties beyond the arm wound in the recon platoon on day two. Several VC KIA, with bodies booby-trapped and left lying about. Wounded Bode? Dead. VC prisoner? Porked. Wounded VC? Dead. Wagner? Malaria, with no sign of improvement. Contrary to our initial SOP, Wagner would be picked up by chopper the next morning, in the wake of the resupply. We would stage simultaneous air strikes in and around the area, conduct the resupply, and slip in a chopper for the extraction. Given the activities to date, and the planned air strikes, the medevac chopper was considered an acceptable risk. As we rested, a large explosion interrupted our meditations, probably the surprise package recon had left the day before in another VC base camp. Said gift was a fragmentation grenade prepared for instant detonation, pin removed, arming handle

wrapped tightly by a rubber band, and placed carefully in a
fire-pit oven. Now, that made for what I call a hot fire.
Winding down, the MGF moved out of the base camp en route
to the DZ that recon was securing for the next day's aerial
resupply.

About 0900 on day five, two A1-E fighters screamed toward our location, each heavily laden with napalm containers
loaded with food, ammunition, and batteries. When over the
DZ, the first plane, with seven pods, dove wickedly toward
our bright orange ground panel. On command, the fighter
released its containers at about five hundred feet. We looked
skyward with great anticipation as the munitions canisters
sped toward our position. Suddenly, poof. Parachutes opened,
and our supplies continued to waft softly to the ground. Perfect. Several jets conducted bombing runs about the outskirts
of our perimeter, and, in the noise and excitement, a lone
medevac chopper dropped into the area, then departed.
Wagner was gone. The second A1-E missed the target, putting
some of the canisters in the trees. Even so, within about an
hour we had cleared the DZ, hid and booby-trapped each con-
tainer, and swiftly left the area, continuing north. As the sky
darkened, we established an operating base, assigned operational areas, and began to conduct a series of night patrols. We
didn't want to be caught off guard. Given the noise we'd created, we thought that a good defense was a good offense. We
planned to work at fifty percent throughout the night. Second
platoon and recon were odd man out. I was tired, but alert as
my Bodes and I departed.

A Leg on the Trail

Patrolling operations were conducted to learn more about
how the VC were disposed in the secret zone, and to pick up
some clues about the movement of NVA forces through the
area. Only five days into the operation, we had already discovered and destroyed two regiment-size base camps or way stations. That solidified our contention that War Zone D was

being used by Hanoi as a major infiltration route. It was
becoming obvious to us that they had been using the area for
many years with relative impunity. Simply put, we were the
first friendly forces ever to inhabit War Zone D. We were
beginning to unlock the mystery about the methods the VC
used to support their NVA comrades. For the first time,
someone was beginning to fix the coordinates of enemy base
camps, and with luck we would catch a large unit resting, then
systematically destroy it with Sky Spots or B-52s, which we
had on six-hour standby.

So it was with some trepidation that my group of Bodes
and I deployed in the dark of night down unmarked trails,
weapons at the ready, trying to smoke out the VC and learn
more about their tactics and techniques. Just like fishing.
Move into an area. Set up. Maintain silence. Wait patiently.
Relocate. I was beginning to think there was little more to
learn that night, as we slogged back toward our base camp. No
sightings. No contacts. No unfamiliar noises. Just one foot in
front of the other. Going home. Raining slightly. Moonlight
glistening against the dripping trees overhead. Just a leg on the
trail. Wait a minute! A leg on the trail? Outside one of the main
entrances to our base camp, at about 0200, there was indeed a
clean, naked, fully distinguishable Caucasian leg lying neatly
across the trail. In single file, one by one, we simply observed
what we saw—what we knew to be true—and kept moving.
Recorded.

As I saturated the ropes to my hammock with mosquito
repellent to guard against the leeches, then liberally coated my
hands and face to ward off mosquitoes, I could not help but
reflect on what we'd just experienced. Eyes closing, I have to
get some sleep, I thought, but still had images of the white leg.
Hard to forget. I was surprised by the timing of this psychological ploy. I was also impressed with the planning and execution required to acquire the leg, transport it into the area, and
carefully place it across the trail on which we would be
walking without being seen or heard. Scary, huh? I didn't even
want to underestimate those guys.

A few hours later, upon awakening, I learned that our

wounded forceman was dead. We wrapped his body in his waterproof poncho, cached it in a tree, marked the coordinates on our task force map, and recorded the eight-digit coordinates in the TF diary. We briefed the Bodes at length, making sure they understood that we would recover the body for the dead man's loved ones thirty days after the operation was over. This was our SOP. We felt it was important to establish and hold true to this requirement for several reasons: recruiting, peace of mind, religious influence, and a sense of fairness for anyone who would have the audacity to join and fight with the MGF.

Elephant Walk

As we continued south we began to labor in the hot, humid environment of mountains on mountains. Even though we were light-to-fight, the weight of our rucksacks, weapons, and ammunition was telling. Those who carried the M-60 machine gun or one of the radios were burdened even more. Ever going up a mountainside, and then down, at times cutting our way through wrist-thick vines at a pace of no more than a hundred meters per hour. Getting nowhere, slowly, we decided to climb straight up one mountainside and onto an elongated ridgeline heading generally in the direction of the objective area we sought. But once on the high ridgeline with the entire MGF, I was surprised to learn that the going would not be much easier. Although the terrain evened out, the vines seemed larger and stronger. No wonder the VC chose such an area to establish their secret base area. Our movement slowed to fifty meters per hour, then twenty-five meters, as we rotated cutmen with huge machetes every fifteen minutes or so.

Just as I was beginning to think that moving to the high ground had been a terrible idea, I stepped into, or rather onto, something resembling a Presto log. When I looked down to get a better look, I realized that the suspicious hardened substance was elephant shit. Thinking back to my logic class with Father John P. Leary at Gonzaga University in 1961, I began to look for any noticeable changes in the ground below my feet. Putting out patrols in several arcing directions, we finally located a relatively open trail that we followed for several thousand meters. Within hours we found ourselves on a huge plateau that opened up into more livable terrain. We had managed not only to travel to our objective area more quickly, but to be immediately rewarded with an expanse of land that looked like it might be home to many large units. Of course, if that was the good news, it might also be the bad news. We established a set of coordinates for reference, but immediately broke down into fighting groups and began to patrol in our assigned sectors.

Was It Him, or Was It Me?

As daylight broke, my Bodes and I found ourselves moving swiftly down an east-west trail toward a suspected enemy base camp identified by a series of small black squares on the map. Something akin to a set of Mexican ruins. We wanted to check it out. As we zigged and then zagged for the better part of an hour, just a thousand meters or so from our objective, the relative silence was interrupted by a flurry of gunfire. Ambush! The VC had let our point man and his 9mm MKII British Sten gun with silencer slip by, choosing to trigger the ambush with me, next in the order of march, and the five or six Bodes following. At the first sound of fire, I got my butt on the ground and began returning fire immediately. The Bodes did the same. To defeat an ambush, you need to counterambush immediately. No thought. No plan. No decision. No maneuver. Just instinct. More noise. More firepower. More balls. You will win or you will lose, but one thing remains constant: if you do not react correctly and instinctively—and this we taught at Ho Ngoc Tao—you are dead. Period.

When the fire cleared and the screams were less audible, I checked myself for wounds. None. I then checked the Bodes who were laid out in the vegetation on either side of the trail. Okay. We then scoured the area for dead or dying VC. Three

dead, three weapons, three sets of gear. There were several
sets of blood trails out of the area. Securing the site, we
quickly prepared for departure. We rigged the bodies and left
them on or near the trail. We secured their weapons and field
equipment. We collected the VCs' unexpended ammunition,
pulled the bullet heads, emptied out the powder, and replaced
it with PETN, which burns at 26,500 feet per second. We then
recrimped the bullet heads and scattered the newly adapted
rounds on the ground. Within fifteen minutes we were on the
way back to our mission support site (MSS). He who knows
he need not stay, lives to fight another day.

We were lucky. I was lucky, because I was the first man in
the killing zone. There was nothing wrong with the VC ambush that could not have been cured by better weapons. They
were simply outgunned. Their aging bolt-action weapons with
a six-round clip were no match for our fully automatic-fire
M-16 rifles, with eighteen rounds per magazine. We could exchange magazines almost as quickly as they could operate the
bolt action and get off another shot. To this day, every time I
pour a beer from my tap, I glance at the wall on which hangs
the French-made MAS-36 rifle with fixed bayonet and clip, an
NVA green plastic canteen with star, and one crudely fash-
ioned homemade field knife. All items are just as they were
at the ambush site some thirty years ago. It was him. Hard to
forget.

Was What You Lost Personal? Did It Hurt?

After I compared notes with Howard, Ovsak, and Chilton, it
was apparent that we were all experiencing a higher level of
activity. Accordingly, Gritz decided this would be a good area
to explore. Also, we were scheduled for our third resupply, by
then a proven concept, albeit controversial, for clandestine
operations. In addition to our regular on-call provisions, we'd
ordered new fatigues, since cutting through the heavy brush
had taken its toll on the black and gray tiger fatigues we called
home. It was day twelve.

The fighters screamed inbound as platoon leaders secured their designated sectors. With three line platoons, one recon, and a small headquarters section, our security plan was by the lensatic compass. Once the center of the perimeter was designated, the rest was instinctive. Howard's first platoon established a perimeter from 0 to 120 degrees, at a distance of 100 to 150 meters, depending on the nature of the terrain. England's second platoon tied in with the first, occupying from 120 to 240 degrees. Ovsak occupied from 240 to 360 degrees. This proved effective and efficient, as no one had to wait for instructions or wait on each other. For added security, Chilton's recon platoon established squad-size listening posts for each sector and at a greater distance, to provide early warning of enemy activity. The headquarters section—Gritz, Kindoll, Sergeant First Class Al Doyle (Wagner's replacement), and a small complement of Bodes—established the command post near the center of the perimeter defense.

Our experience indicated that the operation would take about an hour. Each platoon sent half its assigned strength as a gathering party to extract the sandbag loads of supplies from the napalm canisters. Sandbags were tied together with parachute cord, enabling one man to sling a two-bag load over his shoulder, quickly depart the area, and return to his platoon to distribute the contents. Bags were marked "Headquarters/ Fatigues" or "Weapons" to indicate the point of ownership and distribution. Each platoon hid six containers near the edge of the perimeter, where Jarvis, Glossup, and two Bodes booby-trapped them in place. We "hid" the canisters because we wanted the VC to think we did not want them found. Actually, that was our plan. Since each canister was prepared for instantaneous detonation when moved, we cautioned the Bodes not to go near.

Suddenly, I heard an explosion. It was not likely that the VC had been able to penetrate our perimeter without alerting either recon or one of the line platoons, but anytime there are the sounds of battle, there is some confusion in the ranks. Either we were going to fight our way out of the area, or one of the canisters had somehow prematurely exploded. I was concerned that one of our demolitionists had been careless and was in need of a medic, or worse. I walked over to where England had set up headquarters and overheard him talking into the handset, "Fox, Fox Two. Over." He heard a response. Then, "Fox Two, request status of explosion. Over." When he replaced the handset on the radio, there was a slight grimace on his face as he learned that one of the Bodes, Kien, from the third platoon, had been wounded by an M-14 "toe popper" while trying to remove a bearskin from a VC rucksack placed in the vicinity of one of the canisters. Because parachute silk was a valuable black market commodity, we left the chutes tied to the canisters to entice the VC. Also, the rather small T-7A reserve, green in color, provided excellent camouflage and superior warmth for cool, wet nights in the jungle. Apparently, Kien thought that the ruck, unlike the canister, was safe. Unfortunately, he was wrong, as we left few items of value without some kind of mine or booby trap in place. I returned to MGF headquarters, where both Donahue and Montgomery were busy cleaning fragmentation wounds and treating the Bode for shock. Apparently, he'd tried to loosen the rucksack, and in the process triggered the small but effective anti-personnel mine. The upward force of the explosion had blown out the crotch of his fatigues and severely damaged his groin. Even so, it was important to treat the wound quickly, get him on his feet, and clear the area before the explosion attracted a determined VC response. Believe it or not, as he was waiting to be medevacked with two Montagnard women and two children—we were loath to kill innocent women or children— he was on his feet, walking, and there was a smile on his face. He proudly wrapped the prized bearskin about his body as if for courage. With his wounds, he would need it.

Please Pass the Chicken

As we moved farther and farther from the DZ, slithering down the side of a steep ridgeline, I noticed that the trees overhead were distinguished not so much by their height or girth, but by the way they grew. The horizontal limbs were tied into each other, so much so that it was difficult to visualize where one tree started and another ended. It also made it next to impossible to see much wildlife, although I could hear the chatter of spider monkeys, like LBJ at Suoi Da. Rude little fuckers. The slope steepened and it began to rain softly. We hadn't had much rain lately, so I welcomed any chance to cool off. Just when it seemed there would be no war stories for the day, I stumbled headfirst into a nest of red ants concealed on the underside of the massive, head-high leaves dangling from the crisscrossed branches. Ants attacking everywhere about my face and neck, I wildly swung my hands and arms across my head and down my shoulders, all the while holding my M-16 tightly in my left hand. Hundreds of startled small mouths fought for any piece of flesh they could find as I tried to maintain my balance while still moving down the rain-soaked contour. What seemed like minutes was more likely no more than fifteen to twenty seconds, but the savagery of these red jungle ants remains clearly fixed in my mind some thirty years later. As all soldiers know, there is more to war than living and dying.

Without warning the column slowed, and then stopped. There were no shots fired, nor was it a scheduled communications site. Nor was it a particularly good place to take a break. No, it had to be something else, like the smell of rotting waste, or the sounds of an approaching scout, or some other suspicious sign along the trail. Something was not quite right. Since we were third in the order of march, I walked cautiously toward the front, passing soldier after soldier securing left, then right. Approaching a small clearing, I came to a sudden stop as I watched members of our platoon try to decapitate a large boa constrictor coiled around a sizable branch. Except for its giveaway head, the large, nonvenomous snake was virtually indistinguishable from the branch itself. The boa, the diameter of a man's well-muscled upper arm, had the agility to slide from its perch, drop on its prey, and wrap its powerful body around the neck of its prospective captive. I watched as first one Bode, then another skillfully swung his machete at the giant snake's head as the late afternoon sun lowered itself on the distant hillside. Finally, *whack!* The head fell, writhing on the ground, causing a commotion. They then pulled the huge body, very much "alive" with whatever "nervous" energy remained, from the tree as well. Twenty to thirty feet. *Whack-whack-whack-whack-whack.* As we departed the area, one could hardly fail to notice the intense pride on the faces of the carrying parties, each burdened with a five-foot section of something that, of course, tasted like chicken.

Did You Bring a Map?

After a few hours of much-needed rest, we again prepared to move. I quickly stepped into my boots, then untied my hammock and packed it into an empty ammo pouch. That done, I laced my boots, finishing at the top with a square knot. I then secured my M-16 and my rucksack. The luminous dials on my government-issue Seiko watch said it was 0215 hours, leaving just fifteen minutes until departure. There was still time for instant coffee! Following the explosion at the drop site, we had decided to relocate early to another mission support site to reduce the risk of being discovered. We did not tell the Bodes until it was time to move.

As we inched our way down the middle of a shallow stream, I lightly held the harness strap of the soldier in front of me, both for direction and balance. There was no illumination. It was misting heavily. As the cool river water flowed into my boots, I could not help but think that it was a perfect night to be a guerrilla. The irregular departure was true to the MGF name. We moved slowly but surely, making little noise in the ankle- to knee-deep water. It was not likely that anyone was following us. After about ninety minutes my left foot hit dry land, then my right. We were on the move down a small trail, then up a steep slope for about fifteen minutes. Then, an abrupt stop at our new MSS. Secure by the compass. The time was 0500, and the first hint of daylight filtered through the dense overhead foliage. We slept with our boots on, gear packed and rifles cradled. Sleep was one of the small pleasures in the life of a guerrilla.

At 0830 hours we departed the new area as quietly and efficiently as we entered. For the next day or two we patrolled the same general area. We wanted to know whether the VC were using some of the major east-west trails for high-speed transportation. If so, we could establish a frequent but irregular schedule of Sky Spot bombing missions to discourage the practice. Working again with twelve to fifteen Bodes, we crossed one shallow river, then another, stopping briefly to replenish canteens. As we had not encountered signs of enemy activity, I decided to move off the trail to establish a patrol base. Also, I wanted to check my map, not only to determine where we were, but also to set our direction of movement to the next MSS. We'd been moving in a generally southerly direction, and I knew that within the next few days we would swing to the east, and then north on up to the Song Dong Nai.

Secret missions employ unusual methods to guard against premature disclosure. For BJ-31, we restricted information about our operations to the thirteen-man SF A-team. No one but the Americans knew what our plan was—where we would be going, when, and why—and the two maps Bo and I had were the only ones depicting the entire operational scheme. We simply did not want to have to account for more than those two maps. Of course, the maps were available to all SF team members, but only to review and record operational events and locations for the next day or two. My map depicted the routes of movement, planned resupply sites, and the proposed MSS. Of course, the coordinates for the DZs and the MSS were not marked for location, but entered only in the ledger using a simple substitution code for our commander—J-0, A-1, M-2, E-3, S-4, G-5, R-6, I-7, T-8, Z-9—and committed to memory. You can understand, then, my general fear when I reached down with my left hand to remove my map from the large, open left pocket of my fatigue pants and sensed immediately that it was not there. Trying again, deeper, did not make the missing map return. I knew better than to begin to explore other pockets; they were reserved for other specific equipment—such as the CBN gear in the lower right fatigue pocket—as there was little chance that the map would be anywhere else. Also, a large map—about six inches wide and ten inches long, when folded—was not like a set of house keys.

I quickly checked the pouch of the claymore mine bag strapped about my shoulders. Not there. I started to feel numb. There were few other places the map could have been. Yet, we had made that irregular movement the night before, and hadn't had much sleep, so I was not going to rule anything out. I searched. No, it was not in my rucksack, nor inside my fatigue shirt. It was not on my person, and its safekeeping was mine alone. I started to imagine that our entire unit might be in danger from my one careless act. I said a small prayer to Saint Antony, the patron saint of lost articles. This I remembered from my days as an altar boy at Saint Aloysius grade school. It seemed like the Catholics had a patron saint for everything. But I was sincere, and I truly needed to find the missing map before it fell into enemy hands. What seemed to take an eternity while I searched myself and my belongings was just five to ten minutes in real time. No time to lose. It was 1130 hours.

Without revealing the nature of the mission to the Bodes, I directed the patrol to fade back into the treeline, take up a good security position, and wait in place. After defining the challenge and password as any combination of numbers that added up to ten, I selected two Bodes for what I said was a special mission to locate a communications site. I allowed three hours, knowing we could retrace our movement through the several river crossings, about ten to twelve kilometers, in that time. Regaining my poise, I reasoned that the map must have slipped out of my fatigue pocket at the stream where we had replenished our canteens just an hour or so before.

My heart raced as we moved quickly but quietly over the narrow trail. With one Bode on point, I occupied the center position of the three-man foray. I was beginning to play out in my mind the steps I would have to take if unable to locate the missing map. One had to assume the worst case: VC have the map and were able to decipher its contents. Even though a lot of the information on it was in substitution code, they would have our general direction of movement, so our intended routes would be in danger. Of course, Gritz would be pissed. No one, however, would feel worse than Fox-2.

Got to have that map. Please, God, let me find the fucking map. Moving swiftly and silently, we were quickly approaching the river where we'd just taken water. From a distance I could see the water, and then, as we broke around a slight curve in the trail, I could see the far bank. Still no map. One hundred meters, then fifty, then twenty-five and closing on the near bank of the river.

Dripping with apprehension as we approached, both my mind and my eyes picked up something flashing in the mid-afternoon sun near the bottom of a small rock. It was the map. Undisturbed. Still folded. Thank God. Within an hour or so we closed on the main patrol, rechecked our plans, and moved into an interim security position to get our bearings. Our plans were to patrol for a few hours, set up for the night, then continue near dawn.

Things Are Heating Up—Again

Eager to find some sign of VC activity in the area, we fanned out in a series of cloverleaf patrols. The name of this type of patrol comes from its pattern. Rather than moving directly to a known or suspected enemy location—such as a small village marked on the map—the patrol covers an area on the map where there are several indications from which one could reasonably infer an enemy presence. These indications, or signs, might include a village or two, a major river junction, a formidable piece of high ground such as a hilltop, a major trail network, or an area where VC had been previously engaged. The patrol pattern begins at the stem, and continues as a series of elongated ovals shaped like the overlapping leaves of the clover plant itself. That ensured that the patrol not only covered the entire area of interest—such as four square kilometers—but viewed the area, and its signs, from decidedly different perspectives. Also, because each finishing route is but the start of the next leaf-shaped route, the patrol visits the same general area more than once so that what may have been missed the first time might be seen the next time around. (Of course, an enemy force might see the patrol more than once.)

So it was that we were able to stumble into a VC way station on the "out-route" of the second leg of our patrol after bypassing it on the "in-route" of the first leg. The center of the way station was situated in a clearing about the size of a tennis court. An east-west trail bisected the area from one corner to its adjacent corner. Cooking facilities—a row of five large, earthen fireplaces—indicated that this was another regiment-size base for 300 to 500 soldiers. Fighting positions dotted the perimeter, and an extensive tunnel network facilitated escape routes from the inner to the outer perimeter and beyond.

As we cautiously searched the base camp, we became convinced that it had been recently occupied—fresh boot marks, new litter, the scent of fresh waste, and recently used ovens—but no one was home. We did not enter the tunnel complex because we were small in number and did not want to get trapped in the meandering tunnels, the exits of which were unknown to us, by a force that might have heard us coming and quickly relocated to the outer perimeter, only to prepare for reentry. After posting security at the four corners, particularly at the two trail junctions, we prepared the area for reoccupation. First, we placed booby-trapped grenades in the four or five tunnel traps we found. That ensured we would hear anyone trying to either enter or escape the complex through these trapdoors. Next we seeded the trail near the center of the clearing with an M-14 plastic antipersonnel mine, identical to the "toe popper" that severely wounded Kien. The small, round mines—about two inches in diameter and two inches high—are prearmed and volatile, but usually not lethal in and of themselves. I carefully placed one of the mines in a small hole dug into the trail. Anyone stepping on one of the mines might lose a foot, a leg, or worse. The mine tends to "incapacitate" its human target, requiring immediate medical support that might not be available to a VC field unit. Without proper medical attention within twenty-four to forty-eight hours, the wound begins to take its victim down, often resulting in death.

We repeated the process until we had sown five or six mines, covering them lightly with trail dirt to hide their presence. We then prepared five fragmentation grenades for instantaneous detonation, pulled the pins, wrapped the arming mechanisms with strong rubber bands, and hid them in the earthen ovens. The frag grenade, its case breaking up into thousands of steel shards on explosion, is lethal to the unprotected body within a thirty-meter radius. Instant death for someone near the fire. Our last action before silently departing the area was to record the center-of-sector coordinates, as well as the coordinates along the trail and each of the tunnel traps. The eight-digit coordinates, accurate to ten meters, when translated into bomb targets, would enable us to schedule Sky Spot missions at a time of our choosing. Because we wanted to see if the camp would be reoccupied, we put the bombing mission into our "on-call" file.

As we cleared the area, I heard the distant sounds of small explosions to the north. About five in all. I speculated that they had been VC weapons exploding from the bullets we'd filled with PETN near the site of the last trail ambush. What a pleasure it was to learn that the fruits of your labor were paying off, if indeed those were VC so surprised. We continued south, then east, toward our next MSS.

We rendezvoused with the others about 1800 hours, and I briefed Captain Gritz of our efforts. He was sufficiently interested in the area that he directed me to again explore the way station within the next forty-eight hours. From an MGF point of view, we agreed that we would not tip our hand just then with any bombing missions in the area; we first wanted to learn the results of our efforts to "seed" the area. Bombing—we could do that as we moved north toward the Dong Nai River within the following few days. Also, Gritz had been ordered to produce a prisoner from the area. One who would be alive for interrogation by intelligence agencies.

It Was Simply a Matter of Identification

Early the next morning, we vacated our MSS in MGF strength, moving southeast. Having checked my map, now secured in my claymore bag, I surmised that we'd traveled generally south from Duc Phong about fifteen kilometers, about one-third of our planned route. It was day fourteen of an operation that had been envisioned to run from thirty to forty-five days.

I could say with all honesty that I felt very comfortable working as a guerrilla in a VC secret zone. On the other hand, I knew of a similar effort tried in II CTZ only a month or so earlier. From the reports we got, which were sketchy, the operation was over before it started. Apparently, a poorly trained Montagnard company out of Pleiku infiltrated and had intended to remain operational within a highly contested VC area nestled in the mountains. Within the first week, the unit was discovered, pinned down between two ridgelines on the valley floor, and decimated. My sense of complacency grew weaker as I thought about how fragile guerrilla operations could be. The same kind of disaster could happen to us. I knew that. But we were well-trained, mostly ethnic Cambodian, well-supported, including the A1-E, and had the army's most experienced Special Forces soldier in command. I was convinced that, come hell or high water, we would not be defeated. In the last instance, Bo Gritz would not let the MGF go the way of the previous, ill-advised effort. I felt confident. We had managed to remain in the area for nearly fifteen days, inflicting some damage on the other guy, and our casualties were very low. Something had to be right.

Abruptly, and without warning, the column came to a halt. We had entered a small clearing, without incident, and would set up an antenna to facilitate communications with our higher headquarters in Bien Hoa.

Without boring you with the details, we were able to establish two-way communications with our leaders some hundred miles away. Secure. Using a PRC-74 radio supported by a waist-high, fifty-foot-long wire antenna placed three feet off the ground and perpendicular to our direction of traffic, we sent and received transmissions using Morse code and employing Dianna one-time pads to encode and decode messages. This operation would take about thirty minutes to execute, so we began to secure the immediate area, placing listening posts at both ends of the small trail leading into and out of the clearing. However, within the first few minutes our plans were rudely interrupted by a small VC patrol of five to seven men. The engagement was direct and interactive. The VC attempted to hit the center of our sector, just about the exact location of our radio transceiver. Rude, indeed. This brought on an immediate exchange of gunfire, resulting in zero friendly casualties, two dead VC, one unwounded capture, and several escapees leaving blood trails. Before attending to the escapees—we wanted them back—I directed through an interpreter that the prisoner be secured until I returned. I briefed the three-man security force holding the POW on the ground at gunpoint that under no circumstances were they to eliminate the prisoner. I said, "We need this prisoner alive; we have an order from Nha Trang to capture a POW from this area for interrogation; do you understand?"

Through the interpreter, one of the Bodes said, "Yes, Daiuy." Certain that they understood, I quickly departed to task the first platoon to follow the two escapees and, if possible, capture them. Howard set about immediately to comply. Returning to the site of the POW, I was startled to see that the VC was lying on the ground, faceup, but where his face had been was a two-to-four-inch-deep crater. There were no eyes, no ears, no nose, no mouth, and no throat. Only bloody cavities. Yet the body seemed alive, and it sounded as if he were trying to say something. Emanating from the mouth cavity came a combination of deep, resonating groans and sucking sounds. *"Unxghgh,"* he inhaled. *"Oughgh,"* he exhaled. This he repeated at regular intervals for several minutes.

"What the fuck happened?" I asked the Bode in charge. Silence. Again I demanded, "Why was this prisoner executed." Still, complete silence. At some point I began to notice

the size of his hands. Large. Muscled. His arms were uncharacteristically well-developed. I had my answer. "Cambode,"
I said.

"No, Dai-uy, Montagnard," was the reply.

"Bullshit," I said. "This man was a Cambode." Once again,
silence. Continued silence. I turned the corpse over with my
foot, and my eyes focused on three small bullet holes through
the head. "You fuckers blew this guy away because he was a
Cambodian soldier—a Khmer Rouge, right?" More silence,
then embarrassment. I saw it on their faces. They had been
unwilling to accept that a Cambodian soldier—unlike them,
who had been recruited through the Khmer Serai headquarters
as being loyal to the South Vietnamese cause—had chosen to
fight with the VC movement instead. So they had turned him
over while alive, and fired three M-16 rounds at close range
into the back of his head. The M-16 rounds, which wobbled
slightly in flight, blew off the entire front of the man's head,
completely obliterating his facial characteristics. Having personally recruited the Bodes, having lived with them through
forty-nine days of training at Ho Ngoc Tao, and having seen
firsthand their fierce sense of national pride and their commitment to Special Forces during Black Box, I had come to the
heart of the matter. Strangely, I was not disappointed. Hard to
forget.

When Was the Last Time You Played Kick the Can?

The two VC who had attempted to escape were intercepted
by recon and, with the first platoon in hot pursuit, had nowhere
to run. As we moved into our new MSS, I could not help but
reflect on the man without a face. Unfortunately, the POWs we
had now captured, one of whom was only slightly wounded,
were also Khmer Rouge. I knew this situation would be dicey.
Since Gritz had reported the demise of the prisoner to Huddleston, all efforts to evac a prisoner from the area had been suspended. We were back to POW control and the good prisoner
versus bad prisoner mentality. Also, since we were expecting

our fourth resupply the next morning, after which we would begin the swing toward the Song Dong Nai, one could reason that both of these prisoners were good. Too bad, but whoever coined the idiom "war is hell" was not far off. What is often demanded, and counted, as "normal" behavior on the battlefield, runs counter to the values for human life and the sanctity of the human being that most of us were taught, first by our parents and then by society itself. Even so, the POW situation was bothersome to me.

Bo and I, and Buck Kindoll, took some time out to review our progress to date and to discuss future operational plans. That the prisoners were expendable was a given. The danger posed by the resupply activities, coupled with the VC contact at the comm site, told us that we had better break down again into small patrols, take care of some unfinished business in the area, then move on up north. The VC knew we were in their house, and we knew they didn't appreciate that one damn bit.

It also felt good to spend some time with the others—some good old American interaction—after being mostly with the Bodes under some trying circumstances. I made it a point to do the rounds through each platoon, not only to learn more about what they had accomplished, but to let them know I was damn right proud of them. Also, to inquire whether there was something I could do for them. Jim Howard, Dennis Montgomery, and Dick Jarvis were all sporting pretty good growths of facial hair, but their poise and experience easily showed through. Howard's leadership was an important asset to the success not only of the first platoon but of the MGF itself. He was a seasoned veteran. Dale England, probably the only staff sergeant to command an active duty captain, was his old inimitable self. George Ovsak and Jim Donahue—vintage third herd—were busy whipping up some kind of gourmet meal. I knew that they were all right. Donahue, along with Monty, kept our force healthy and ready to rock-and-roll. Ken Chilton—"Charles K"—provided the necessary leadership for the recon platoon, a most demanding job.

Between operations, I spent more time with Ken, mostly because we were both officers and we got along so well. He

was a real workhorse. He, Lowell Glossup, and Joe Cawley
were busy scouting out the routes they would use after departing the area. All three looked like they were worn to a frazzle,
but their minds and spirits were sharp. Cawley was one of the
team's humorists. Jarvis, Glossup, and Pat Wagner—the man
medevacked earlier with malaria—were all close seconds.
After making the rounds, I returned to the second platoon,
where England and I planned our destiny. We knew that it was
only a matter of time before we would return to the clearing to
see if anyone had come home for dinner. Although tired, I was
anxious to find out. I was keyed up. It must have been around
midnight before I was able to get some rest. I could hear the
faint sounds of battle, but they were too far away and too muffled to identify.

In the process of clearing the MSS early the next morning,
about twelve to fifteen hundred meters south of our designated
resupply we moved onto an almost indistinguishable path that
ran intermittently through the base camp itself. Toward the
western end, a trail junction offered the possibility of two-way
traffic. We turned east. As I approached the turn, I began to
hear some commotion up ahead, as if there was some kind of a
scuffle. There were voices talking, laughing, and other sounds
of the sort one would expect to hear during a street fight. Since
we were in single file, separated by ten to fifteen meters, I had
to wait until I was at the spot in question before I could learn
what was going on. When I arrived and looked down, I saw
the two Cambodian prisoners sitting at the base of a large tree.
Their arms were stretched backward and their hands were tied
around the back of the tree with det cord. Their feet, without boots, of course, were also slung back around the tree,
exposing only their torsos to the front. Their mouths were
gagged. The ritual taking place reminded me of the game I
used to play as a kid growing up in the Gonzaga University
district of Spokane. As each of the Bodes approached the prisoners, he delivered a swift and potentially lethal kick into the
various parts of the human anatomy exposed. The prisoners'
heads were bleeding profusely, with darkened eyes, broken
noses, puffy cheeks, and ripped mouths. Their bare chests

were swollen beyond all comprehension, and their private parts, partially exposed through soiled shorts, were severely damaged. Once again, the Bodes were showing their intense disrespect and hatred for their own kind fallen from grace. But that was neither the time nor the place to change thousands of years of Cambodian culture, however horrific the demonstration. Hard to forget.

This Hill or That?

The quality of life of the guerrilla is, at best, variable and irregular. The mission support site, while not able to offer all the comforts of home, is nevertheless home to the guerrilla. An ever-changing address, but home. A chance to interact with others after a long, hard day at the office, some time to unwind, get something to eat, attend to personal hygiene, and get some rest. And clean and oil weapons.

So, as we were in the process of securing our twelfth set of quarters since leaving Duc Phong, I welcomed the temporary break in operations. I was bone tired, and needed to clean up. The resupply mission was again successful, but the patrolling operations were uneventful. The wet boots and socks, eternal crotch itch, hands and face caked with mosquito repellent, horrible body smell, and constant morning breath were beginning to take their toll on me. Since it was late afternoon and we seemed to have some time, I set about to refresh myself.

Personal hygiene was a dilemma. On the one hand, there was every well-intentioned reason in the world to stay clean and healthy, if only to live and fight another day. On the other, there were all the seemingly insignificant ways you could get into trouble without being able to pinpoint the cause. But the effects were real. They could be measured in increased VC ambushes, signs of trackers, and, not altogether unlikely, VC or NVA dominance of the battlefield in position or numbers. As in any game of chance, you had to reduce the odds of capture and destruction. So, for the MGF there were no showers, no hot running water with soap, and no Dempsey Dumpsters

for the trash. Even so, how you cared for yourself was every
bit as important as whether you did or not. A single mistake
could have endangered the mission, not to mention the MGF. I
reached into my rucksack to remove three pairs of boot socks
I'd managed to wash while wading in river water. I set them
on my hammock lines to dry. Given the intense heat and high
humidity, underwear was a liability. Socks, boots, and loose-
fitting fatigues. That was it. From an ammo pouch, I pulled a
small tube of toothpaste, squeezed a dab on my finger, then
rubbed my teeth. No residue to spit on the ground. I just swal-
lowed. I then removed a small green plastic bottle of Phisohex
and, pouring water from my canteen, massaged my groin area
to fight bacteria. This I did about once a week. The total
amount of water did not exceed one cup, and the surgical
cleanser could be measured in drops. I covered the dampened
ground with leaves to disguise signs of my presence. So much
for hygiene. Then it was time for some rest.

Or so I thought. Within minutes Buck Kindoll informed me
of a problem in need of an immediate solution. We were lost,
or so it seemed. The night before, we had seen what looked
like cooking fires near the top of an adjacent hill. We suspected the fires were coming from a VC base camp. So we had
a perfect opportunity to bomb the shit out of the suspected VC
unit very early the next morning, and then send recon to assess
the damage at daybreak. The problem? There were conflicting
opinions among us as to the map coordinates of the hilltop in
question. Little wonder. I had often thought of that part of War
Zone D as a "bucket of balls." Golf balls. Numerous hills,
most of which were the same size and the same height, competed for the same space. The suspected VC base was about
the same size and elevation as the hilltop on which we'd established our MSS. If we were wrong—the hilltops were only
four to five hundred meters apart—we would have, in effect,
ordered our own destruction. That was a serious problem
indeed. We had to resolve the question of our own location
before we could send in the coordinates for the strike. We had
about two hours of daylight within which to make a decision.

Our decision would be in God's hands, as we were either going to be right or terribly wrong.

In the military, when there's a problem to solve, there's a three-step process. First, define the problem. Okay, the problem was that we didn't know where we were on the ground, so were unable to identify our exact location on the map sufficient to providing eight-digit coordinates for a bombing mission. Second, look at the facts bearing on the problem and analyze the alternatives. For our purposes, we were on one hilltop and the VC were on the other. This hill or that? Third, make a decision. Well, we set about to analyze the alternatives, under some pressure, because we were sure as hell going to blow the shit out of one hilltop or the other.

We dispatched three patrols, each operating independently and with a one-hour time limit, to walk the terrain between our location and a shallow river nearby in the valley to our west. Then we put together a four-man map study group to carefully analyze the terrain depicted on the map, from all perspectives, toward another independent solution. Finally, I offered a third course of action. Do a resection problem using both the map and the existing terrain. Gritz thought this was a good idea, so we had five independent efforts trying to solve the problem, and one hour to get it done.

I circled our proposed location on my map with a grease pencil, making sure I did not cover up either our own location or that of the VC with the thick black lines. By map inspection, I found a dominant mountain range well outside our operational area—perhaps twenty kilometers away—running generally north and south. Perfect. All I needed was a tall tree in the area that I could climb. Done. Very close—within twenty-five feet—so this would be a true test. At twenty-six, I was an animal. Still, as I pulled myself higher, branch by branch, I began to experience some anxiety. I began to wonder if I was up to the task. Near the top there were fewer branches, and although the tree was slim, which aided the monkey climb, there were not many foot- and handholds. Just above me was a small branch I could use as a secure foothold, and from which I could do my work. My heart began to race as I eased myself up and over the limb.

With my feet holding firmly to the branch just below me, I tied myself into the tree at the waist with the twelve-foot length of five-eighth-inch nylon rope and snap link I carried on my harness for use as a Swiss seat during rappelling operations.

Once secure, I looked down at the surrounding terrain with awe. Beyond, I had a breathtaking view of the distant mountain range. I estimated my height at seventy-five feet. Tightly clutching my folded map with my left hand, I lifted the compass out of its pouch with my right. The end of the compass was secured at the thumb loop with a two-foot length of parachute cord, the other end of which was knotted below the drain hole of the compass pouch itself. This was a common technique for safeguarding the compass. I had also tied a two-foot cord onto a small steel ring punched through my map, securing the other end to my web gear. So much for logistics. But, really, for those of you who are into instructionals, nothing a guerrilla carries is not secured. For two reasons: if you lose it, it probably can't be replaced during the operation; perhaps more important, if you lose it, the enemy is likely to find it, and eventually find you.

Pushing the compass out from my waist, I pointed it in a straight line toward one of the two prominent peaks also identifiable on the map. I looked through the viewfinder. Holding the compass steady, when perfectly still and intersecting the mountaintop, I took a reading of 45 degrees. I plotted the back azimuth, 225 degrees, on my map, not with a grease pencil, the thickness of which would reduce the accuracy of the plot, but with a sharp lead pencil. Next, the second peak. Azimuth? One hundred twenty degrees. Back azimuth? Three hundred degrees. I made sure that the lines of the back azimuth were extended for a thousand meters through the point of intersection on the map. I had my answer.

It was about 1730 hours as we gathered to make one of the most important decisions of our lives. Bo wanted to know what the three patrols found. Only one patrol placed the MGF on

Hill A and the VC on Hill B, four hundred meters to our northwest. Two patrols found the opposite. The map study group, consisting of Gritz himself, Kindoll, and Howard, thought we were on Hill A. Two and two. My resection problem confirmed that we were on Hill A.

To my knowledge, no one slept that night as we waited and watched for the Sky Spot mission to be flown. Because we were but three hundred meters from the leading edge of the target area—normal safe distance for bombs was six hundred meters—it was important that the bomb run be parallel, and not perpendicular, to our MSS. That was a lot to ask, by CW, from a hundred miles away for a mission that would be directed by radar to the target at an altitude of fifteen thousand feet. I thought we were right, but still, I was nervous. There was a lot that could go wrong, but only one option, perfectly executed, that would score a touchdown. And we needed a touchdown, for sure.

About 0200 hours, we heard the bombs from the first flight into Hill B. So far, so good. The fighters must have flown the correct line, as we experienced no short rounds. But the ground shook. The mission continued. Flight two, then three, and finally four. Then silence. When the sky cleared, we could neither see nor hear anything from Hill B. The boys in blue had completely obliterated the entire area with their five hundred- and thousand-pound bombs. The air force had just blown the bejesus out of the Cong. What can I say? My mother always said I was lucky.

A recon patrol departed at first light, but the terrain was so difficult, partially due to the river that split the hills, that the first reports of bomb damage did not reach the MSS until about 1000 hours. Not before, we surmised, the VC had removed most of their dead and wounded. Results? One regimental base camp destroyed, with an undetermined number of blood trails leading out of the area.

I thought we were lucky to be alive.

Double Your Pleasure, Double Your Fun

Our fourth resupply went off without a hitch. The pilots who flew our missions out of Pleiku had come to master both the unconventionality and the art of the operations. The only snafu to date had been a few parachutes in the trees, but not once had we encountered a systemic problem with either the drop of the canisters or the simultaneous air strikes in and around the area. Also, given our level of activity, four days of food, ammunition, mines and booby traps, and batteries and other special items, was about right. Prior to our infiltration, we had prepared an extensive, coded list of items available to us and that we might need. Because of our daily exertions we discovered, about day twelve, that the indigenous rations we had selected, mostly for their lightweight benefits, were inadequate. Soldiers were getting fatigued and at times felt undernourished, driving a new requirement for the old C-rations, some of which had rested peacefully in their heavy tins since World War II. To my knowledge, this was the only unforeseen adjustment we had to make throughout the operation. It was day eighteen.

From the DZ, England and I moved back toward the west and the way station. By then we felt we owned the trails, and so found ourselves moving quickly and quietly on one of the trails marked on the map. If we were lucky, the main trail would intercept the unmarked and much smaller trail we'd used two days earlier while departing the VC base camp. It was about 1630 when we reached the eastern edge of the clearing, about two hours before dark. Not much time.

We first discovered the way station from the west, so we now encountered the same area with a different view of the clearing. We used arm and hand signals to spread our formation from the customary ten to fifteen meters between individuals to about thirty meters, and to assume a low profile. If for some reason we were discovered and outnumbered and/or outgunned, our SOP was to break out in buddy teams of two, and RV at a designated rally point. We inched toward the center of the clearing, to about the location where we'd seeded the trail with antipersonnel mines just days earlier. There was evidence that at least two of the mines had detonated, and there were blood trails north along the trail. A couple of rucksacks lay just off the trail.

Ever so cautiously we low-crawled north, not wanting to be seen or heard. The speed of the maneuver was less important than its silence and lack of signature. We drove our bodies forward slowly with our knees and elbows, cradling weapons lightly in the crook of our forearms, as England radioed a sitrep to Gritz. Up ahead, about 150 to 200 meters, I heard a low metallic sound. Like a shovel on rocks. My eyes focused on those of the Bode to my left. When I was certain I had his attention, I stopped momentarily, showing him a full view of my left forefinger crossing my pursed lips. Then, two taps of the same finger to the lobe of my left ear, followed by an exaggerated pointing of the same finger up ahead. Finally, a sweeping motion of left hand and forearm forward, as a signal to continue the movement. Ever so slowly, so silently, trying to improve our position without being discovered. I wanted to raise my body to get a better view, but my heart pounded as the sounds were now more distinguishable. I didn't dare give away a position it had taken the better part of thirty minutes to achieve. Fortunately, we reached a small rise in the ground, causing our heads to be about twelve inches higher.

With an outstretched open palm, I motioned a halt. I guessed that we were within fifty meters from whatever it was we were going to see. Not wanting to risk being heard, I pointed to my chest, then my eyes, to signal that I would raise up to get a look. The Bode nodded his understanding. Not wanting to queer the deal, I laid my weapon on the ground at my right side. I raised myself slowly, trying to control my breathing. When my head reached a height of two feet, I glanced forward. For nearly a minute I watched, through knee-high grass, two blue-shirted VC with shovels filling what looked to me like a foxhole. Both were inviting targets, and well within desirable range, but we needed to eliminate both VC at the same time.

I glanced to my left. About twenty meters away the experienced MGF guerrilla was watching my every move. I pointed forward to the location, then showed two fingers, waving them from side to side to improve his peripheral vision. When I saw him nod in the affirmative, I pointed directly to the trigger mechanism of my M-16, then to him. Again he nodded his head up and down. Now for the hard part—who shoots whom. I again displayed the two-fingered V, reaching my arm well forward, indicating the two VC. With a small stick in my right hand, I pointed first to the leftmost finger, then to him; then to the rightmost finger, then to me. I repeated the signals, and he affirmed his understanding. Now for the timing. Gripping my own rifle in my right hand, I showed him the five fingers of my left hand. I left all five up for a five-second count. Pulling in my thumb, I showed four fingers for another five seconds. Five seconds later, three fingers, then two. With one finger exposed for only one second, I withdrew the finger, took aim, and, continuing the count in my own mind, fired at the VC to my right at zero. My fellow guerrilla did the same. Unbelievably, we both acquired our targets, fired within a second of each other, and hit our men. But really, how much different had that been from playing cowboys and Indians in a vacant field twenty years earlier?

As soon as we'd fired, we raised up to confirm our kills. To my surprise, I could see nothing but dirt. I motioned our Bodes forward. As we neared, still unsure of what had happened, I saw two shovels near the fringes of the hole, but still no VC. Then it dawned on me. They were both in the hole. How efficient. Walking up now with a foolish sense of boldness, peering into the hole, I saw there were four VC. The "foxhole" had been a shallow grave for two VC killed by trail mines. It was now to be the final resting place for all four.

We had no sooner finished filling the hole than shots rang out. We were under attack from the north. It was now about 1730 hours, and the first shadows of a long, hot day began to reduce our ability to acquire targets. Still, we pursued the enemy. The volume of fire told me we were at even strength, but we had the coveted M-16 rifles.

As we drove them up and out for about two hundred meters, the return fire lessened and then stopped altogether. We had apparently run them off. Returning past the grave site toward the center of the way station, we secured in a tight perimeter. "Fox, Fox Two, over."

"This is Swamp Fox, Over." It was Kindoll.

"Fox Two, four VC KIA. VC attack stopped. Coming home."

"Fox Two, negative." This time it was Gritz. "Remain in the area for a while. See if they won't return, over."

I tried to prevail. "Negative, we drove them north, we are small, and it's too dark to acquire a target, over." We were two thousand meters from the MSS, and, if hit by a larger force— and they certainly knew where we were—we would be at a distinct disadvantage.

"Fox Two, this is Swamp Fox. I repeat, hang around to see if they return. Swamp Fox, out."

We had our orders, but to this day I can't say I was happy about them. On the one hand, I admired Bo's capacity to take the fight to the enemy. He was fearless. And in case you're wondering, he really wouldn't ask anyone to do something that he wouldn't be willing to do himself, and often did. He always pushed the envelope of the possible. Of course, his experience usually proved him right. Really, there is no room for pussies on the battlefield. On the other hand, we didn't know the enemy strength or disposition in the area.

Concerned for our tiny force as a whole, we established a perimeter defense of the area and reminded the Bodes to keep the noise down and the lights out. Our breakout plan was still in effect. The Bodes responded like well-trained experienced soldiers. Two hours later, as night fell, and with no visual or audible signs of the VCs' return, we picked up our marbles and headed for home. Hard to forget.

Earthquake!

Sometime early the next morning, about 0200 hours, I woke from a deep sleep to the rolling thunder of what sounded like an earthquake. I nearly fell out of my hammock. Although you could not hear the F-4s approach, even when directly overhead at fifteen thousand feet, the results were deafening. The way station was being rendered inoperable, compliments of the air force and U.S. taxpayers who, from the noise alone, bought, paid for, and delivered enough ordnance that night to put a sixth floor on the Pentagon.

Hey, What's the Haps?

The next couple of days were uneventful, at least for the second platoon. It was possible that the VC were growing wary of our MGF, and although it was their home into which we'd invited ourselves, one could hardly blame them for their lack of hospitality. Yet one had to wonder just when we would be seriously challenged. How would we begin to know when we were surrounded by a superior force? Would the first signs appear during the daytime or at night? We were operating around the clock, and we were most unpredictable. In a sense, we were just moving through the area. No single target, no pitched battles for terrain. No defensive posture against which they were able to develop a strategy. No heavy weapons or pieces of equipment for them to see, hear, or cite as a critical target. No expressed desire to stand and fight. Elusive. Mobile. Small. Light. Unpredictable. Disciplined. Independent. Camouflaged. Quiet. Confident.

We began to think we were out of business. Was it the terrible destruction of the base camp? Was that what was now occupying their minds? Caring for their dead and wounded? I guess that made sense. If the situation were reversed, we would have had to declare a state of emergency, call for reinforcements, react to heavy casualties, get out the dead and wounded. Evaluate the whole reliability of continuing operations. Maybe they were going through some kind of crisis management. Why not? Perhaps we had destroyed their confidence, their will to fight. Or perhaps they were sending for reinforcements—getting ready to counterattack—in the wake of heavy casualties. The suspense was killing me. I wanted to know. I thought of Sun-tzu.

The Right Time and the Right Place

There was never any assurance that any of us would get out of the secret zone alive. What you had was what you had. No more. No less. If for some godforsaken reason you were betting on the outcome, that was simply a personal matter. If you were thinking about your "life after" BJ-31, you would not have been called for delay of game, but certainly for offsides. For such reasons, Staff Sergeant Cawley was called front and center by Captain Gritz late in the afternoon of January 26, 1967, while the MGF was assembled in our MSS deep within enemy-held territory. Cawley might die during his mission, but not without knowing that he would go down wearing the gold bars of a second lieutenant.

Nothing was taken for granted. Gritz read a few lines from Howard's Bible, then prepared to pin the new rank onto Cawley's shoulder tabs as the rest of the team looked on with the earnestness and attention an occasion like that so deserves. Without Joe's knowledge, the day before our FAC had dropped a miniparachute with an envelope containing the commissioning second lieutenant's orders, bars, and the coveted crossed-rifle insignia of the Infantry. He was taken completely by surprise.

As Gritz stepped forward, someone—probably Glossup—spoke up, standing Gritz on his heels. "Sir," he said anxiously, "with Staff Sergeant Cawley about to become an officer, this may well be our last chance to properly address him with a revered hymn."

Bo said, "I guess you're right."

At that point Glossup led the chorus in a refrain uttered only for special people under special circumstances. "Hymn, hymn, fuck him." After just a few rather loud words and a raucous bit of patter, Gritz spoke the words that promoted Staff Sergeant Joseph Cawley—recon section leader, cross-trained medic, and communications specialist—to the rank of second lieutenant, United States Army, Infantry.

We spent the rest of the afternoon preparing our thrust into the Dong Nai River region, and eventually a crossing of the Song (River) Dong Nai itself. The Bode leadership was not happy when they learned about our plans to enter the Dong Nai river valley. They were convinced that the area was the home base for several VC units. In addition, the steep, elongated stretches of mountains on either side of the valley offered both long-range observation and excellent fields of fire. The small northeastern valley exit emptied into the steep banks of a river that would have to be crossed. To be sure, no unit, guerrilla or otherwise, would want to be pinned down in the lowlands, entrapped, and destroyed, save the few small teams able to pass through the encirclement in the dead of night. The Bodes were very unsettled by the thought of the impending missions, and their anxiety soon became obvious as the word spread through the ranks. It was not a good sign of things to come.

Night of the Living Dead

Captain Gritz had a plan, both to deal with the uncertainty expressed by the Cambodian leadership and to increase our chances of staying alive as we moved through the Dong Nai valley region. He broke the MGF down into two groups. Group one, consisting of his command element plus the first and third platoons, would operate through the mountain range on the left, or northwest, of the valley. Group two, under my command, made up of the second platoon and recon, was to move through the mountain range on the right, or northeast, of the valley. Both groups were to operate extensively along the ridgelines, avoiding the low-lying areas of the valley to the extent possible. We were to rendezvous two days later near the valley's exit. That done and the word out, the level of dissatisfaction seemed to dissipate. Recalling the carnage suffered by friendly forces operating in the II Corps debacle, and Dien Bien Phu, one could hardly blame the Bodes for being cautious about exposing themselves to attack from above.

As recon departed the MSS on local security patrols in and around the area, I briefed group two on our departure and route the next morning, stressing that we would be moving along the ridgeline to avoid detection and, if we were lucky, contact the VC on terms not to our disadvantage. As the sky darkened I slouched in my hammock and closed my eyes, vowing never to wake again.

As in the real world, there are times in combat when what you think and what you see are dissimilar. Minds can and do play tricks. Eyes can be deceived. When a soldier is exhausted, what he experiences is real enough, but his senses can be misleading. Have you ever awakened to a dream, only to challenge its authenticity? You are riding a bicycle with small wheels through a city street, trying to dodge the traffic from your seat perched hundreds of feet above the ground. Your grasp of reality tells you that you are doomed. There is no way you can continue to avoid the onrush of cars and trucks below, particularly when you're hard-pressed even to see them with any certainty. The only thing you can confirm is that you're going to crash and burn. Well, that also happens to someone who has lived with death and destruction for weeks on end deep within the homeland of forces he has yet to challenge. What one person records as gospel, another labels as folly.

So it was when I awoke that night to the faint glimmer of lights moving ever so slowly toward our security position. With a great deal of caution, I lowered myself from my hammock, reaching for the M-16 positioned muzzle up near the tie lines. It was automatic. Trying to comprehend the seemingly filtered lights approaching, I began to wonder if anyone else was awake, or whether anyone cared. I knew I mustn't make a sound. Radio off-squelch, of course. Silence. Heart rate about to explode. Real questions about whether or not to initiate fire.

No. Otherwise, the marauding force would have the drop on a sleeping enemy whose inner perimeter had just been penetrated. Contact others, by feel, certainly not by radio? No. Too risky? Lights now approaching to within fifty meters or so. Very real. Hard to imagine. I know what I see. Looks like flashlights with red filters. Do VC have such things? Yes. Is this our recon force reentering our perimeter? Don't know. Challenge? No, what if I am wrong? The enemy would open fire instantly. Death and destruction. Clinging to the back side of the tree to which my hammock was tied, I sought cover while continuing to peer toward the lights. Had the VC finally been able to locate the MGF situated on a rectangular hilltop about two hundred meters long by about a hundred meters wide? Was this how it was all going to end? How to react? Remember the dream. In the dream, there is no reaction because you know what the final result is going to be. You just accept it. And then, fortunately, because it is but a dream, you wake up, and put on the coffee. But now everything is at stake. And it may not be a dream. It may be real. What to do?

If it was a dream, it was real. And if it was real, it was a dream. I chose to do nothing but remain silent. I was wide-awake as I watched the VC unit walk through our inner perimeter, hoping against hope that no one would make a sound and thus give away our precarious position. I watched the unit fade in the distance. My mother always said I was lucky. Hard to forget.

Anyone for Corn on the Cob?

With recon leading, group one moved like a long, green lizard along the higher reaches of the ridgeline that bordered the Dong Nai Valley below. Only sporadically were the lowlands visible from the thickly vegetated masses of jungle vines, banana trees, and three-tier jungle growth. This bothered me, since I wanted to know what was going on both in the highlands and in the lowland approaches to the river below. If the VC were living in the area, there would be the signs of activity one normally associates with the health and welfare of people. Food. Water. Shelter. Security and defense. Farming. Fishing. Well, we were not going to find out about those by limiting our operations to the steep, rugged, over-grown jungle highlands. For that reason, I asked Ken Chilton to continue to move through the high ground, letting him know that the second platoon, under platoon commander Dale England and platoon sergeant Kim Lai, would cover the valley below. I advised him that we would move on parallel axes, maintaining radio contact, and, should one or the other make contact with a superior VC force, we would be mutually supporting. This way, I reasoned, we could have our cake and eat it also.

The Dong Nai Valley was a large, lush, relatively open and continuous stretch of lowland grasses, with rivers and streams that emptied into the Song Dong Nai. It was not long before we began to find all of the life support systems of a VC village. There were boat docks along the river, acres of corn about to be harvested from well-regulated and well-irrigated fields, and storage sheds containing mountains of rice. It was not hard to deduce that this was not only a large VC community—as in political structure—but an area that would recruit, train, and deploy a VC force, not only for local security, but for expanded operations within War Zone D. Tunnels were everywhere. No VC were to be seen. They were good at that. They could be present, but not in sight. Kind of like a casket with the cover sealed. We had a decision to make.

How Well Can You Fight on an Empty Stomach?

It seemed to me that we could choose either to look for the VC or to deny them the food stores necessary to sustain life and fight effectively in the jungle. I decided on the latter. Why? Well, from my experience, the VC were good at staying away when they wanted seclusion, and when they wanted to avoid contact with a potentially superior force. I say "potentially" because the VC knew that we had the ability to make their lives miserable by calling in Sky Spot bombing missions and, perhaps more to their dislike, our option to use the B-52s. The huge bombers could lay down a carpet of thousand-pound bombs about one kilometer wide by three kilometers long. That's more than 27 million square feet of total death and destruction. Pretty scary, huh? I think that under the circumstances I would have chosen to hide. What did they have to lose? I mean, besides food?

From early morning until sunset we used every means available to us—save the B-52s—to destroy the local VC food supply and keep them from transporting it to market via the Song Dong Nai. Fighters made continuous bombing runs against the living structures, tunnel complexes, and rice storage containers. The dehydrating effect of the warm winds and the relatively dry corn fields were a combination easily taken advantage of by our lighters and incendiary devices. As the sun sought refuge behind the mountain ranges just beyond our area of operation, we pulled up stakes and moved on, continuing north toward the rally point with group one. As we left I could have puked just to look back at the devastation wrought by so worthy an effort. War is hell.

Sucker Punch

As the second platoon spent the day in the kitchen, recon had a busy day at the office. From Chilton's radio conversations, I learned that recon had located a large VC base camp nestled quietly in the high ground to our left. Chilton recommended, and Bo approved, a Sky Spot attack on it later that night or early the next morning. Our plans were testing the VC in two ways: as the result of our destroying their crops, they had less to eat; the bombing mission ensured that they would have to look for another place to hang their hats. Tough shit!

Hide and Seek

The next couple of days were uneventful, at least for the second platoon. The two operating groups had come together on January 27, or day twenty-two, and continued north looking for a suitable river-crossing site. Recon's BDA confirmed seven VC KIA and the large complex destroyed. A special piece of equipment—a small inflatable raft—arrived with our resupply on the twenty-ninth. We were only a few hundred meters from the west bank of the river, and Gritz wanted recon to make a preliminary crossing to "test the waters" and observe activities on the other side before crossing with the rest of the MGF. Unfortunately, whoever packed the raft in the canister failed to include the inflater. Not good. To improvise, we took turns blowing the raft up by mouth, using the end of a PRC-25 radio antenna as a medium. Nearly ineffective. On one of my turns, I got the feeling that if I'd blown any harder, my nuts would explode. I was not alone.

Around 2230 hours recon reported some activity on the river. Apparently, during the hours of darkness, motorized sampans—small, narrow, wooden boats—could be made out through the heavy river mist, but not heard. We concluded that the boats were "running silent," with the flow, and would use the motors only when required to buck the current on their return. We also reasoned that they were patrolling the banks for clues to the ominous guerrilla force that had been wreaking havoc in their homeland. That would be us.

Wanting to observe for myself, I walked down the steep embankment from our MSS to the dock below. As I approached, quietly, I sensed a sampan floating toward the same dock. One of the Bodes and I positioned ourselves on the well-maintained wooden platform, our rifles at the ready. Radios were off-squelch, as I didn't want an unexpected message to give away our location, nor did I want to stir up trouble only days before a major crossing. Without being able to see the sampan—nor, I surmised, could they see us—I could feel them getting very much closer. It was almost pitch-black.

As my friend and I waited, silently, totally immobile, the

boat drifted into the dock. We were but ten to fifteen feet apart. Neither of us was entirely certain about what was happening. Neither of us wanted to lose the edge. We waited, and waited. Several minutes went by, and, for some reason, there came a moment when I wanted a violent outcome. But I resisted. About thirty minutes went by before the sampan pushed off, once again floating freely south. Thirty minutes later I decided that they were indeed gone and out of the area. My heart began to return to normal, my breathing slowed, and I wiped the sweat from my forehead.

Crossing the Song Dong Nai

In our original concept for BJ-31, there was to be no crossing of the Dong Nai River. We were to conduct operations alongside it, from south to north, for ten to twelve kilometers, but had not contracted to cross the river itself. However, as we worked our way into the Dong Nai Valley it became apparent to us, and to our sponsors, that the large VC forces living in this part of the secret zone would have to maintain control of both sides of the river to ensure their own security. Also, it seemed reasonable that the VC moving through War Zone D—possibly from the VC Ninth Division—would also occupy the operational terrain that spanned the Dong Nai. For these reasons, Blackjack Kelly and his intelligence staff wanted us to cross. There was one other reason: we wanted to search for and destroy the largest concentration of forces we could locate. We wanted to make a difference. The Song Dong Nai would test our courage to conduct daylight operations in full view.

There are rivers. And then there are *rivers*! The Dong Nai was a monster. How big? Well, perhaps you remember our near-fatal operation outside of Trai Bi, the afternoon our CIDG force tried to cross the Bien Hoa? That was a river. Twenty to thirty feet across, not too deep, and flowing at about six to eight knots. You know, the kind of river you just walk up to, secure, rig your shit, cross with a small force, secure the far side, then cross with the rest of the grunts. And, you may recall, we just about bought the farm. Of course, some of us did, one machine gunner while making the crossing. The Dong Nai would require a more deliberate plan and some high-powered logistical items that our small light-to-fight MGF would have to request and/or prepare from natural materials near the crossing site. At our crossing point, the Dong Nai, narrowed by the almost breathtaking beauty of the adjacent jungle wilderness, was several hundred feet across, too deep to gauge without a depth finder, and was flowing somewhere between ten and twelve knots. Our immediate challenges were three: (1) decide on a vehicle to support the crossing; (2) complete the crossing quickly, certainly before nightfall of the same day; (3) provide adequate security during the crossing to soldiers on both sides.

Any way you try to slice it, this was going to be a very dangerous operation. Even though all Green Berets are excellent swimmers, the width of the river and the speed of its current would challenge even the best. But most of the Bodes could not swim. It was not considered safe to cross on a rope as individuals, as the use of tethers would be too slow and, given the weapons and other equipment, the lack of personal safety ties would result in unacceptable losses from drowning. No, we would need a safe, fast, effective method that offered a single best chance of securing the force throughout the crossing. It became obvious that we would need a full day to prepare and a full day to conduct the crossing. That posed special security problems, as we seldom stayed in one spot for more than twenty-four hours. This operation was to be an exception. God help us if we got pinned up against the river by a superior force, with limited escape routes.

Minimum essential equipment consisted of the small rubber boat used to conduct a recon on the other side, and a thousand-foot coil of rope, both of which were dropped several days before the crossing. Gritz ordered Chilton's recon platoon to patrol to a distance of two thousand meters from the river line, in an arc spanning 180 degrees. That would provide some security against the worst-case scenario of prediscovery by a larger force. If warned by recon, we would have a couple thousand meters within which to escape the area in three directions, by platoons.

Howard's first platoon secured the southern approaches to the river. England's second secured the western routes into the area, and Ovsak's third the area to the north. With security in place by 0700 hours on D-1, Jarvis and Howard teamed to build an eight-foot-square raft from the gigantic bamboo trees that dotted the steep riverbanks and surrounding forest. On patrol to the west, I could hear the not-so-faint *whack*ing of bamboo from the MSS, which was located near the crossing site. I wondered if the VC were getting the same report.

Sometime that afternoon, I was informed by England that Gritz and two others—Cawley and Montgomery, if I recall correctly—had managed to cross the rope to the other side, but not without some anxious moments. With one end of the half-inch rope tied securely to a large tree at the near bank, Cawley lost his fatigues during the crossing, or had to abandon them in rough currents. Gritz, blown off the rope early, returned to shore, then reentered the water to try again.

The swimmers used parachute cord tied to the heavier rope to facilitate pulling it across the river. Even so, the current was so strong that the swimmers were forced downriver several hundred feet and, by the time they recovered, had little rope to spare from the thousand-foot coil. Had they reached the point of no return and been forced to drop the end of the parachute cord, they would have had to gut it out to the far side, then reswim the river back to the near bank, without having the safety of a rope, to try a second crossing—or someone else would have had to pick up the slack. Of course, during all the time the crossings would take, the VC in and around the area would have been able to generate a legitimate spoiling operation of their own. Fortunately, the swimmers made it, and though exhausted, were in position to set up a listening post for the night. Only if things seemed square would we commence the crossing of the main force the next morning.

I've Got a Ticket to Ride

The cool night gave way to the early morning sun as the first of four main elements slipped into the water. With Gritz on the other side, I positioned myself at the crossing site while the remainder of the second platoon continued to secure in sector. It was day twenty-eight, February 2, 1967. With minimum security on the far bank, and the distant sound of single-shot rifles somewhere to the northwest, the recon platoon quickly and quietly loaded onto the rope-and-raft ferry the rucksacks, weapons, and radios—all wrapped in water-resistant ponchos—of the first squad of eight men. Those eight would constitute the first real security force on the far bank. Perhaps more important, the initial run would be the first real test of the crossing concept itself. With the bamboo raft filled to capacity with equipment and tethered to the crossing rope with ten-foot rope ties secured to aluminum D-rings, the soldiers pushed off from the waist-deep water and propelled the ferry into the waters beyond.

About twenty minutes later I saw through field glasses that the initial trial was a success. So far so good. Pulled by a rope tied to the stern, the unburdened raft was then on the way back. The operation continued well into the late morning as the size of the security force on the near bank slowly shrank while a formidable new support site was built on the other side of the river.

As I walked into the murky water and took my position in one of the last loads to cross—third platoon would be the last—I was overcome with a powerful sense of awe. Apparently, the force was with us, as we had been able to plan and execute a most vulnerable—most dangerous—mission in broad daylight in the heart of a VC stronghold. I could only hope that our being undetected, or at least undeterred, was not a bad sign. What if the VC had been watching, calculating, trying to suck the MGF into an untenable posture somewhere down the line? My ears could not escape the ominous sounds of combat as I forcefully kicked my legs to maneuver the large, heavily weighted platform toward the distant shore.

Part of Bo's security plan for the other side was to schedule another resupply. With the close proximity of the fighters and an FAC overhead, the VC would have been risking their lives to interfere. Their best chance would have been at the near bank, toward the end of the shuttle, when we would have been powerless to react. Their second best chance was at the far bank early in the operation, when there were limited forces to secure the crossing site. But neither ambush occurred. Why?

When I got to the other side, our resupply was well under way in the midafternoon sun. The DZ was located about three hundred meters north-northeast of the entry point. When I arrived, someone—Donahue, I think—handed me a not-so-cold-but-oh-so-good can of beer. Possibly as a reward for making the other side in one piece, our benefactors threw into the drop several cases of Budweiser, one can for each member of the MGF. Fortunately, the beer seemed to be in one piece even though, for some unexplained reason, a large number of canisters had screamed into the soft, thick underbrush with undeployed chutes. Regardless, I guzzled the brewski in seconds, and in my first official act in the new neighborhood—perhaps hyped by the first alcoholic beverage in several weeks—I put out the word to trash the hood. In a complete display of irregularity and undisciplined discipline, I suggested that the empty beer cans be strewn about the local landscape as if to say, "Fuck you! Just *fuck* you! We are here in your homeland, and if you try to fuck with us, we will blow your shit away."

As the last of the fighters cleared the area amid the screams of yellow-eyed monkeys, I stripped to my shorts and began to rid my body of the scores of bloated leeches trying to suck my veins dry. That bit of housekeeping accomplished, I finished some canned peaches, drank from a canteen of purified water, then prepared to move on. As we departed, recon had a brief skirmish with three VC. Two KIA and one CIA.

The night of February 2 was unforgettable. Weary from the crossing, but pumped up by its success and the follow-on resupply, I lay in my hammock for what seemed to be hours, sipping very slowly from a canteen of black coffee laced with bourbon someone had so thoughtfully added to the resupply. Alone with nature. At peace with thoughts of my family and friends. Alone with my best but unspoken wishes for my daughter Kim, who would turn two just three days later.

What I missed more than anything else was the comforting knowledge that I would be able to see my family again. I had prepared about twenty letters in the days before we left Duc Phong, leaving them with the C-team personnel officer for release every other day. I wanted Donna and the kids to know that things were okay with me, even though I knew that I might never see them again. I made up casual stories about being confined to the "safety" of an A-team camp, unable to conduct full-scale operations on a daily basis. I talked "happy thoughts"—about the elephants, monkeys, and snakes—taking pains to spell out to Lori and Kim, through their mother, the beauty of the jungle. And to Donna, how much I missed her warmth and her smile. That seemed to be the best I could do under the circumstances. If you have been to Vietnam or you know someone who has, this revelation should not come as a surprise.

Before nodding off to sleep, I had the unhappy premonition that we would be seriously challenged in the days ahead. We were getting tired, and it seemed that it would be only a matter of time before the VC had their say. I said a small prayer, then lay motionless on my back, gazing at the stars overhead peeking through a break in the forest's endless foliage. My last thoughts were of my love of God and how privileged I was for having been able to know Him.

Do You Believe in Fate?

Our luck with prisoners was consistently bad. Heretofore, either we did not want to tip off our position by evacuating captured VC or, as was the case at the comm site, the Bodes had disposed of the evidence. Recon's latest acquisition would be the third time we were to have the chance to evacuate a healthy POW from the secret zone. With any luck at all, the

frightened soldier being secured near the small pickup zone
for the near arrival of a C-team chopper would answer the
mail. On the other hand, the conditions were not favorable for
an extraction. The mid-morning temperature hovered in the
high nineties and, partly because of the nearby river, the
humidity was out of sight. Those circumstances do not make
for good lift. And, unfortunately, the only PZ in the area was
less than fifty meters square and nestled in and among several
tall trees.

Anticipating a worst-case scenario, Gritz himself carefully
passed the requirement to C-3, giving strict instructions not to
complicate the mission with extra personnel whose added
weight would further degrade the UH-1H's lifting capacity.
Normally, helicopter pilots rotated slowly through a series of
descending turns until able to stabilize their two skids firmly
on the ground. But given the local conditions—high trees,
small PZ—this mission would more resemble dropping a
giant yo-yo fifteen floors straight down an elevator shaft. Like
the yo-yo, the aircraft would "sleep" for the ten seconds it
would take to load the prisoner, then lift straight up to the top
before acquiring the necessary clearance to level off in normal
flight. Scary, even under ideal conditions.

After talking down the C-3 chopper pilot into the deep
recesses of the PZ, ready to secure the prisoner for an immediate takeoff, I was unpleasantly surprised when an overweight captain stepped from the chopper to inquire, over the
deafening roar of the Huey, about the nature of the mission.
Murphy was alive and well. As two Bodes secured the bad
guy into an outside seat, I hollered, "Captain, get your fucking
ass back into the helicopter and get the fuck out of here."

As the chopper lifted off, we could make out the sound of
an explosion just off the PZ. We had all but cleared the area
when the chopper returned to earth. Shit, I thought to myself,
just what the fuck we need. The pilot, hearing the sound of
rifles getting closer, looked worried. He said, "I can't lift off
high enough to clear the trees with the weight I'm carrying." I
told him to drop some weight. Of course, as he dumped half
his fuel, I was thinking about that sorry-ass assistant S-3.

The second liftoff was not much better. Several minutes passed as the pilot-in-command and his two door gunners tried to lighten up. Out went the armor plating from both front seats. Next the door gunners threw out half the machine-gun ammunition. With the stripped-down helicopter, one pilot, two door gunners, one prisoner, and the sorry-ass officer, the Huey climbed away. Hopefully, for the last time. I held my breath as the huge brown machine reached the fourteenth floor, where the skids became tangled in the stiff branches of one of the trees, then appeared just to freeze in place. Then, like a yo-yo suddenly worked loose from its string, the chopper once again dropped straight down, hitting the ground with such force that it barely stayed upright.

If you are writing your own ending, you may be having a hard time deciding which one of the five people aboard was odd man out. In my mind it was a toss-up between the un-invited officer and the VC prisoner. As the chopper cleared the trees for only the first time, we pulled in security and prepared to depart the area. Avoiding the trail network for fear of an ambush, we slowly inched our way to the northeast. In the near distance I heard the muffled sound of a single shot from a silenced Sten gun.

A Test of Leadership

From the first mention of the Song Dong Nai, the Bodes began to puke. The valley was said to house several large VC units, but the MGF prevailed. Crossing the river raised their level of anxiety. Recon's discovery and destruction of a large VC base area, and the second platoon's successful engagement with a VC unit on the move, upped the ante. Since crossing the river, all elements of the MGF found themselves in contact with VC hunter-killer forces and methodically uncovered several way stations. Our enemy casualty figures were increasing threefold, while friendly casualties were virtually nonexistent. We were on a roll. Why, then, on the afternoon of February 4, did David, the trusted MGF chief interpreter, ask for a meeting with Captain Gritz? I wanted to know, and so made sure I was in attendance.

"Captain Gri," David said, "Cambodian say they want to leave. They say that they have been away from family for long time. They want pay for family. They say that Tet is religious holiday that require they be home to worship. They say they not afraid of VC, but many VC force live in this area."

Of course, I could empathize with the Cambodians. We *had* been out a long time, taking lots of risks, and VC units on that side of the river seemed more formidable. I had thought for some time that it was only a matter of time before we stepped in some shit. I said nothing.

"You tell the men that we are soldiers, and that we are just doing what we are told to do by Colonel Kelly. Meet me back here at 1500 hours with the Cambodian leaders with their answer," Gritz said in measured tones. It was 1400 hours. David had the unenviable task of convincing the Bodes to stay.

As we gathered for the 1500-hours meeting, two F-4 fighter-bombers dropped 250-pound bombs within five hundred meters of the command post. The ground shook as the mighty jets roared overhead, circling for yet another run. Raising his voice to be heard, Bo asked David for an answer. "Captain Gri," David reported, "the leaders say they fight very hard for the MGF. They say they kill many VC for Captain Gri, and they like Captain Gri because he is fearless leader. Still," David continued, "they say they must go now, so they can return to camp in two day." Looking at my map, we were ten to twelve kilometers out of Duc Phong, with a *river* to cross.

As the jets screamed overhead, their wayward ordnance seemingly getting closer and closer, Bo said the only words he would speak on the subject, choosing them carefully and speaking them slowly so that David could translate each sentence, one at a time. "You tell the leaders that I understand. They have made great sacrifice for themselves, for their family, and for Cambodia. They are free to leave. I appreciate their commitment to the MGF. I am honored to have served with the Cambodians. Cambodians are honorable men. Cam-

bodians hate VC like American. Cambodians are fierce fighters. We miss Cambodian freedom fighters. We wish them
well. American must stay."

He then paused for what seemed like an eternity. "Tell them
United States Air Force have massive bombing campaign in
area. We do not know where bombs go, but air force know
where MGF, and air force not bomb MGF. Tell them be very
careful."

Several minutes passed as David conferred with the Cambodian leaders. Then, "Captain Gri," David offered, "Cambodian leader say Cambodian stay with MGF."

I had to give it to Bo. He was a leader. Yes, we talked in the
interim. He asked me what I thought. I admired him for that.
That's how he was, and that's how he is today. Always willing
to ask someone he respects for input. On the other hand, those
who command no respect quickly find the door. For the
record, I said, "Jim, it really doesn't matter if the Bodes leave
or not. There isn't anything in our mission that we can't
accomplish with just the Americans. We're small, either way.
Either way, we're elusive, light-to-fight, know our strengths
and weaknesses, and we're mobile. It doesn't matter what the
fuck the Cambodians decide to do. But I like the Bodes. I hope
you can convince them to stay. For themselves. For the MGF.
For Cambodia."

Winding Up or Winding Down?

For the next two or three days, we worked at platoon level,
continuing to move north-northeast, away from the river.
Whatever the projection, it seemed clear to me that we were
not going to cross the Song Dong Nai again. This new area
appeared to be more built-up, containing more base areas for
local VC-tenders. Also, more way stations for larger VC or
NVA movements. All platoons were now reporting an increase
in enemy activity. More Sky Spot missions were flown, more
bomb-damage assessments were conducted, and more VC
were being killed. That much we knew.

I think that by this point in BJ-31, we were really starting to earn our pay. We were able to help the intelligence staff define a "pattern" of activity within the secret zone. Our reports were becoming longer, and more frequent. We were able to confirm the presence of numbered units that had previously been unknown or mere speculation. Maybe it was time to pick up our marbles and go home. With so many reported enemy operating bases—so many sets of accurate coordinates—maybe, just maybe, it was about the right time to let the boys in blue bring in the B-52s en masse and just blow the fuck out of War Zone D. "Just maybe" was starting to play on my mind, but perhaps what I had been saying to Bo about the Cambodians was about right: more soldiers meant more soldiers to feed, to wound, to treat, to bury. It meant more ammunition, more water, more lapses in noise and light discipline. More of this and more of that. Maybe it was time for less. Maybe Bo was wrong to order the jets to scare the Bodes.

The thoughts I had were beginning to scare me. The thought of returning from BJ-31 alive was beginning to play cruel tricks on my mind. Before then, I had been content, never allowing myself to wonder if the mission was about over. Football fans are well aware of the number of times teams lose in the final minutes using a prevent defense. Must start thinking in real terms, I told myself. Now I was really starting to frighten myself. When you begin to cross that line from guerrilla to staff puke, all bets are off. I even began to start to think that, for some unexplainable reason, I was not good enough to get out. That I was among friends, and that Dong Nai would be a good place to die. Home. Among friends. Like Tiny. Jesus Christ, doesn't this ever end? Is life just going to be about death and destruction? I knew the answer, but was still thinking that I was afraid to come out. Coming out meant either risking another crossing, or bringing a lot of helicopters into an area swarming with units with numbers. And I so much wanted to live.

Life and Death in the Balance

When Bo told me on February 5 that we were to be extracted two days later, it was all I could do to mask my emotions. We'd been operating in two groups, and would remain as such for the night of the fifth. My body started to shake. What a wonderful birthday present for Kim, I thought, even though I knew it would be many years before I could tell her that. Maybe you can see my tears on these pages as I try to wade through words that continue to strike me with a sense of humility and pain me with a sense of emotional discomfort. There, I will be okay, I think. On the night of February 5, I would not allow myself to sleep, as if I could have done anything to prevent it. I was awash with the thought of leaving. But now that leaving was a reality, I began to entertain all of the negative thoughts one could imagine about the risk of getting out alive. It was almost as if I had learned how to cope with the jungle, with daily death and destruction, with the unwholesome improprieties of war, and that now made me afraid to change. War was like a bad habit, maybe, one really hard to break, even though you know it's not good for you. Scary!

Friendly Fire

Bo assembled the Americans about 0700 on the morning of February 6, and basically told them what he had discussed with me the night before. "Prepare your platoons for extraction by helicopter some time around 1000 hours tomorrow morning," he said. He added, "Today may be the most dangerous day of your life." From the thoughts I'd had the previous day, I knew exactly what he was talking about. "Make sure the Bodes understand that we cannot let down our guard, that the VC will be watching our every move, and that we will be most vulnerable when we're in the process of out-loading our troops onto the helicopters. Before we can leave, we need to accomplish two more things. Recon will locate a PZ suitable for three flights of five, and run the PZ. Also, we need a prisoner. Platoons will patrol in sector. Yed will run the command post."

To say that there was a sense of joy and fulfillment in the air would be an understatement. There was also the very real concern about not being one of those who *almost* made it. Strange things can and do happen to those who lose their focus and forsake their discipline. None of the Americans I saw were going to make any serious mistakes on that final day, nor were they going to let their guard down during the extraction itself. Nor, I surmised, were they going to play it safe. No prevent defense there. Not in the MGF. This would be a "balls to the wall" effort to find a PZ and capture a fucking prisoner. Period. I admired the people I helped to recruit. They were awesome. They and their families, and their loved ones, should be proud.

So it was with some surprise, and an uncommon sense of urgency, that I reacted to the sounds of automatic rifle fire not more than a hundred meters from my command post.

Then came the report. "Fox Two, Fox Four. Over." It was Chilton.

"Fox Two, over." I responded.

"Fox Two, contact, VC platoon. Over."

"Fox Two, roger. Over."

"Fox Four, out."

Instantly, yet another report. "Fox Two, Fox One. Over." It was Montgomery.

I asked, "Fox One, are you in contact? Over."

"Roger. Over."

I had the uneasy feeling that the recon platoon was in contact with Howard's first platoon. As the next radio started to break squelch, I asserted myself. "Break, break. Fox Four, Fox One, cease fire! Cease fire!" I was relieved that no more shots were fired but expected there to be some casualties, since American leaders characteristically operate near the front of the small unit in order to gain a better perspective, and to quickly control the action. Such was the case. Although none of the wounds was serious, all four Americans had been hit. They could have been killed. War is hell. The rest of the afternoon, medics treated the task force wounds. Broken wrist, thigh hit, leg scrape, and shoulder. So much for the prisoner. As the warmth of the afternoon sun gave way to the night's cool air, I thought to myself, Fuck the prisoner. Just fuck him. Bo agreed. No POW.

What Can You Not Believe?

For the second night in a row, I was unable to sleep. Little wonder. Soldiers have lived forever just thinking about one day and a wake-up. As I lay there letting my mind wander, I could not help but think that there was a part of me that didn't want to leave. Did not want to let go. It was as if, throughout the thirty-two days in War Zone D, I had become a part of the secret zone. One with the zone. Just me and the zone. The zone and me. One. Inseparable. I was the zone.

When your biological clock is set for anytime, you just manage to awake at the right time. No big deal. As I flicked my lighter at the last heat tablet I would use in War Zone D, I knew deep down that I was lucky to be alive, and that barring some catastrophic problem at the PZ, I was going home. Still, it was hard to believe. Smokes, jokes, and hot coffee were the order of the day for those inclined. Personally, I was wired. A lack of sleep and an overabundance of good fortune kept me ticking like the Energizer bunny. I really was having a hard time letting go.

The whir of the first flight of choppers dipping toward the PZ made my heart flutter. First lift-off. Neither an accident nor an ambush. Second flight, in and out. My turn. About ten minutes into the operation. I was buoyant but nervous. I climbed aboard uneventfully, and as the bird I was on lifted slowly into the free blue skies above, the trees and other dense jungle growth below were getting smaller and smaller. Suddenly, a hard left turn. I knew what that meant. As the chopper picked an azimuth to the northwest, and the Song Dong Nai appeared faintly below, I knew we were but minutes from our destination. It was then that I put my hands to my face, lowered my head toward my knees, and started to cry. What I had refused to let myself believe was becoming a reality. I had wanted to believe for a long time, but was now just starting to get used to the idea of some newfound freedom, for me, and for my friends. Yes, we were going home. To Duc Phong. It was day thirty-three, the last day. But would that be the end, or just the beginning? You be the judge.

Terra Firma and the Power of Coke

Have you ever had the feeling that you'd died and gone to heaven? That's the feeling I remember having as I was walking from the helicopter over the cracking hot, dust-blown dirt trail toward the team house and someone handed me an ice-cold Coke. I will be forever grateful to that someone who cared enough to be there, snap a picture, and quench my thirst. The little things in life really do become the big things, the things worth remembering, the things that are hard to forget. As for the Coke, its icy tang hit my parched throat and rippled through my body with such an exhilarating force that my body began to shake. I thought, Welcome to the real world.

Some Unfinished Business

The MGF returned to Bien Hoa on February 9. Lieutenant Colonel Huddleston and Blackjack were there to congratulate us. That meant a lot to me. Blackjack presented some awards, after which he posed with Task Force 957 for the first and only time.

The strikers were paid and put on leave. Many of their families and friends were there to greet them. Later in the day we back-briefed Colonel Kelly in the C-3 TOC, after which Lieutenant Colonel Huddleston treated us to a lavish party featuring a gorgeous blond, blue-eyed Swedish stripper. Without going into details that might be of little interest to readers, but some of which may be remembered by team members, it's fair to say that those of us who attended had a good time. We even got the front-row seats. Over the next few days, we gathered in the TOC to complete an After-Action Report that would be sealed for twenty-five years in a Secret file.

On February 14, all thirteen Green Berets stood tall in the III CTZ headquarters in the presence of General William C. Westmoreland, commander of all forces in Vietnam. He and twenty-one other generals listened to our briefing. As the facts were being revealed, General Westmoreland had to feel good about his decision to authorize the creation of the MGF, and about the results. Following the briefing, he said that our operations—Black Box and BJ-31—played an important part in securing vital defense secrets and impeding movement of NVA units from North into South Vietnam. I felt good about that.

After entertaining several questions from the senior officers in attendance, Westmoreland asked the members of the team to stand. He then asked each directly if he would ever go back. Of the thirteen present, six said yes.

Bo and I put several of the team members on in-country R&R while he and I worked out of the TOC, completing reports, and writing up award citations for team members and letters of appreciation for those who bravely and expertly supported the two missions. In a Special Forces field unit, in 1967, administrative support was limited. For example, there were no typewriters—the awards had to be printed out by hand—and there were no copying machines for making duplicates of the awards.

During that period, Lieutenant Colonel Huddleston asked me if I wanted to extend for six months to recruit, train, and command another MGF. Although I was one of the six who had told General Westmoreland that I would be willing to volunteer to go back, I said no. I felt a little bit like the Bodes. I just wanted to get paid and return to my family. I have never regretted that decision.

So it was coming down to the last few days. I was scheduled to leave on February 22, which meant that I would be flown to Camp Alpha in Saigon on February 21 for outprocessing. I was prepared to relax on the twentieth, get my shit together, and take a hot shower and shave, something I had not done—shaving—in about forty-five days. My combat gear was strewn all over the landscape, at Suoi Da, Duc Phong, and some at Bien Hoa. I could not have cared less. Maybe someday it would just follow.

A Bridge Too Close

On February 18, while Bo and I were working in the C-3 TOC, Huddleston walked in to join us. The S-3 Operations officer and the S-2 Intelligence officer were with him. He said that U.S. Intelligence had learned that about twenty trucks per hour were pouring over a bridge just inside Vietnam on the Laotian border. The trucks, moving only at night, were thought to be carrying supplies and ammunition in support of a new NVA campaign to begin within the next thirty days. Taking out the bridge would disrupt their plans. He asked Bo if he wanted the mission.

When Huddleston and the staff officers had departed, Bo, Buck Kindoll, and I began to analyze the requirement. The bridge was not thought to be heavily guarded, so there was no reason to go in with vastly superior forces, I told Gritz. Besides, the mission had to be conducted within one of the next two nights to quickly cut the flow of armaments. Recalling the Bodes from their two-week leave would have been difficult at best. "Bo," I said, "this is a mission for a small group of highly trained men who work well together."

He said, "Yed, you can't be serious."

I responded that I was. I continued, "It will take about eight people, including a commander, deputy, two demolition specialists, one communications specialist, one medic, and two light weapons specialists. In and out," I said. "Chopper in with guns blazing to clear out the security at the bridge site, fast-rope rappel onto one of the bridge approaches, place the demo with four flights of F-4 screaming overhead, blow the bridge, and get the fuck out of Dodge."

Bo said, "Yed, even if I agree that's a good concept, you can't go, you're going home."

I thought briefly about his effort to take the heat off me, but responded quickly, as if I had regained some badly damaged courage: "Bo, I'm a part of this fucking team, and if this fucking team conducts this mission, I want to fucking go."

"Okay, Yed," he said. "Let's get out the maps, and put together a concept we can use to brief Lieutenant Colonel Huddleston."

We worked on the concept for the rest of the day. Providing the support was available, we would blow the bridge the night of February 20. From departure from Bien Hoa Air Base to return, the work would be accomplished in about six hours. In sequence, we laid out the ground tactical plan first, including the security at the bridge site and the placement of the demolitions. Next in the backward planning sequence was the air infiltration plan, then the air movement plan, followed by the air loading plan.

Other supporting plans, such as the air support plan, communications plan, medical evacuation plan, and emergency response plan—all to be integrated and briefed to all units involved—were in the process of being finalized when the C-3 Operations officer walked into the TOC. "The mission's off," he said. "Further intelligence indicates that the bridge is three miles inside the territorial sovereignty of Laos."

Going Home, for Real

Military personnel assigned to Vietnam during the buildup— a period of ten to twelve years—knew about the Freedom Flight. The return to the Real World was a daily occurrence for hundreds of soldiers, sailors, airmen, and Marines. From Cao Lanh to Khe Sanh, from the paddies to the mountains and all points in between, the Freedom Flight, a large silver streak dashing across the sky, visible to most for only a few moments, would someday become a reality for those returning to their families. If you were lucky, you were whole, physically if not emotionally. If you were a career soldier, your days at home often served as a cruel interlude because you were probably going back. As I finally boarded the large commercial airliner in civilian clothes and saw the warm, friendly smiles of the stewardesses, I felt safe. And lucky.

San Francisco, Here I Come

During the long flight back to the States, I had given little thought to the adjustments that were in store for me when I reentered my family after twelve months in the bush. I thought that whatever adjustments might be necessary would just happen naturally, you know, like coming home from a long weekend, or an overnight fishing trip. Besides, I was about to land in San Francisco. I had written to Donna and our two girls, then two and three, but could not be sure whether she got the news. First order of business was to call, letting her know that I was booked for a flight into Seattle—she and the girls were living in Puyallup, near her family—the next morning. It was wonderful to hear her voice. Next, I wanted to find a restaurant with a bar. It was early morning, and I had a long time to unwind from my ordeal. I deserved it, I thought. That done, I walked in, sat down at the bar, and told the bartender I was returning from Vietnam and that it was good to be home.

He offered his welcome home, saying that he frequently served returnees. "Could I take your order?" he said.

Without looking at a menu, nor was I in the mood to sit at a table, I said, "Two steaks for starters, and two drinks on the side."

"What kind of steaks?" he asked.

"I have always thought it's hard to beat a New York strip," I replied.

"Drinks?"

"Rusty Nail, of course."

IV

Postwar Adjustments

My heart pounded as the flight from San Francisco began to make its descent into Seattle-Tacoma Airport. I pictured the warm, smiling faces of Donna, Lori, and Kim, standing near the arrival gate as I walked quickly down the jetway to meet them. Lori would be just shy of her third birthday (March 15), so she would be walking on her own but would probably be holding her mother's hand. Kim, having just turned two on February 5, would also be walking on her own, but free and clear of adult assistance as she struggled for her own sense of independence.

During the two-hour flight I reread the many letters received from Donna over the past year, by then dog-eared and soiled from the many openings and closings. I also studied the pictures she had sent of the two girls, whose memories of their father would be based mostly on what their mother had told them and the figments of their imaginations.

Jarred by the unsettling noises of the wheels coming down, I began to experience a sense of anxiety and fear I found uncomfortable in the wake of what I had built up in my mind as a modern-day Renaissance. As the captain announced our arrival, I caught myself staring, not only at the cool gray skies and the snow on the ground, but deeply into the hollows of my own soul. How could anyone who had just spent over thirty days in War Zone D fear a reunion with his family?

The Moment of Truth

The final steps were just as I had pictured, and hoped, they would be. As I caught the first glimpse of Donna and the two girls, I began to well up inside. I was home. A soft, warm embrace. Then almost kneeling, clutching the girls to my side, still holding on dearly to those feelings that had been building since Bo told me we were being extracted. There were many expressions of love, warmth, and affection. Also, a soothing sense of relief as my worst fears were beginning to subside. As we slowly made our way through the wind and snow-swept roads toward Puyallup, I knew that everything was going to be all right.

Who Is Daddy?

In the weeks that followed, our hectic lives revolved around family and friends. Donna's parents lived in Puyallup, where most of her (three) brothers and (four) sisters were still at home. Conversations seemed to center on what was going on in their lives, as all were eager to update my memory bank with their activities. And I loved them for that and was a willing participant, even content to sit back and watch the world revolve around me. There were few, if any, questions about Vietnam. Perhaps they sensed that I was unable, or unwilling, to discuss in any detail what I had done. Or, perhaps like so many millions of Americans, they had tired of news about Vietnam. Whatever the reasons, I was beginning to learn that life was something that occurred *after* Vietnam. There were so many people to see, and so little time, it was little wonder that we were unable to spend much time together as a family. Oh, we were all there together most of the time, but there were few precious moments when we—Donna, Lori, Kim, and I—were alone together. When just we, the four of us, had time, or took the time, to renew our love and friendship. It was clear to me that the girls looked to their mother for direction and support. Under the circumstances, one would not expect anything different, but for some reason I *did* expect something different, and that feeling of not being consulted was confusing and uncomfortable. I began to feel underappreciated, even resentful, knowing full well that what was happening was not a conspiracy. Nevertheless, I was overcome with the very real idea that my two young daughters had come to depend on their mother and were unable to identify with their father.

Can You Ever Go Back?

Although I had talked to my parents by phone shortly after my arrival in San Francisco and several times while closing out of Puyallup, it was hard for me to contain my anxiety as we approached Spokane from the high western reaches of Sunset Hill. Having only days earlier watched the last packed boxes being placed on an American Van Lines truck headed for Chicago and our next assignment, I got goose bumps just thinking about seeing my dad and my mom once again. With two weeks of leave left, I was coming home to the Inland Empire. To the city of 180,000 people in which I'd been raised. To my own brothers and sisters.

En route, we had stayed in Ephrata with my brother Bill and his wife Kathy and their large family. Rejoicing with my older brother was always good for the soul. For one thing, he always had a cold beer. For another, he had served his country in the Navy during World War II. As a young communications specialist serving on the aircraft carrier *Intrepid*, Bill had come close to losing his life, along with many of his comrades, from Japanese suicidal kamikaze (Divine Wind) pilots who knowingly and willingly dive-bombed their fighters into the steel structures of the ship itself. All in the name of stopping American aggression, or so they thought. For some reason, I could never get Bill to open up about the war. It is something very personal and very painful to him. During the Fourth Annual Yedinak Family Reunion, in August 1996, Bill finally offered the few revelations I've mentioned. But not before.

The Heart of the Inland Empire

Few cities, if any, can match Spokane for its rugged beauty and for its four distinct seasonal changes. As we approached my parents' home in the heart of the Gonzaga University district, it was snowing lightly. The temperatures were seasonably colder than in Seattle, and the snow was likely to stay on the ground.

My parents adored Donna from the very first time they began to know her, and she loved them dearly. The girls were comfortable with their grandparents, and they with the girls. The next week would be one of the very best in my life. All of my brothers and sisters, except Anna Marie, who lived in Chicago with her husband Dick Kirmse and their children, lived in Spokane. Alice, my older sister, lived nearby with her husband, Chuck Moyer, and their children; Patty, my younger sister, lived with her husband, Dave Brown; Tom and Dorothy, both younger, still lived at home. The first few days were an endless round of love, friendship, and fellowship. Of course, I got a chance to bullshit with my best friends, Denny Higgins and Mike Shanks, who marveled that I came back alive. Also, my dad took the time to be with me, to relive some of our stories about fishing and camping. I don't recall telling him about the profound influence he had been on my life as a guerrilla. I don't think that would have made him terribly proud.

Did You Forget to Pack Your Bags?

About the morning of the fourth or fifth day, my dad asked me what was in the box I'd sent. I replied, "What box, Dad?"

Taking me to the back of the house and into his office, pointing to a standard army footlocker, he said, "This one."

I told him that I had no idea but noticed that it was addressed to me in care of my parents. We lifted the heavily weighted footlocker to our waists, then walked it into the living room. Dad said that he had thought maybe I'd sent home some china from my R&R in Hong Kong. I guess I'd failed to tell him that I changed my R&R plans in favor of the MGF.

Of course, I had no idea about the combination, and so broke through the lock with a hammer. On opening it, I recognized my web gear with ammunition pouches filled with M-16 magazines. Some of the magazines still contained live rounds. My bush knife was strapped to the left harness with green tape, and all of the other equipment seemed to be untouched.

Just then my mother pointed to four oblong, steel-cased munitions. "What are those, Steven?" she asked.

Lifting one of the live grenades carefully from the belt, I told her what they were. Thinking back, I then realized that my field gear had been left unshipped because of the impending bridge mission. One of my friends apparently closed the lock, posted it for air freight, and mailed it home.

So what does one do with four live military fragmentation grenades in the middle of Spokane, Washington? Call the military? And say what? The police? Bury the grenades? Where? I thought of the Bien Hoa River northwest of Trai Bi. That was the answer. Somewhere at the bottom of the Spokane River, about five miles north of the Washington Water Power industrial plant on Mission Street, lie the components of eight grenades. My dad and I drove to the location the same day, on or about March 1, 1967, where I carefully separated the arming mechanisms from the grenade bodies, then threw each set of components well into the middle of the river. After I answered my dad's questions about the safety and security of such a plan, he departed the scene knowing that the grenade bodies could not explode without an arming mechanism and that the arming mechanisms alone were useless. Improvisations of a guerrilla.

Back to the Future

As I was walking back toward the radio site, I reentered the small clearing where the two Bodes were securing the VC prisoner. He had no face. The hideous sounds coming from his mouth cavity seemed to be crying for help. *"Unxghgh,"* he inhaled. *"Oughgh,"* he exhaled. I listened for what seemed like minutes. Was he still alive? As I began to question the Bodes, I awoke. It was day ten.

How Could You Not Remember?

Webster's New Collegiate Dictionary defines psychology as "the science of mind and behavior." To psychologize is to explain or interpret (events) in psychological terms. As a student of psychology while studying for my undergraduate degree, I had to design, conduct, and publish a report on a psychological experiment. Interested in perception, retention, and forgetting, I wanted to verify that people more often tended to remember information perceived as "more threatening" or "less acceptable."

Accordingly, to one (experimental) group of college students in a darkened room with pencils and paper, I presented a list of ten words, tachistoscopically on a screen at two-fifths of a second. Seven of the words were "neutral," such as *tree, car,* and *house*. Three of the words were "value-laden," such as *sex* or *death*. After each brief exposure of a list, students were given twenty seconds to write down each word they recalled from it. Guessing was discouraged. A second set of ten words was presented, under the same conditions. Then another, and another. All in all, I presented a hundred words to the group, then tabulated the results.

The following day, nearly the same word lists—differing only by the substitutions of "neutral" words for the "value-laden" words—were presented to another (control) group of college students under the same conditions. As expected, statistical analysis showed that the value-laden words were seen and recorded more frequently than the neutral words. The results were statistically significant.

The results of the psychological experiment, although produced under scientifically controlled conditions, suggest nothing that cannot be observed by each of us from the pages of everyday life. From your own experience, you no doubt find it easier to remember—and forget—certain events that impact your life: a death in the family, baby, wedding night, first kiss, serious accident, promotion, divorce, injured pet, and so on. If there are certain everyday events that are less memorable, it follows that there are specific memorable events that are hard to forget. It isn't that the capacity of the human mind necessarily fluctuates over time. More likely, the human mind is predisposed to save, for easy retrieval, selected information already patterned and stored in the human brain or information acquired directly through the five senses. What one sees, hears, touches, smells, and tastes—perceptual information—is categorized and stored according to the relative importance assigned to it by the brain. This conceptual information is subject to recall, during waking hours and, if particularly frightening, subconsciously in dreams. War presents many events to soldiers that are perceived as threatening or frightening. How a soldier acts, reacts, or fails to act or react on the battlefield, builds a repository of potentially frightening or threatening events that are profoundly memorable. Unfortunately, some are hard to forget.

Family, Friends, and Society at Large

During my first few weeks at home, I struggled to find my place in my family, among my friends, and within society at large. Having read extensively about the nature of insurgency while training at Fort Bragg, and having just completed a combat tour, I had little patience with those who, in 1968, felt we had little reason to be in Vietnam. The disparity between my persuasions and the well-publicized feelings of those who differed would continue to be a very real annoyance for many years to come. While the headlines increasingly focused on groups (like the Communist-inspired academic elitists at Berkeley, the self-righteous Students for a Democratic Society) and events (like Jane Fonda's openly conspiring with the North Vietnamese) that decried our very presence in Vietnam, I sickened at the thought that these recriminations would reach our soldiers, who, by an act of Congress, were compelled to do their duty. How fucking demoralizing when the very fucking people you are there to "protect" are shitting in your mess kit.

At the local political level, the mayor of Spokane proclaimed a day during my visit as "Steve Yedinak Day." To this day I can recall my embarrassment when I first learned of that, and my reluctance to attend a ceremony and speak on a local TV newscast. Now I know that they were trying to show their respect and help me assimilate. But I was not ready then to acknowledge my achievements to my country—not while soldiers were still dying. Not when people at home were questioning our involvement. I wondered if I was the only one who felt that way. Why had I chosen to repress my true feelings? Was I alone?

At the same time, I was proud of my uniform, perhaps too proud. When my dad, whom I loved dearly and respected even more, asked me if I would wear my uniform in court while my younger brother Tom argued a driving charge, I declined. My dad's disappointment aside, I was not about to tarnish everything I stood for just to seek a judicial favor. Apparently, my dad thought that the notoriety surrounding my return to Spokane would influence the outcome. I was not about to find out, and my dad knew better than to ask a second time. To this day, I worry that I may have let my brother down and deeply hurt my father for failing to meet his expectations of me.

My friends assumed they knew too much about the war. A steady diet of Vietnam on the six o'clock news was, apparently, enough for them. One war for all. Not a single war for each one of the hundreds of thousands of soldiers, sailors, airmen, and Marines who were called. No one asked what had happened to me—how I felt. About what I had done, or failed to do. No one fucking asked! But if they did—if they really tried—I wasn't ready to respond.

The Nightmares

I don't know if I'm ready for this. On the other hand, I may never be ready to soberly address the issue of the recurring nightmares I experienced for twenty years—beginning with the faceless man ten days after my arrival home—until sometime in 1988 when, without much fanfare, they just stopped. I don't know why.

A dream is a series of thoughts, images, or emotions occurring during sleep. Sometimes dreams tend to satisfy a wish. Nightmares used to be thought of as the result of an evil spirit's oppressing people during sleep. Today we generally view nightmares as frightening dreams accompanied by a sense of oppression or suffocation that usually awakens the sleeper. The experience, situation, or object having the monstrous character of a nightmare often produces a feeling of anxiety or terror.

In all, I had one recurring dream of the "normal sort" and fourteen insidious nightmares. Only the American Celebration seemed out of place. As you may remember, when training at Ho Ngoc Tao had come to an end, with the help of the Bode leadership we ate and drank our way into oblivion. The dream focused on the round table with large serving dishes piled high with oven-baked beefsteaks topped with peanut sauce—a Cambodian favorite—and fresh langoustinos, the American team and Cambodian leaders, and, of course, the eighty-six-case pallet of beer. When the dream ended, I was always alone, sitting there at the table about four o'clock in the morning. An exact replica of the actual event, with one exception. There were no words. Just a picture. About an eight-second time exposure. No anxiety or terror. This dream occurred once or twice a year for about five years, then stopped. Other forms of dreaming occurred over the next five to ten years. These tended to produce some anxiety but were neither persistent nor animated.

For years, as I walked my security post around the inner perimeter of Suoi Da in my dreams, my mind's eye searched for the two Vietnamese girls Lieutenant Trang offered as bribes for overpayment of the CIDG strike force. My thoughts bored into each of the occupied dwellings I passed, wishing that, for some unexplainable reason, one of the young girls would emerge. No such luck. It was during this dream that I learned that I am never, ever, able to behave in a dream differently than I would were I awake. Although I wanted those girls in the worst way, I had passed up my chance for such a liaison during Trang's visit to the Suoi Da team house as I was reviewing payroll records. As a result, I always returned to the team house sexually frustrated and very much alone.

For years I experienced the anxiety of mines on the trail. It was always the same. The column of troops would suddenly stop. As a leader and adviser, I watched myself quickly move toward the front of the column. Confirming the existence of two tomato-can mines, I would conduct a clinic on how to cautiously probe for the mines, carefully remove them from the hardened trail, and bury them. Although the fear of detonation was omnipresent and I awoke in terror, the mines never blew up.

For years I witnessed our CIDG troops moving through the grassland clearing. As shots rang out from our left flank at about five hundred meters, I had no idea that soon I would be looking into the soft, warm eyes of a young girl, her camouflaged body shredded by small-arms fire as she gasped her last breath. From this dream I learned that my nightmares unfold in the same precise sequence as the frightening situation they represent. The link between the nerve cells and my brain on that sad afternoon must have been strongest as my mind recorded the image of the helpless girl, as I always awoke soon thereafter.

For years I lived with the old man with the .45 caliber pistol in his right hand, slumped in death over the table inside the small jungle hootch. I never discovered the reason for his death, nor for which side he died. I was always sad when I awoke. From this I learned that if, in fact, dreams provide an escape from the full impact of reality—like a pressure

cooker's pressure valve releasing built-up heat and energy—
they tend to work at inexplicably maddening rates.

Dreams can be physically and/or emotionally challenging.
For years I lived with the possibility of losing one of the only
two maps depicting the details of our operational plans. The
realization that I no longer had the map was terrifying. Retracing my movements back through the network of VC trails
was always filled with high expectations and high anxiety.
Although I always found the map, every episode presented the
same challenges, and the heightened anxiety over failure.
From that dream, I learned that I never learn anything during a
dream that I had not learned during the actual event. Nor is
the information provided to me prematurely. Unfortunately,
each time I initiated my search for my map, I had only my
expectations—but no knowledge—that I would find it.

For years I lived with the fear of being blown up by friendly
bombs because we were unable to know where we were, on
this hill or that. The fear and anxiety of climbing a very tall
tree to confirm our location never diminished over the ten or
twelve years I lived that event. Interestingly, that nightmare
always concluded as my feet touched ground. There was no
transfer of the important information I could have provided.
Just that I could no longer fall out of a very tall tree. Apparently it was concern for my own safety that governed my
thoughts. Just as interesting is the fact that I have never been
afraid of heights—including sixty-five parachute jumps—and
even today tree pruning and removal are a business line for
me. Or is the dream a demonstration of my need to continu-
ously prove to myself that I can overcome such a fear? Who
knows?

Eight nightmares recurred for nearly twenty years, about
four times per dream per year. As each occurred, it was as if I
had just lived the actual event in most of its gory details.
Seeing the nightmares unfold, in slow motion, produced an
anxiety that persisted for minutes after awakening. It was not
necessary to record the dreams, as they were apparently
indelibly inscribed in my subconscious. The persistence of the

eight nightmares proved to be a major motivating factor in wanting to tell my story. While many events herein are memorable, the following episodes are hard to forget.

Burn, Baby, Burn!

Shortly after witnessing the corpse of the young girl, and the old man who had taken a stand, we found ourselves in an untenable position. We were surrounded by a superior force, and there didn't seem to be much we could do about that situation except die with dignity. When you know you are about to die, and your parents have done their job, you say your prayers. At that moment in time, you are able to ask for the forgiveness you know you have never earned. Torching the hootch was an afterthought, a last-gap effort aimed at survival. That the crimson rooftop was seen by the lead fighter, through the dense green foliage hundreds of meters below the cockpit, was a stroke of luck. On the other hand, perhaps it was a case of an inexperienced combat soldier overestimating the threat. Regardless, this nightmare was, first and foremost, at the very front of my dream cycles for about twenty years.

The Risk of Supporting One's Government

On the scene, and in my dreams, the faceless man was but another casualty in a horrendous ideological struggle. Why was he fighting for the Khmer Rouge? I guess for the same reason I was fighting for the United States. On the other hand, we in the military had our detractors, but there were few confirmed cases of treason in America. There were hundreds of thousands of Cambodians who openly opposed their government and who took up arms against its political positions. There were also thousands of Cambodian soldiers—hundreds of whom were our recruits—who knew that their current government's position was horribly wrong. At the time, I didn't give a shit for the Bode who had his frontal features blown clean from his head, but thirty years later his motivation seems an important question. Not only was he killed in battle, but he was purposely disfigured so that his own kind would never suffer the indignity of having to recognize him. Go figure.

I think that this nightmare persisted not because of the horrific presentation of the faceless man and his grotesque utterances, but because of my empathy for a man who, like me, was inextricably caught up in his government's political agenda.

A Man Without a Leg

The leg-on-the-trail image unfolded like a picture postcard, one reminiscent of the Budweiser Christmas card commercial featured annually on television. As we snaked our way slowly along a narrow trail, overgrown in places with thick jungle grasses, it was important to stay focused, not only on the trail but on the distant shadow walking fifteen meters to my front. Though War Zone D was a long way from Yosemite, Ansel Adams would have enjoyed the contrast of the pitch-black night softened by the filtered beams of moonlight dancing about the rain-soaked sky. This event was anything but frightening, until, of course, the leg appeared as if out of nowhere. Even more startling than the realization that the VC were able to employ that form of psychological warfare, deep within the secret zone, was our apparent lack of interest, as the long green column just kept on moving. A five-second exposure frozen in time forever. Not once, in all the times I endured that nightmare, was I able to escape the reality that somewhere— perhaps somewhere nearby—there was a man who, tortured for information, was forced to witness the brutal and excruciatingly painful severing of his own leg.

The Destructive Force of U.S. Mines

When you first begin to experience the U.S. edge in weapons technology, it is hard to not be impressed with the awesome destructive power of our command-detonated mines. The first time I practiced with the M-18A claymore mine at Fort Bragg convinced me that if we were to lose the Vietnam War, it would not be to inferior battlefield weapons. I had never seen anything quite like it. I could bore you—or impress you, as the case may be—with statistics, but why? All you really have to know here is that when I hit the two VC trail trackers square-on with the claymore, they seemed to disappear. That is, until my eyes were drawn high into the trees rising peacefully above the trail below. What I could not come to grips with then, I cannot come to grips with to this day. It was as if two humans had been dumped into an industrial blender on full power, then spewed carelessly upward for hundreds of feet to their final destination. The multicolored trees became the focus of that nightmare. And though I no longer suffer the grim reminder of my actions on the trail ten thousand miles from Newport News, I shall never forget the imprint of their souls on my mind.

Of course, I never discussed the contents of this dream, nor its mother some thirty years before, with anyone. After all, I was a hardened combat veteran—hard as nails, as uncaring as anyone could be—so what's the point? Fuck those guys. They were wrong then, and they're wrong now. Except . . .

It Could Have Gone Either Way

I just poured another beer from my tap—Miller Ice House—and as I did, as always, I glanced up on the wall at the MAS-36 French-made rifle he was carrying. Also his North Vietnamese green plastic canteen with an embossed green star, and his homemade field knife crafted from spent shell casings. At this point I am crying. Not because I blew his shit away during an ambush, but because I have grown to understand that but for superior weapons technology—the M-16A1 assault rifle versus the MAS-36—it could have gone either way. In case you're wondering, I only recently recovered the "ambush ensemble" from my attic—about the same time the nightmares stopped. Here's the point. If you have such memorabilia in your attic, and if you are still having nightmares, take the weaponry out of the closet and display it, if not proudly, at least with the understanding that the asshole was trying to blow your shit away. And, apparently, you did okay. It has helped me recover from a sight worse than death. Hopefully, it may work for you. Go ahead, I'm serious. Try it.

The Struggle for Survival

When I first began to study dreams as partial fulfillment of my master's degree in counseling from Loyola University in Chicago and read Freud's *Interpretation of Dreams*, I didn't recall anything that would help me explain the recurring nightmare at the foxhole. Unlike the other nightmares, that one *was not* an actual portrayal of the event that occurred in early 1967. As you may recall, we entered a clearing, and saw two VC burying two more VC killed by mines we had sown three days prior. We worked our way up for a clear shot, then porked 'em. Walked up to the burial ground to investigate the results, which were final. Case closed.

Unfortunately, this was one of two or three dreams that caused me the most terror and anxiety for nearly twenty years. Although there was no close combat with the VC during the actual situation, the nightmare featured a momentous life-and-death struggle with knives. My heart raced as I danced around the "campfire," rife with the mystic smell of rotting flesh, fighting two others for the right to make a wish. The surrealistic image of three hombres in full camouflage but without rifles never ceased to scare the shit out of me. Not once did I have any idea about the outcome. And there were always two against one. At times over the years, the knives would give way to wooden batons, like those carried by urban cops. Not once did any of the three of us try to escape. We all knew why we were there. Kill, or be killed. Also, that was the only dream in which I seemed to have superhuman powers. Often, though I would be unable to dodge one of the combatants, I was able to leap over his head—something far in excess of my capabilities—to avoid destruction. This scene proved to be the most persistent. Never did I lose. Why? Also, in several of the other nightmares, I experienced "real blood," but not in this one. Why? Finally, there was never any aftermath. When the last VC was slain, he always fell neatly into his earthen memorial, and the dream stopped.

Where Is the Reality When You Need Answers? Or, Does It Really Matter?

Donahue thought they were distant lights. I thought they were a VC infiltration. Not once during Blackjack-31, nor in the thirty years that followed, did Jim and I ever discuss this incident. In *Mobile Guerrilla Force*, published in March 1996, this award-winning author for whom I have the greatest respect wrote that he had witnessed a bank of red-filtered lights engulfing our mission support site late one night in the heart of War Zone D. He recalled that at first he was terrified and could not find an explanation for the distraction. In reviewing his manuscript, I was forced to admit that, even in combat, when one's instincts reach their peak, there will be honest differences of opinion about the same event. For me, I was terrified then, and for about twenty years afterward I rewitnessed the same insidious invasion with extreme anxiety. I am willing to acknowledge that, indeed, fatigue is a constant companion of the field soldier. As if that would have made any difference. I know this will sound crazy to many veterans, but maybe—just maybe—there is a need for members of the same unit, having participated in the same operation, to just air it out for a day or two following, just so such important questions can be discussed. You know, from day one through whatever. Just a thought. To this day all I know is that a VC infiltration

unit walked through our MSS for about thirty minutes that
night, and the only thing that saved us was my decision to
remain calm and hold my fire. As far as I knew then, no one
else witnessed that near disaster, nor was the penetration significant in light of our impending missions.

He Wasn't Heavy, He Was My Brother

He was black. He was young. He was a member of a group
disproportionately drafted for the Vietnam War. He lay beside
me in the field hospital. Had he lived, he would have had
his whole life in front of him. Had I died, he would have
remembered me. We had a bond. We were combat soldiers.
We were together, for a couple of days, and for eternity. From
the start, I knew he was dying, so we didn't talk much. I
wanted him to live, and I prayed for him as if he were one of
my daughters. I agonized over his treatment. Ice packs, followed by a warm blanket. The doctor's prophetic remark that
if they could reduce his temperature to acceptable limits, he
would probably die from pneumonia. On the third day, he
died. He wasn't heavy, he was my brother.

V

Hard to Forget

If you were with me in Ho Ngoc Tao, and deployed with the MGF on Black Box and BJ-31, you no doubt feel a certain sense of pride and accomplishment. It means that you served with the very best in the glory days of the Green Berets. You were dedicated. You were focused. You were determined. More important, you achieved your mission. The price you paid for your dedication, focus, determination, and achievement, however, was not without its high rate of interest. The war zone—the killing fields—without the warm touch of the ones you loved, took its toll, and you may never be the same. What you and they experienced, during the same time frame, was eons apart.

And that, my friend, is what slows your recovery. As you were doing everything in your power to stem the tide of Communist influence ten thousand miles away, when you noticed not, an insidious mental aversion began to nest deep within the farthest recesses of your mind. There it lay dormant, in a subconscious state, lest it be seen for what it was and exorcised as an evil spirit. For you and for me this sense of ambiguity, this ambivalence—the eternally conflicting emotional states involving our love for peace and our indulgence in war—may well still be there as we try to recover from our sordid lives of death and destruction. As we try to make sense of what we were asked to do. As we try to make peace with ourselves, and

237

then, perhaps, the rest of the world. Not you, you say? Well, then, me.

I owe each and every one of you a long-overdue debt of gratitude for being there. For being a friend. For caring. For doing your best to ensure that our operations, while bold and imaginative—and certainly, while not risk free—had a better than even chance to succeed. Yes, as Bo was fond of saying, "We did it exactly right." From my perspective, under his leadership, we were not only the first Special Forces A-team to conduct successful *guerrilla* operations in the Vietnam War, but, perhaps more important, members of one of the finest fighting forces ever assembled. And, to be sure, we all owe a long-overdue debt of gratitude to our Cambodian brothers who trained so valiantly and fought so courageously. *De oppresso liber.*

If you were one of the loved ones of a member of Task Force 957, Mobile Guerrilla, you will always have a special place in my heart. You can be proud, not only of your loved one's accomplishments during those most difficult missions, but of your strength and desire to keep the home fires burning. There is nothing that contributes to a combat soldier's courage and his willingness to endure on battlefields ten thousand miles from home more than knowing he is loved at home. And yes, you had your own cross to bear.

If you served in Vietnam, God bless you for your service to our country. In whatever capacity assigned, don't think for one minute that your contribution was unimportant. Hold your head high. You don't owe anybody a nickel. You know and I know what you did was the right thing to do at the time. And you never have to apologize for doing the right thing.

If you were a loved one of someone who served in Vietnam, hold him, or her, in high regard. Don't be afraid to ask them how they felt about the war. What it was like to be so far away from home. What was their job? How well did they think they accomplished their job? Failings? Were they afraid? Of what? How they felt about coming home. Going back a second time? A third time? More? How they felt about themselves as the war dragged on and the people at home were getting restless.

Were they sorry they went? Why? Why not? Ask open-ended questions requiring some thought and dialogue. Ask follow-up questions. Let them know how you felt about their absence. About your own struggle.

If you knew someone—a friend, a neighbor—who went to Vietnam, fight the temptation to think of them as losers. Open up a dialogue. Ask questions. Don't assume that the Vietnam War is over for them. Ask them if they have ever gone to the Vietnam Memorial—the Wall—in Washington, D.C. What were their feelings when they approached the pathway leading up to the magnificent stones holding the names of those who made the highest sacrifice? If they haven't gone, why not? Will they ever go? Too far? Don't let them off the hook. Remember, they once went ten thousand miles just to help our country and its people remain free.

If you wanted to go to Vietnam but for some reason were not able, don't be hard on yourself. It was not to be. On the other hand, seek some compassion for those who went, and understand that many, if not all, are still somewhere in the healing process. Don't be impatient.

If you never went to Vietnam—if you actively or passively avoided the draft—forgive yourself. Also, understand that those who went deserve consideration for their effort. Don't be afraid to hire them, talk to them, be their friend.

If you know someone who never went to Vietnam—who actively or passively avoided the draft—forgive them. Let it go. Don't be afraid to hire them, talk to them, be their friend.

If you were one of those who, early on, donned your Green Beret and came along for the ride, I thank you for your willingness to share our experiences. I hope I've been able to maintain your interest.

Life Moves On

Welcome to the mythical time period known as AV—After Vietnam. As I write, the year is 22 AV—that's right, it has now been twenty-two years since the establishment of Ho Chi

Minh City, known in a previous lifetime as Saigon. Unfortunately, most of us have managed to hold on to the same questions, answers, fears, and dreams associated with our existence before Vietnam—BV. I think that letting go means forgiveness. I truly believe that forgiveness, alone, will set us free. Forgiveness of self as the instrument of death for hundreds of thousands of families, and of the destruction of their meager possessions. Forgiveness of self for leaving our families and other loved ones, perhaps at a time when we were most needed at home. Forgiveness of our adversaries, who fought so bravely for their own ideals. Forgiveness of those who were reluctant to embrace our government's position on Vietnam. And, of course, forgiveness by our detractors, for those of us who went.

If somehow self-forgiveness for actions over which we had little control seems to make sense, it follows that we must also seek the forgiveness of those we left behind. Unfortunately, for many reasons, our commitment to serve placed an unhealthy burden on those for whom we had promised our greatest love—our wives and our children. Our absence alone put our wives and children in the unenviable position of having to fend for themselves. Perhaps more telling were the personal changes experienced on our return. Those of us who were emotionally scarred—my observation is that most of us were—could not effectively respond to either societal demands or family needs to our own satisfaction, or to theirs. To the extent that this was true, many of us built up, and harbored over the years, a self-defeating reservoir of anger and guilt owing to our failures and feelings of inadequacies.

One of our nation's greatest combat soldiers, David H. Hackworth, recently posted this note on an Internet Web site*: "The Vietnam War scarred me more severely than any of the eight Purple Hearts I'd received during almost eight years of combat." "Regarding Vietnam: Stories Since the War," can be found at URL http://www.pbs.org/pov/stories. The sponsors

---

*Produced by POV Interactive in association with PBS Online, inspired by Maya Lin, the designer of the Vietnam Veterans Memorial.

suggest, "Perhaps today, twenty years after the war's end, we are ready to listen to each other's stories." For a Web site initiated in November 1996, I am not surprised at the response. By January 14, 1997, just two months or so after its founding, as I sat at my computer and pecked away, 610 subscribers had posted their personal stories on forty-one different topics about Vietnam, fifty-six of them devoted to kicking the trauma resulting from the war itself. Many of them brought tears to my eyes, as I felt the pain the writers suffer so very many years after the war's completion. The depth of their emotions suggests to me that, perhaps, the producers are right. Maybe we are ready to listen to each other's stories, and in so doing, to ameliorate our future outlook.

On a most personal level, to the extent that one should, or could, accept responsibility for the happiness of others, I regret that I was unable to be a closer partner for Donna after Vietnam. I have long sensed that I was unable to meet her emotional needs for closeness and intimacy. The apparent anger and resentment I continued to express for years had a most damaging affect on our relationship and, of course, on our children as well. For this I am truly sorry, and at this late date, beg their understanding and forgiveness.

In 22 AV and beyond, we have an opportunity to put it behind us. Not our memories, and perhaps not our nightmares, but certainly our hatred for our fellow man. Most of us believe that we will only live one lifetime. If that is true, it is incumbent upon each of us to live out the only life we will ever know in a spirit of peace and harmony. Peace within ourselves, and in harmony with our brothers and sisters. There should be no exceptions. Can that be so difficult?

Interestingly, I think it is so insanely difficult because, for some unexplainable reason, most of us feel that because we went to Vietnam, we have entitlement unto ourselves that was never intended for those who did not serve. I felt that way for many years. Perhaps many of us think that because of our physical and emotional scars we deserve special treatment. On the other hand, I am just as sure that for some unexplainable reason, most of us feel that because we stayed home, we have entitlement unto ourselves that was never intended for those who served. In reality, we all have the same entitlement—life, liberty, the pursuit of happiness, freedom of religion, etc.—to the same degree, and Vietnam has not one goddamned thing to do with it. If one million black men can organize themselves in pursuit of personal reconciliation, then, by God, tens of millions—those who went and those who didn't—ought to be able to take unto themselves a personal act of forgiveness of self and others, for the sake of all humanity. If you are willing to forgive yourself today, as I have done, you will have accomplished an important first step. However, it will not be easy. In fact, it may well be one of the most difficult things you have ever asked yourself to do. For me, the act of forgiving oneself incorporates a concomitant moral responsibility to forgive others as well. Even Jane Fonda and our current commander-in-chief. A pretty tall order, right? Absolutely, but I cannot think of a better way to slough off the anger and resentment I have been hiding for years. Can you? I really think that this is about forgiveness, friendship, and survival. When I was distraught and out of sorts, a very dear friend of mine reminded me that a rising tide lifts all boats.

Adjustment Is a Lifelong Process

If I believe that the freedom to live a life without hatred for our fellow man requires an act of personal forgiveness, and a concomitant forgiveness of others, it is important that I understand that this commitment, while an important first step, is but the first step in a process that will take the rest of my life. Those who have had to deal with substance abuse know very well that their single best chance of full recovery is in knowing they must forever abstain. Any other behavior—indulgence of a single nature—jeopardizes the recovery program. Likewise, those who have the need, and concomitant courage, to forgive, must understand that their single best chance of full recovery is in knowing they must forever abstain. Abstain from sowing their own personal brand of hatred as if it didn't make any difference to the rest of us. Any other behavior—indulgence of a single nature—jeopardizes the recovery program. If this were not true, there would be little need for the structure that is an integral component of most, if not all, recovery programs. Basically, there is strength in numbers. Also, there is something supportive in knowing that there are others with the same affliction. Finally, there is a need for honest feedback so that we may evaluate our progress. I have found that others, particularly those who care, will validate our inclination for self-respect. If they really care, they will participate in the healing process.

Talk to Someone—Write a Book

Convinced that forgiveness was the key to a major life adjustment requiring a lifelong commitment, and faced with the risks inherent in operating alone, I knew that I needed help. I realized that I was in a state of denial that anything was out of place in my life. Somehow, I managed to construe the safekeeping of my notebooks, diaries, pictures, letters, memorabilia, awards, citation, and worn slips of paper hidden neatly in my desk drawer as an honest effort to put Vietnam behind me. I suspect that I am not alone.

One vet at an SF convention told me that the only people he can talk to are other Vietnam vets. When I asked him to elaborate, he confided that they were the only ones he could trust. The only ones who would know, and appreciate, his situation. The reason for killing. The perceived inadequacies in his own personal life. I suspect that this train of thought is similar to that of blacks in America who don't think that we, who are white, will ever be able to understand from where they are coming, where they're going, or the routes they have chosen to travel. When our sons and daughters, who were too young to know much about Vietnam, ask us about the war, we tend to clam up, or find an excuse to withhold our experiences from them. When our wives and other loved ones probe for information, that they might know us better, we shrug our shoulders as if to say that it's no big deal. Or, worse, we put them off forever with a couple of pat answers with which we feel comfortable. You know, some of the factual things that say little about the way we felt and perhaps still feel about Vietnam.

I know one such son who has been trying to get in touch with his father for many years, without much success. He tells me that his dad just doesn't want to talk about it. What a shame, for both the veteran, who has much about which to be proud, and the son, who would dearly love to know his father better. My advice to the son was, "Don't take no for an answer." Be persistent. If the father were to read this, I would say to him, "Talk to your son. He has every right to know about your decision to go to Vietnam, how you felt about that choice, what you did or failed to do, what you learned along the way, and what you think you missed while you were gone. The strain it may have put on your marriage and, perhaps, on your family. Maybe not all the gory details, but certainly enough information to quench his thirst for knowledge and to validate your self-respect. And, my friend, if you continue to refuse, you have yet to take the first step toward a lifelong journey to a full recovery. In the process, you will deny your grandson, or granddaughter, the privilege of knowing that you sacrificed a portion of your life that theirs might be better." They need to know that you did the best you could under the circumstances.

I have discovered that it's so important to talk to your loved ones—spouses or significant others, sons and daughters, brothers and sisters, fathers and mothers—and, if you're fortunate, to a best friend or two. Of course, there are other avenues.

Those who are so inclined may be challenged to write a book. For me, writing this book was tied to my personal sense of respect and survival. I say "was" because, over the years, the process of writing has proved to be therapeutic. As I near the end, I realize that, for the effort, I have become a much stronger person. I no longer feel as though I have to apologize for my actions in Vietnam. I have also learned to forgive myself for my absence on the home front. Writing proved to be a personal challenge that forced me to look deeply into my mind, my heart, and, perhaps, my soul. When I began to write my account, several years ago, I had doubts that I was equal to the task. Although in time I became more comfortable with the process of writing, the content was beginning to frighten me. Forcing myself to deal with the realities of what happened was painful. Weeks, and in some instances months, would pass without my putting anything on paper. Recalling, from the deep recesses of my mind to the forefront, the memories attributable to the young girl, the old man, the defenseless position near the burning hootch, the leg on the trail, the faceless man, the foxhole, the beautiful young girls with the silky black hair, the mines on the trail, the crimson-colored trees, the VC ambush, the moving lights, the lost map, the tall tree, the pallet of beer, and the soldier dying from pneumonia, forced me to deal with those events so closely, and so painfully, that I began to wonder if the treatment was worse than the cure. I discovered that the human mind is very creative, resilient, and deceptive. Just about the time that I thought I could drum up no more emotion over Vietnam—after all, the nightmares had been dormant for nearly ten years—I began to unravel as my mind offered this information to me when I asked, with surprising clarity. I realized, then, that the details of these terrifying events were still lurking deep within my subconscious mind, draining psychic energy that may have been useful in another venue. Dealing with the demons in the light of day, on the open page, where they are plainly visible to the naked eye, and discussing them with my family and friends, has convinced me that I am on the road to recovery.

If you are a Vietnam vet, and feel the need to escape the ominous torments of war, record all of the specific events you can remember onto paper, where you can see them. It will not be an easy task. Many of the things you might include, you will argue, are not relevant. But your feelings are relevant. And so is the close association you will begin to experience about the story line. When you start to feel the anger build, don't be afraid to express that anger on paper. It doesn't matter if this effort takes a day, a week, a month, or a year. Add and subtract items at will. When you have a definitive list of things you want to include, continue the attack. All that matters is that you write your story the way you want, the way you need to have it told. It really doesn't matter whether you publish your account or not. You will be writing it for yourself, and perhaps for the ones you love. If what I have suggested has merit for those who went to Vietnam, it may have merit for those who did not serve. Millions of stories behind the requirements to be strong and raise a family need to be told. An open dialogue about Vietnam, even at this late date, may serve to bridge the gap of understanding among spouses and family members. The wife of one veteran recently confided to me, with a great deal of resentment, that "he wasn't home, and I had to raise the kids all by myself." Sensitive to her dilemma, I answered with a great deal of compassion that "for every mother who has been left alone to raise the children by herself, there was a father who, for the unfortunate circumstance, was denied the opportunity." Such a scenario suggests that there may be spouses to this day who, for the lack of open and honest discussion, paralyzed by anger, guilt, and resentment allowed to grow and fester for thirty years, may need to tell their stories to each other. If you are reading this and think this might be you, summon every bit of courage you can muster and begin the process of unraveling your own personal demons. If you know someone—a loved one—in the same boat, begin to ask the kinds of open-ended questions that may help the hostilities rise to the surface, where they might be examined more clearly. A lifetime of agony and grief is too long to wait, too high a price to pay, for reconciliation and resolution.

Don't Be Afraid to Pray

Whenever life becomes difficult for me, I turn to prayer. I seldom ask for solutions, only that I might better understand the problems. My prayers take many forms. Writing this book, for me, is a form of prayer, because it tends to improve the way I feel about myself. It has also tended to strengthen my relationships with others. I pray that my account may, in some small way, cause you to feel better about yourself or someone you love.

Many of the activities I enjoy—handball, diving, skiing, racquetball, blading—are forms of prayer. They put to use and improve those skills and abilities that I have attained, and help me to maintain the level of fitness and well-being that God may have intended. Helping others, sharing one's time, talents, and treasure, are all forms of prayer. Sometimes I pray that others might better understand me, my thought process, and what I'm trying to do with my life. There are also times when I ask God to let me better understand myself and others.

My current work life as a small business owner focusing on home improvements is, perhaps, the most meaningful prayer answered to date. As an army infantry officer, my energies were focused on better ways to kill people and destroy things. Using my head, my hands, and my heart in a more positive way has helped me to heal some of the wounds owing to such a negative agenda. Don't get me wrong—I'm not saying that I'm the least bit sorry that I became a most resourceful "destroyer," as I made those choices knowing full well that freedom is a precious, and potentially diminishing, commodity. But a "kill or be killed" existence has its downside, and in retirement I am thankful that I'm able to be more constructive.

Of course, there are many other forms of prayer. Some are dutifully caught up in religious content. To the extent that you find yourself inclined to formalize your beliefs, be encouraged. There is something healthy about knowing you're able to ask for the love and support of a higher being. As a practicing Catholic, I feel blessed that I am not traveling on life's main road, and on the thousands of side roads, alone.

You May Need a Friend

Beyond my need for spiritual friendship and the love of a higher being, a relationship built primarily on faith and mystery, I longed for that certain someone who was willing to listen without being judgmental. Appropriately, friendship has its historical roots in the verb "to love" and is akin to the word "free." The more I was willing to talk, the more my friends listened, and with each agonizing story told, I began to experience both a love and a freedom that I had never known. Freedom from the anguish and torment brought on by years of silence and quiet despair. Freedom from the fear of being not wanted or being misunderstood. Freedom from the fear of not belonging, of being alone, with my thoughts and with my life.

My friend was kind, patient and enduring, sensing that I was ready to move on with my life. My friend encouraged me to write my story. And my friend was generous with her time. Most of all, my friend helped me to regain my self-respect, to believe in myself once again. Without the love and support of my friend, I may never have summoned the courage to visit the Wall. Those who have been privileged to spend some time at the Vietnam Memorial, in Washington, D.C., know what kind of emotionally draining experience awaits those who have yet to go.

My friend was empathetic, feeling my pain as the blood from my soul poured out onto unwritten pages. When I was in need, drowning in self-pity, my friend reassured me that what I'd done was done for the love of country and fellow man. My friend refused to give up on me, even when I was about to give up on myself. And, in my greatest moment of need, my friend stood by me, holding my hand, laughing with me, sharing my tears and fears, my intermittent joy and growing levels of self-respect and happiness. My friend helped me to regain my balance.

Don't Lose Your Balance

Few words in the English language have as many relatively sophisticated meanings as does the word "balance." In its purest form, balance requires an equal distribution of weight. Equality of ideas. Maintaining one's perspective. To lose one's balance is to vary from one side or the other. My father taught balance as a prerequisite—a sine qua non—to a meaningful life here on earth. You may provide your own interpretation, but what I'm talking about is the willingness and ability to see both sides of an issue or argument, rather than giving in, without equal representation, to personal bias and hypocrisy. That's not to say that each of us is not entitled to his or her own opinion about Vietnam. Balance, however, requires that we give due consideration to the argument of others. Try to see their point. Refrain from condemning them, and their position, because of our past disagreements. And if you're thinking that because Vietnam is in the past, and because we cannot undo the personal choices we made or the beliefs that led to them, I only ask you to consider where we have been on this issue for the past thirty years or more. There must come a day, hopefully sooner rather than later, when we're ready to listen to each other's stories.

For me, the time is now. I have made a personal decision to redirect all of my anger and resentment, heretofore reserved for those who failed to serve, to some other more constructive use. I hope and pray that those who failed to serve will reciprocate. We will all be better for this resurgence of will, this attempt to regain, and maintain, our balance. Once we have slain our own personal demons and are willing to face the light, we will need someplace to stand.

Learn to Stand on Your Own Two Feet

There are times in our lives when, incapacitated, we must begrudgingly lean on others. Those who have endured the physical wounds of war have been fortunate to have had such a caregiver. Most of us, however, bearing only the emotional scars of war, were capable of helping out at home. Yet, for reasons I don't fully understand, I became married to my job and, unwittingly, subservient at home. I allowed myself to become dependent on the one person with whom, before Vietnam, I shared some sense of responsibility. I was content to just sit back and let my wife take care of me. I think that many of us who established military careers were content to just sit back and let our wives run the show. I'm referring to the home theater and all that involves. Outside the home, we had our careers, we had our jobs to do, and we considered that important. How could we be bothered with the simple, the mundane, and the unimaginative? With combat as our background, we had our plans to prepare for the general, operations to conduct for the colonel, and, when other excuses ran short, we had our men to support.

That's how I began to justify twelve-to-sixteen-hour days, and less time spent helping Donna with the children and everyday chores. Upward mobility. Up or out. Promotion or pass-over. Two pass-overs and you were history. Take care of your mission, and take care of your men.

Unfortunately, there were times when my job, and my unit, came first. Vietnam was such an occasion. That accounts for two years. There were more times, however, when I used my job as a convenient excuse for spending time at the club—oh, those work relationships were important, and fragile—and sleeping on the home front. I felt so highly accomplished that there was some danger in my animal magnetism. Like a proud and powerful tiger, faced with the prospects of being caged in the city zoo, I ambled far and wide in my quest for new prey—more responsibility, more authority, and more goddamned tickets to punch!

Was I alone? Why did we do this?

Because we were, many of us, mesmerized by the very system we were committed to uphold. We allowed ourselves to become inextricably linked to our fellow officers, warrants, enlisted, and our units. We began to think alike, talk alike, be alike. Our anxiety and fears about being promoted on time helped to create an addiction, of sorts, to the machine. The Pentagon. The largest single employer in the industrialized world. When we tried to speak out, we were cited for our lack of loyalty, our inability to cooperate and get along, our lack of teamwork. Back in line, yes sir, no sir, we were praised for our selflessness, our willingness to work long hours and our ability to support our superiors. Then, when we noticed least, we were the system.

Unfortunately, you can't win a race on an oval track with a funny car. And you can't be very helpful at home when you are never there or, when you get there, you are just too fucking tired to get it up. No wonder many women claim to have raised their families. They did. Without much help from those of us who were too fucking busy chasing our careers. For many it would have been easier to accept had we been chasing skirts. Many of us, so caught up in attending to the colonel's hemorrhoids, or the general's piles, were unable to develop a much needed sense of balance in our lives, nor were we able to learn how to stand on our own two feet.

So we leaned on our wives. We leaned on our children. We leaned on those for whom we had the greatest love and respect, all the while telling them, or failing to tell them, that we were doing it all for them. After all, isn't the simple definition of success in American society an adequate income? Money for shelter, food, clothing, activities, and schools? If we took at home, in some remarkable demonstration of equanimity and benevolence, we gave at the office. Filled our squares. Got our school seats, pleased our commanders, sucked up to our staffs, and screwed our soldiers in the process. Why? Because our soldiers sorely needed someone— perhaps a leader—who was able to stand on his own two feet. Someone who, for the sake of training, refused to paint the rocks, tag the windows, or commit to some silly demonstration for the Assistant to the Deputy Assistant to the Under Secretary of the something or other.

Well, after all these years, my friend has encouraged me to stand on my own two feet. And, with God's help, I will.

Time Is a Great Healer

Dad, you were right. Time is a great healer. In the days since I last saw you, resting peacefully on a hospice bed with a blackened tongue and a knowing glance, I began to realize that there would have to be some changes in my life. Yes, Vietnam took its toll on me. But so did my failure to get a battalion, your death, and a failed marriage. I now realize that it is time to make repairs. I'm trying to lose that edge. I'm learning that life moves on, and adjustment never ends. Also, the importance of talking things out and the value of prayer. I could not do this without the love and support of my friends. Although I have stumbled a few times, I'm more steady and have learned to stand on my own two feet. Yes, I still get angry at times, and I do feel some resentment about what might have been, but on balance, the years have been relatively kind to me. I know I am but a work in progress and it will take time, but as you taught me from my first days, time is a great healer. By the way, I'm going to say that to others—I'm writing a book.

Final Thoughts

If not from the start—and I have my doubts—then shortly thereafter, our leaders, intentionally or otherwise, deceived the nation about Vietnam. One has only to examine the Vietnam War's "famous last words" to understand why there is division among us:

1. "I fully expect only six more months of hard fighting." (General Navarro, French Commander-in-Chief, January 2, 1954)
2. "With a little more training, the Vietnamese Army will be the equal of any army." (U.S. Secretary of the Army Wilbur Brucker, December 18, 1955)
3. "The South Vietnamese themselves are fighting their own battle." (U.S. Secretary of State Dean Rusk, April 1963)

4. "South Vietnam is on its way to victory." (F. E. Nolting, U.S. Ambassador to South Vietnam, June 13, 1963)

5. "I feel we shall achieve victory in 1964." (Tram Van Dong, South Vietnamese general, October 1, 1963)

6. "Secretary McNamara and General Taylor reported that the major part of the U.S. military task can be accomplished by the end of 1965." (White House statement, October 2, 1963)

7. "Victory is just months away." (General Paul D. Harkins, Commander MACV, October 31, 1963)

8. "The Vietnamese can handle this problem primarily with their own effort." (U.S. Secretary of State Dean Rusk, February 24, 1964)

9. "I think the number of U.S. personnel in Vietnam is not likely to increase substantially." (U.S. Secretary of Defense Robert S. McNamara, May 14, 1964)

10. "We are not about to send American boys ten thousand miles from home to do what Asian boys ought to be doing for themselves." (President Johnson, October 21, 1964)

In spite of having been badly misled, most of those who were eligible and were asked chose to serve their country; many did not.

Shortly after getting settled into my first post-Vietnam assignment, as an ROTC instructor at Loyola University in Chicago, on a wintry Christmas morning in 1967, Donna gave birth to our one and only son, whom we named Jeffrey Steven. Given a war whose end was nowhere in sight, I began to wonder just what kind of a world our three children would be asked to endure. When, in the spring of 1968, I witnessed college students pouring champagne on the U.S. flag, then setting it afire, I began to sense the hatred with which many people viewed the war. Within months the entire world watched Chicago burn during the Democratic National Convention after Mayor Richard J. Daly issued his highly divisive "shoot to kill" orders aimed at arsonists and looters. When, during the next school year, I learned that some on the law school faculty were, without compensation, providing advice to young students on how to fill out the paperwork to avoid the draft, I began to suspect that we were becoming an elitist society.

A much-publicized quote from the widely admired President John F. Kennedy, whose actions were directly responsible for getting our nation into the Vietnam War, revealed just how much societal leverage politics placed in the hands of the so-called "best and the brightest," the vanguard of the Eastern Establishment. Kennedy said, "There is always inequality in life. Some men are killed in a war, and some men are wounded, and some men never leave the country, and some men are stationed in Antarctica, and some men are stationed in San Francisco. It's very hard in the military or personal life to assure equality. Life is unfair." As I witnessed developments at Loyola, I felt compelled to finish his thoughts: And some men are too important to take out of college? Business? Politics? Academia?

Let's face it, the draft was unfair. The draft, the legal instrument in place to process those who would go, sent to Vietnam disproportionate numbers of the poor, the uneducated, and the minorities, while it protected those whose resources enabled them to avoid service to their country.

Those who did serve can find comfort in a famous quote attributed to former General of the Army, Douglas MacArthur: "The soldier, above all other men, is required to practice the greatest act of religious training—sacrifice. In battle, and in the face of danger and death, he discloses those divine attributes which His Maker gave when He created man in His own image. No physical courage and no greater strength can take the place of divine help, which alone can sustain him. However hard the incidents of war may be, the soldier who is called upon to offer and give his life for his country is the noblest development of mankind."

Also, in one of my favorites, words attributed to Theodore R. Roosevelt: "It is not the critic who counts, nor the man who points out how the strong man stumbled, or where the doer of deeds could have done better. It is the man who is actually in the arena, whose face is marred by dust, and sweat, and blood. It's the man who strives valiantly, who fails and errs, again and again, but if he succeeds, he knows his triumph, and, if he fails, he fails while daring greatly so that his soul shall never be with those cold, timid souls who know neither victory nor defeat."

Yes, we may have been misled about Vietnam. And, for our own reasons, we may have had some regrets or doubts. Some of us may still harbor regrets or doubts. But at some point we have to give way. There must come a day when those of us who went must be willing to break bread with those who didn't. And those who didn't go must be willing to open their minds to fully accept those who took the arena. Our nation demands as much.

In my search for the truth—Yedinak versus Vietnam—I am forced to admit that for many years I looked outside myself for the answers, somehow looking for some indication from others that there was nothing morally objectionable about what I did and that the torments of war would not persist forever. After my first tour, I experienced an inner rage, directing my anger at society in general and at what I saw as the many instruments of evil; for example, the Loyola law school mentors who were advising their students to avoid the draft. I was outraged by the idea that I had grown up with people who were about my age and appeared to be deserting their country. I thought to myself, Is *this* what America stands for? Is this what I have to look forward to, a division of souls between those who went and those who didn't? I don't think that I was alone.

An ROTC instructor, I became ambivalent about training my replacement. As one of two advisers to the cadet Ranger unit, I shared my time and skills with Advanced Course students from whose ranks the army would select its infantry officers. As a natural result of that, I was deeply saddened to learn about the serious wounds from which one of our cadets was recovering in Camp Zama, Japan. Second Lieutenant Gutowski was one of the brightest, most accomplished young men in the cadet brigade. I will never forget him, nor his beautiful young bride of about three months.

They had graciously invited Donna and me for dinner in their small northside apartment just weeks before he reported to Fort Benning, Georgia, for infantry training. We were close, as he wanted to become a Special Forces officer. When we received the first of two telegrams, we were apprised of serious wounds to both of his legs and his stomach, wounds sustained during his first combat engagement and for which he was then receiving emergency treatment in Japan. I knew what that meant, but said nothing. The second telegram, days later, announced his death. Performing Survivor's Assistance Officer duties for his young bride, while an honor and a privilege, was one of the hardest things I have ever had to do.

Nor was that the only reminder of the insidious nature of the Vietnam War during my three years at Loyola. I served as a "guardian angel" in eighteen combat deaths, each a grim reminder that death was but a phone call away. I was beginning to wonder which was worse, being there or being home.

There were the parents of a twenty-eight-year-old army infantry captain killed in battle. Because we were the same age, shared the same occupation, and were physically the same size, they wanted me to have his professional uniforms, books, and some of his civilian clothing. They saw in me, him. They were desperate for a replacement. Even after the allotted ninety days' assistance, after which all questions are to be asked of another agency, they continued to call me. I felt so very sorry for them. They were such nice people, and they had lost their only son.

On another occasion I was asked to notify the single mother of a son killed in combat, at her place of work, a southside Chicago factory. Asking the personnel officer for a quiet, empty office, I waited for her to appear, as did he. When the middle-aged woman came into the office, I asked her to please be seated. In the required dress green uniform, I quietly announced the death of her son, expressing to her the deepest sympathy of the Secretary of the Army. She seemed to take it well, but the young office manager began to attack U.S. war policy, and me for bringing her the bad news. Not wanting to further upset the woman, I remained silent, hoping he would desist. He continued to speak out, at one point saying, "As far as I am concerned, you are the symbol of what is wrong in America, and indirectly are responsible for his death."

Sensing no relief was in sight, I asked him if he and I could adjourn to another office. But I reassured the woman that I would escort her home, as she was unsettled. She nodded as we left the office. Once in the other office, out of earshot of others, I waited for the manager to take his seat. When all was quiet, I turned to him and said, "What you did in front of that woman, one of your employees, was inexcusable. Just when she needed to be reassured that her son's death was not in vain, you tried to tear down the very institution he had committed himself to support. You, my friend, are a coward. And if I ever hear that you have continued to talk to her, or anyone else, about this case, I will return, not in uniform, and I will break your fucking neck. Do you understand me?" He said he did, and that he was sorry he had come unglued. I accepted his apology, and with a word of sorrow for my own dismal behavior, left the office. On reaching her second-floor flat near the elevated tracks, I sat and waited while she excused herself for the rest room. Three or four minutes passed, and I sensed that something was wrong. My suspicions were confirmed when I noticed that the bathroom door was open and there was no one inside.

I quickly walked out the open back door, down the rickety gray steps, and onto the tracks themselves. I was horrified to see her running down the tracks, screaming, directly into the path of an oncoming train. Had I stumbled, there would not have been enough time. I spent most of the afternoon with her, talking quietly about her son's sacrifice. When a friend was with her and after I sensed she was out of danger, I left. As the years passed, I awakened often to a vision of the distraught mother screaming her way down the tracks toward the roaring engine of an elevated train. Hard to forget.

Cairo, Illinois, lies at the southern tip of the state, and was a predominantly poor black community that kept pretty much to itself. I will never forget how gracious were the parents, relatives, and friends of the young soldier we were about to bury. In stark contrast to the young office manager, there was not one among them who didn't know that their loved one died a heroic death on the battlefield in Vietnam and had made the extreme sacrifice for the betterment of all mankind. That's just how they chose to see it, and from my perspective, they were as right as the driving rain we endured on the way to the burial ground. It was befitting, I thought, that this young infantry combat veteran would be laid to rest in the kind of grave and environment in which he fought.

As we opened the back door of the well-used station wagon and lifted the simple homemade wooden casket onto our shoulders, the sounds of thunder and flashes of distant lightning seemed to be claiming a right to one of their own. As we sloshed our way down the ankle-deep mud road with the casket—we could not get the vehicle within a hundred feet of the grave—I heard the sounds and felt the distant call of the war-torn jungles left behind. The weather reminded me of tactical operations during the monsoon, with high winds and driving rain all but obliterating sight. While the nondenominational minister led us in prayer, we used ropes to slowly lower our hero into his final resting place. Thinking back to the cremation performed for the South Vietnamese peasants only months earlier, it was not hard to escape the reality that in much of rural America people lead more simple lives and, when the time comes, deal more modestly with death. Soon after, we left, while three men backfilled the opening with shovels.

On the short ride back to their home, the rain gave way to a brief hint of sun, perhaps a sign that the gods were pleased. The early morning burial left plenty of time for family and friends to gather at the home of the only son that family would ever know. As we ate and drank together throughout the afternoon, I felt heartened that I was being treated as one of the family. Later in the evening, during the cab ride back to my hotel, I marveled about how differently people accept the death of a loved one. Hard to forget.

I could never quite find relief from the episode of the mother with a supposedly weak heart. While awaiting her return from a nearby southside market, I had the presence of mind to summon both police and an ambulance, which were standing by out of sight. As her sister and I waited anxiously on the front porch, I was preparing myself for the worst-case scenario—she sees me and, instinctively knowing why I'm there, drops comatose to the ground, requiring immediate medical support and hospitalization, with a police escort. As the relatively young, badly overweight, black woman approached, I caught myself leaning toward the parking area, not wanting to waste time. I had been led to believe that, in heart arrest, every second counted. When she drew near without collapsing, I felt more comfortable. She was the first one to say anything, as it was our policy to first verify the relationship, then quietly urge the person to be notified to the inside comfort of their home. Seeing my uniform, she spoke calmly: "It's Kevin, isn't it?" I once again expressed the deepest sympathy of the Secretary of the Army. As we talked inside, there was no evidence whatever that she lacked the stamina to withstand the horrible news. Not then, nor anytime during the three months that followed.

Perhaps the most bizarre case I administered involved a man who, after days of nagging, promised his wife that she could see the remains of their son contained in the "unviewable casket." He indicated to me that he was a Korean War vet, and that he had "seen everything," so I relented, making arrangements with the mortuary that he, and he alone, could see the damage wrought by land mines. Only after he'd personally witnessed the scattered assortment of bones held loosely together by bits and pieces of darkened flesh would I consent to showing his wife, and then only on his say-so. But after almost vomiting into the opened sheets and blankets that contained the unrecognizable dead matter, he turned his head away, saying, "No fucking way. I had truly forgotten how terrible war can be. My wife will never see this. Close the casket, for good." Hard to forget.

For those of you who are new to this, one reason that motivated some loved ones to personally view a badly damaged body was merely to verify that the government was about to bury the right remains. For some there was just enough publicity about cases of mistaken identity to warrant such investigation. In some cases, loved ones heard from friends who reported "seeing him alive," or had other reasons for wanting to confirm their suspicions that indeed the dead man could be someone else. From a soldier's perspective, I can say that the system is almost always right, but there have been times when, for reasons of secrecy, I have witnessed the caching of a body that would later be returned. Soldiers have always found comfort in a code of ethics that ensures the return of remains from the battlefield. Before the body, or bodies, is cached, all of the correct information is recorded, so that even in the worst cases the information is available, even if the body is not.

But there are those who have to see the body. Such was the case involving the combat death of a young man with two brothers. The mortuary was packed with family and friends. About waist high, the closed casket rested peacefully along the back wall, nestled neatly into a corner. I would otherwise not have noticed, as people were moving quietly about the room, filling up all the available spaces, but I thought I heard something drop. Although I was not officially responsible for safeguarding the remains, I was alerted to a potential problem in the same manner that a mother might sense that the spaghetti will follow the fork to the floor. I quietly maneuvered myself toward the corner. Once there, I turned slowly, in time to witness the attempted removal of the top of the casket by the two brothers. Knowing their concern, I whispered, "Your brother is a hero who sacrificed himself so that you might have a better life. Please let him rest in peace." They desisted, with apologies, and I think we were the only three who were aware of the problem, and the solution. They promised me that there would be no further attempts to open the casket. I believed them, and was equally sure that this would prove to be a most memorable event. In fact, hard to forget.

Of course, readers are free to determine whether, or to what extent, events described in this book have any interest for them. But what continued to interest me about Vietnam were questions about the morality of the war and the ethics of my behavior. So many people thought the war was morally objectionable that, I wondered, could they all be wrong? What if they had been right all along? Or, if wrong, why was something that happened so very long ago still at the forefront of American thought? Was there room for different opinions about the morality of the war and how it was fought?

When I returned from Vietnam, having been shielded from outside news for many months by the close nature of special operations, I was not prepared for the abhorrent actions of many citizens who opposed the war. To preserve my own sanity, I began to look long and hard for the answers that would, somehow, justify my part in the destruction of so many lives. At some point the background noise stopped, like the faint whine of a computer's hard drive on the completion of a search. In my own mind, I concluded that what I did at the time was in keeping with the highest standards of military conduct while limiting the potential spread of communism across the Asian continent. But the critics?

Yes, if ever there was a need to silence the critics—and, for me, I suspect there was—there was also a requirement that I begin to look inside myself for some of the answers. At some point I discovered that it was one thing to somehow rationalize the criticism of others, but quite another to resolve my own propensity for self-doubt. I was forced to recognize that throughout my military career I was my own worst critic. Simply put, I was too hard on myself, and in retrospect too hard on others. My mind would look for, find, and record for posterity the slightest imperfections in my work. Sometimes a single instance of a plan gone awry required immediate resolution. Or else. Or else I felt inadequate. Trying again forced improvements, but in the long run I could never quite meet my own expectations. At that point, I felt I no longer needed the evaluation of my work by others. Shit, I could have written a *book* about my own failings and, no revelation to those who know me, my life was, and for the most part is, an open book.

It took me a long time to convince myself that there was no such thing as perfection, nor, for us humans, will there ever be. This was not an enviable position in which to find myself.

To escape that insanity, I began to relearn one of psychology's—indeed, one of life's—valued principles: that we tend to see in others those things we see, and fear, in ourselves. Put another way, we humans tend to project onto others those failings we harbor in ourselves. Why? Because we're more comfortable with the outcome. It is far easier to be critical of the perceived hatred of others—maybe, those who failed to serve—than to accept the possibility that our own hatred and anger may not be justified. I forced myself to acknowledge that I had so convinced myself that the answer to my dilemma was "out there," I had cleverly managed to refrain from looking "in there." I was so hopelessly committed to bringing about changes in others—for their own good, of course—that I forgot to closely inspect my own inner workings. As a result, I often projected onto others my own imperfections. Once I began to see that the road to recovery required changes from within, and once I had decided to change those things about myself that I liked least, I felt a tremendous relief that I was, indeed, by the grace of God—and the kind words of my very dear friend—on the road to recovery from a lifetime of emotional war injuries that had been, to that point in time, hard to forget.

The next step in my search for personal growth was to begin to reverse the processes of my irrational thinking, which proved to be so debilitating. For most of my life I looked to others for approval of my behavior. Much of that thinking was just an honest outgrowth of what is recognized by the military chain of command. Those of us in the military *had* to seek the approval of our superiors because if it was not given— officially, in efficiency reports—we were denied education, choice assignments, promotions, and—in the worst cases— even retirement. Unfortunately, this need for approval became so ingrained in us that even in retirement we seek the approval

HARD TO FORGET   263

of others in what I believe to be an unhealthy way. Then there was the need for perfection, to be totally competent in everything I did. This, followed by the idea that if something was not perfect, then someone—myself or others—had made a mistake and, accordingly, must be blamed for it, punished. If things didn't go my way, I was crushed. Things that happened in the past would continue to affect me in the present. There seemed to be no statute of limitations. And rather than admit that life *is* unfair, that there are no perfect answers that will work for each and every one of us, I chose to continue the search for the flawless solution. And finally, there was a time that I not only looked to others for my own happiness, but somehow felt responsible for the happiness of others.

To the contrary, rational thinking, or cognitive therapy, requires more. Instead of believing that I needed approval by everyone for everything I do, I began to realize that no one is universally loved, nor is his or her work universally accepted.

Instead of looking for perfection in my work, I now realize that I am a capable, confident person doing the best I can. When I make mistakes, I can learn from them, but should not become overly disheartened by inconsequential failure. I'm learning to accept that there are many things I do very well, and of which I can be proud. For my remaining days, I will choose to accentuate those things that tend to bring me peace and happiness.

Instead of perceiving the actions of others as wrong—something for which they should be punished—I'm learning to think that in life things frequently go wrong, and in most instances it is nobody's fault. In those instances where my own deeds or those of others are clearly wrong, causing someone else personal grief and hardship, both ownership and full restitution are important, but the deed ought not to be perceived—except in the most egregious cases—as deserving of a death warrant.

Instead of believing that it's catastrophic if things in my life do not go the way I want them to go, I now recognize that, although unpleasant, it's not the end of the world. Sometimes things do go my way, sometimes they don't. In either event, I have learned not to engage in useless worry and guilt about those things over which I have little control. I am also learning that I like myself better when I exercise less control over the behavior of others.

Instead of thinking that because something in the past affected me it will always affect me, I have learned to alter my outlook considerably. I have come to understand that, although there may be pieces of the past that come back to haunt me, I can learn to keep an eye out for them and to cope with them better. And, of course, my commitment to no longer hide in fear of my nightmares, but to choose instead to talk to someone, will not escape even the most casual reader.

I have also come to accept that life, far from fair, is imperfect to the same degree, give or take, that we are imperfect as humans.

Finally, I have stopped looking to others for my own happiness, nor am I any longer willing to accept responsibility for the happiness of others. I have chosen to believe that only I can make myself happy, and that, realistically, I can be just about as happy as I choose to be. Yes, I can be more open, I can learn to be more assertive—without being controlling—in asking for what I want, but in the final analysis, I have a great deal to say about my own sense of accomplishment here on earth, and true happiness after that.

My father—dear God I miss him—was eighty-eight when he died in June 1993. At the age of eighty-seven, before his health failed, he took a ten-thousand-mile fishing trip to Alaska—by car. He was blind at the time, having been unable to see for many years. He was also writing a book about his life, a book he was unable to finish. That he was "writing" a book—slowly talking into a voice-activated recorder—whether he completed it or not, meant a lot to me. My brothers and sisters and I always enjoyed hearing about his exploits in the Merchant Marines, how he met my mother, and how, during the Great Depression, they all pulled together. Because he was willing to share his life with his seven children—the good, the bad, the scary—we will forever be able to recall the things for which he stood. His unfinished manuscript said that "the road one travels is often more rewarding and interesting than the destination itself. There are thousands of forks in the road to destiny, and from birth to death, and beyond, the various stages of road provide great variety." Dad's life personified the spiritual insight embodied in author Scott Peck's classic definition of love in his best-seller, *The Road Less Traveled*. Peck wrote that "love is the will to extend one's self to nurture one's own, or another's, spiritual growth." Dad always talked about the importance of taking the high road.

Well, Dad, if you are reading along, you can see much of yourself in this book. I hope you like the approach I have taken to put the unhealthy aspects of Vietnam behind me. Thanks for your dedication to your family. You were my hero. Without your love and support—and your love of fishing—I might never have had the courage, or the experience, to write this book.

If my dad was my teacher, my mother was my alter ego. She was like a cheerleader who, sensing the need for encouragement, helped others to get the most out of themselves. She seldom took credit for anything she did herself, more often attributing success and good fortune to the luck of the draw. Although an expert bridge player, she would go out of her way to convince others that, owing to his bold and imaginative style of play—usually without the cards to go along—my dad was the better player. When I screwed up as a teenager, she was the disciplinarian, not afraid to punish, but quick to participate in the healing process. She had a sense of reality about her. She knew that if I persevered, I could graduate from high school, and she was optimistic about my chances to get into Gonzaga University. Until then no one in our family had graduated from a university. She never gave up on me, always willing to accept that, though imperfect, I would learn from my mistakes. Although my suspension from the university hurt her deeply—it was the only time I saw my mother cry—she didn't make me feel unworthy. She was there to witness my resurgence of energy and reinstatement in the ROTC program. When I was commissioned as a second lieutenant in the army infantry, she was overjoyed, but nothing made my mother happier than my engagement and subsequent marriage to Donna.

Mom, if you're listening, I did the best I could under the circumstances. I will always think of you as one of my guardian angels, and will always love you for trying to understand me. And for letting me be me.

All things considered, except for a few bumps in the main road, and a couple of turns onto questionable side roads, all interesting and rewarding, I have to this point lived a most memorable life. A life based on an established faith in God, strong family values, and life-giving principles. Three wonderful children who still love me, now grown and married, all of whom have prosperous lives of their own and spouses whom I dearly love. Two Vietnam combat tours from which I safely returned. A well-rounded education. Two retirements, one from the army, the other from five years in the corporate world. Thirty years of marriage to the same, most remarkable woman. My own, more constructive business, for which I no longer need a watch. Several special friendships, people who stuck by me through thick and thin. People who really cared for me when I was most in need, and with whom I still share a common bond. One, an SF vet like me, who always listens to my stories and with whom I have been diving for years. Another, a Navy vet, my next-door neighbor for seventeen years, who urged me to continue this effort when I had serious doubts about whether I wanted to, or could, complete the task. And, of course, there are other special friends, whose names in print might prove a source of embarrassment to them, but without whom the real war—the one after the fighting stopped—might still be raging. To them I owe a special debt of gratitude.

And now, of course, I have a book, the completion of which has meant more to me than I ever thought possible. A book that has been on my mind—in both my fears and tears— for thirty years. A book that I hope will have broad appeal. A book that took fifty-seven years to live, and four years to write. A book about forgiveness, friendship, and survival. A book that, in time, will help me escape the torments of war. A book that will be hard to forget.

Yes, I have a lot about which to be thankful. But then, my mother always said I was lucky.

Epilogue

The 1997 Thanksgiving Day trip to Lowell, Massachusetts, was one of the most difficult drives I have ever had to make. Only one week earlier, in Philadelphia, where I had been asked to speak for the Americans attending a Khmer Krom convention, I had reunited for the first time with Kim Lai and several other Bodes who fought with the Mobile Guerrilla Force I had recruited in 1966. About nine-thirty the following night, Lai, the sixty-four-year-old former platoon sergeant, who was only a few feet away from me when his second platoon discovered the black box, excused himself, saying he was very tired. Kim Lai then lay down on the sofa of his longtime friend, Son Thay Hien, our machine gunner, who had hosted an afternoon brunch, and fell asleep quickly. Forever.

As I began to exit I-495 toward rural Route 3 and the Lowell connector, my mind sorted through the speech I had delivered on November 22 to forty or fifty Khmer Krom— Free Cambodians—who had come from as far away as Seattle to learn whether, or to what extent, we Americans would support the Khmer Krom Council's movement to establish equal rights for Cambodians who had cast their lot in life with the U.S. in Vietnam.

This is what I said:

Cambodian friends and warriors, Soc Si Bi [Hello]. I am honored to be with you. I speak for all Americans

269

who are honored to be with you tonight, tomorrow, and forever.

I also see some soldiers, who because of their sacrifice so many years ago, could not be with us tonight. In our hearts, let us say a small prayer that they will smile on us and listen to our words of admiration and thanks for their courage.

Since we served together, much has been written about the courage, and sacrifice, of the Cambodian soldier in Vietnam:

In his 1976 book, *A Soldier Reports*, General William C. Westmoreland, former commander of American forces in Vietnam, praised the Cambodians with the Mobile Guerrilla Force for finding the black box of the U-2 spy plane that crashed into the jungles of Nui Ba Ra in 1966. So important to the United States was this mission that U.S. President Johnson was immediately notified of its recovery.

In his 1983 book, *Inside the Green Berets*, former Deputy Commander of the Fifth Special Forces Group, Colonel Charles M. Simpson, details the significant support and sacrifice that CIDG soldiers—including thousands of Cambodians—gave to the United States during the Vietnam War.

In his 1988 book, *No Greater Love*, Mobile Guerrilla Force medic Bac Si Donahue wrote: "In order to gather our indigenous force, we relied on an underground Cambodian organization known as the Khmer Serei . . . because of their inherent discipline, physical strength, stamina, good nature, tactical prowess, ability to conduct silent operations, and intense hatred for the Vietnamese."

Donahue continued: "[The Cambodians] were a people without a country—the Vietnamese didn't want them in Vietnam, and the Cambodian government under Prince Sihanouk wouldn't allow them to live in Cambodia. But when America and Special Forces called, . . . the Khmer Serei raised a force of two hundred of its best men . . . who became known as the Mobile Guerrilla Force." The date was 1966. But most of the Cambodian heroes here tonight—more than thirty years later—who fought with Special Forces are still without their families.

Donahue wrote his second book, *Mobile Guerrilla Force—With the Special Forces in War Zone D*, in 1993. He dedicated that book "to those Americans and Cambodians who fought with the Mobile Guerrilla Force." Donahue documents for the first time that it was a Cambodian soldier who first found and reported the location of the black box. Some of the Cambodians who recruited for or fought with the MGF on the Black Box operation may be here with us tonight: Tan Thach, III Corps Khmer Serei, who helped to recruit the MGF. Rinh, chief Cambodian medic, who was wounded many times, but still stayed with the MGF. After the overthrow of Cambodia's Prince Norodom Sihanouk, he graduated from the Cambodian Military Academy and was promoted to the rank of captain. Rinh avoided capture for years, walking back to Cambodia, then back to Vietnam, where security forces from the Cambodia National Front arrested and jailed him. Rinh convinced his captors that he had never worked for the Americans, so was released. Rinh later made it to the Thai border, where he applied for permission to immigrate to Seattle, Washington, where he found part-time work as a medical interpreter.

Kim Lai, platoon sergeant, second platoon, MGF, who also fought with the Third Mobile Strike Force in the overthrow of Prince Sihanouk. Kim Lai became a captain in the Cambodian Army, but when the Communists overthrew Lon Nol in 1975, Kim was captured by the Khmer Rouge. He escaped execution but was sent to a Communist re-education camp. Kim also escaped from prisons in 1976 and 1979. In all, Kim was wounded nine times before immigrating to the U.S. in May 1984. Kim currently lives in Lowell, Massachusetts.

Son Thay Hien, machine gunner, second platoon, MGF, lost a leg while fighting the Khmer Rouge in Cambodia. In 1975, Son walked back to Tay Ninh on one leg, where he was jailed by Vietnamese authorities. Released by the Vietnamese in 1981, two years later he walked to Thailand. In 1984, Son immigrated to the U.S. Currently he lives in Philadelphia.

After my days with the Mobile Guerrilla Force, I returned to my family, but I could not escape the torments of war. I thought I had forgotten about Vietnam, but I kept seeing the young girl in VC pajamas killed while fighting for her village near Suoi Da; the old man in his hootch, still holding in his hand the gun he used to blow out his brains just before the VC arrived. Many more horrible sounds and sights of war. Too many nightmares. I know I am not alone. I know most of you sitting here tonight have your own nightmares. Some things that are hard to forget.

After twenty-five years I started to write my own story. My book, *Hard to Forget: An American with the Mobile Guerrilla Force in Vietnam*, will be published in August 1998.

My book talks about the courage and the sacrifice of the Cambodian soldier.

I also wrote that Donahue's story about the black box is true. An unknown Cambodian, with Kim Lai's second platoon, was the first person to locate the secret device.

To him, to all of the Cambodian strikers who fought with the Mobile Guerrilla Force, and to all Cambodians who fought with Special Forces, we Americans offer our public thanks and gratitude for your courage, focus, discipline, and good fortune. Without the Cambodian, there was no Mobile Guerrilla Force. Someday I hope this book, and others, can be translated into your language so that you and your loved ones can begin to realize the credit you deserve.

Thank you for being a friend. For caring. For doing your best to kill VC, to destroy VC bases, to take care of each other, and for taking care of your Americans.

We were not only the first Mobile Guerrilla Force to conduct successful guerrilla operations in the Vietnam War, but perhaps more important, members of one of the finest fighting forces ever assembled. *De Oppresso Liber.*

At this point, I asked Tan Thach, Rinh, Kim Lai, and Son Thay Hien to stand, then invited the rest of our Cambodian brothers to rise. I saluted them with:

You are the greatest warriors who fought with the
    Special Forces;
You can be proud of your courage and your sacrifice;
We love you like brothers;
Chey Yo! Chey Yo! Chey Yo!
Puc a puc a Ho Chi Minh

The room thundered with excitement as I bellowed loudly
into the microphone, three times, "Chey Yo!"—the battle cry
of the Cambodian soldier. I knew instinctively that it embodied our collective desire to recall where we met, where we
fought together, and who had been our main target. All of the
Bodes and those American warriors present—Tom Johnson,
the SF captain who took my post at Suoi Da when I volunteered to start the Mobile Guerrilla Force; Dave Christian, a
Vietnam vet who bled on Cambodian soil and author of *Victor
Six*; Jerry Burr, Paul Grillo, and Phil Downey, all of whom
fought with the Third Mobile Strike Force, the issue of the
MGF; myself; and Jim Donahue, MGF medic and award-
winning author—all of us then picked up the chant, repeating
it over and over again, "Fucka Fucka Ho Chi Minh," until we
had confirmed our roots and were quite sure we knew we were
together again. Forever.

During the half hour that followed, we listened intently as
Thach Tan Dara, chairman of the Khmer Kampuchea Krom
Council, outlined the Kampuchea geopolitical issue. After the
United States invaded NVA sanctuaries in Cambodia in the
spring of 1970, although there was substantial opposition
within the United States to President Nixon's decision, there
were few U.S. scholars who could offer reliable information
and analysis on the expanded war. Cambodian scholars have
concluded that the United States chose not to be involved in a
problem it did not understand. Even after more than twenty
years of U.S. involvement in a war in Indochina, there continues to be little understanding about the existence and nature
of the Khmer Kampuchea Krom. In that vacuum, Vietnam is

trying to prove its right to the occupation of Kampuchea and Laos. That is the major issue facing Free Cambodians today.

The Khmer Kampuchea Krom are South Vietnam's indigenous people. Born in the southern regions of South Vietnam, known to soldiers who fought there as the III Corps and IV Corps Tactical Zones and encompassing the major cities of Tay Ninh (Raung Damrei in Khmer), Bien Hoa (Kampong Sraka Tre), and Saigon (Prey Nokor) in III Corps and Can Tho (Prek Russay), Soc Trang (Srok Khleang), and Bac Lieu (Pol Leav) in IV Corps (also known as the Delta), the Khmer Krom consider themselves to be one of the unrepresented people of the world. As Cambodians of Vietnamese origin, the Khmer believe those political regions in what is, at present, known as South Vietnam, constitute Kampuchea Krom, part of the Khmer Empire formed during the ninth through thirteenth centuries.

Because of their political and religious beliefs and their aspiration for full independence following the Vietnam War, hundreds of Khmer Krom political, religious, and military leaders were imprisoned, persecuted, and murdered by the Vietnamese. Also, thousands of Cambodian soldiers, like Rinh, Kim Lai, and Son, were caught in the cross fire, fearful of imprisonment and persecution whether in Kampuchea (Cambodia) or Kampuchea Krom (South Vietnam).

Aside from a favorable resolution to the political struggle that may take decades to achieve, or may never be resolved to the satisfaction of the Khmer Krom, the Cambodians of Vietnamese origin who fought with U.S. forces want the same rights as are accorded to all Vietnamese citizens: they want to be able to return to their country without being imprisoned. They want to locate loved ones scattered by the ravages of war. They want to bring their loved ones to their new country, a country whose freedom they have grown to love but whose actions to care for those who fought for freedom fall perilously short of their expectations (and mine).

The following morning at a breakfast meeting, we Americans decided to establish an advisory board to the Khmer Kampuchea Krom Council, electing Jim Donahue, who heads the Veterans Employment and Training Service in the State of

New York, as our chairman. Jim had worked painstakingly and methodically with Americans and Cambodian leaders to insure that we could meet on this occasion. We confirmed our intent to develop, publish, and execute a plan designed to meet the expectations of our Cambodian brothers, their families, and the Khmer Kampuchea Krom Council, which has offices in Australia, Cambodia, Canada, France, and the United States.

As American Friends of the Khmer Krom (AFKK), the pre-liminary goals we outlined focused on the accomplishment of objectives designed to alleviate some of the concerns that had been the subject of our discussion with the attendees:

1. Immigration reform. Make it easier for Khmer Krom vet-erans and their family members to immigrate to the United States.
2. End government-sponsored discrimination against the Khmer population by the Vietnamese government.
3. Link Vietnamese foreign aid to human rights reform.
4. Assist individual Khmer Krom veterans with special problems.
5. Raise funds that will be used to achieve the above listed objectives.

Before we concluded our meeting, Thach Tan Dara distrib-uted a detailed account of the Khmer Krom plight written by Bunroeun Thach, Ph.D., and provided an Internet address for the Khmer Krom homepage (www.aracnet.net/~kampkrom) for those interested in learning more about Khmer issues.

The festivities at Son's home in Philadelphia provided to our brothers-in-arms—for the first time—the opportunity to socialize with their longtime friends, as soldiers of disparate rank seldom socialize in a war zone. I was humbled and grati-fied that after so many years we were together once again. We shared stories that, we thought, were all but forgotten. We laughed. We cried. We held on to each other as we had never been able to do before. As I complete this manuscript, the thought of those moments together is overwhelming. Before leaving, we assembled for pictures, and as we departed—all but Downey, who had driven Kim Lai's car to Philadelphia—remarks about Kim Lai's strong appearance and apparent good health dominated the conversation. Having survived in a country that experienced near genocide following the war—the killing of at least three million Cambodians at the hands of its own rulers—Kim had to be a survivor.

During the six-hour return trip to Newport News, I experienced an inner peace that often accompanies the end of a long personal struggle. I could only begin to wonder how I had been blessed, finally, with the capacity and the will to look into the eyes of those whose images I had repressed for so many years. There was so much love and understanding in Philadelphia that I needed to experience, but until then had failed to act on.

Downey's call came about midnight, only minutes after I walked through the front door. As I listened to him say that Kim Lai had died and as he described the failed attempts to resuscitate him, I said a small prayer for Kim, his wife Yeuth, and their two children, Sophia and Philipina. And, of course, for Phil, who had a mountain to climb. As I dried my eyes, I was first annoyed, then relieved, as my mind forced itself to recall a line from Robert Browning's "Rabbi Ben Ezra" that I had read in the *Daily Press* only a few weeks earlier: "The best is yet to be—that part of life for which the first was made."

Kim Lai has had a profound impact on me and, I believe, on all those with whom he came in contact. The hundreds of Cambodians and Americans who prayed by his side after his death had witnessed in life his gracious smile, his cultured manner, and his meek personality. A select few of us had witnessed his fierce fighting spirit and his hatred for the VC. This unbridled warrior, whose will to live outweighed the risks he willingly accepted while fighting alongside his American friends, will remain in my mind all the remaining days of my life. I pray that I will be so fortunate to survive on this earth, as did he, until which time he could be, once again, with his friends.

Hard to forget!

TEAM SERGEANT
A Special Forces NCO
at Lang Vei and Beyond

by Willaim T. Craig

The son of a career enlisted man, Bill Craig was a hard-bitten Korean War veteran and Special Forces brawler. Now here is his unvarnished account of a military career that catapulted him to team sergeant, the pinnacle of achievement for a Special Forces operator.

During Tet 1968, Craig's camp at Lang Vei was overrun by NVA, who parked a Soviet tank on his command bunker and dropped grenades down the air ducts. The riveting description of the breakout that followed and the raw courage of men fighting to save their comrades is an inspiration for anyone venturing into harm's way.

Published by Ivy Books.
Available in bookstores everywhere.

THE PROTECTED WILL NEVER KNOW

by Leigh Wade

Special Forces operator Leigh Wade outwitted death through five harrowing tours in Vietnam. In 1965, he volunteered for duty with the newly arrived 173rd Airborne and participated in the first battalion-size helicopter assault in Vietnam. In early 1966, after joining the highly classified all-volunteer C-5 unit, he engaged in unconventional warfare and clandestine ops in Cambodia.

Unlike many of his comrades, Wade lived to tell about what he saw. Captured in these pages are the combat, courage, and carnage of moments spent trapped precariously between life and death.

Published by Ivy Books.
Available in bookstores everywhere.